CANADA

GROWTH OF A NATION

Stan Garrod
Fred McFadden
Rosemary Neering

Fitzhenry & Whiteside

Contents

Picture Gallery *4*

The First Canadians *18*

Peoples of the Northwest Coast, Plateau, Plains, Arctic, Subarctic and Eastern Woodlands

Exploration *50*

The Vikings, Cabot, Cartier, The Northwest Passage, Champlain

Eastern Settlement *68*

Acadia, New France, The Hudson's Bay Company, English Colonies on the Atlantic Coast

Struggle for a Continent *106*

The Conquest of New France, The American Revolution

Life in a New Land *126*

United Empire Loyalists, Quebec After the Conquest, Pioneer Life

War and Rebellion *152*

The War of 1812, The Rebellions of 1837, Durham's Report

Expansion *174*

The Great Migration, Red River, The Pacific Coast

Confederation *192*

The Debates, The Conferences, The Fenians, The British North America Act

Joining the Pieces *210*

The First Riel Rebellion, Manitoba, B.C. and P.E.I. Join Confederation, The NWMP, The Indian Treaties, The Railway, The Northwest Rebellion, The Klondike

Turn of the Century *246*

The National Policy, Industry and the Labour Movement, Women in 1900, The Laurier Era, Immigration, Regional Development, International Affairs

Photo Album *290*

Glossary *298*

Index *302*

Acknowledgements *304*

EDITOR-IN-CHIEF: Robert Read
EDITORS: Barbara Hehner, Sheba Meland, Elizabeth Reid
DESIGNER: Brant Cowie/Artplus
ILLUSTRATORS: Dominic Amato, Alan Argue, Neil Harris
CARTOGRAPHER: Julian Cleva
PROJECT COORDINATOR: Elizabeth Reid

Every reasonable effort has been made to find copyright holders of illustrations and quotations. The publishers would be pleased to have errors or omissions brought to their attention.

Printed in Canada

CANADIAN CATALOGUING IN PUBLICATION DATA

Garrod, Stan, 1946-
    Canada, growth of a nation

ISBN 0-88902-199-6

1. Canada — History. I. McFadden, Fred, 1928 —
II. Neering, Rosemary, 1945 —

III. Title.

FC170.G37   971   C80-094430-8
F1026.G37

Fitzhenry & Whiteside

CANADA
GROWTH
OF A
NATION

Garrod
McFadden
Neering

Fitzhenry
&
Whiteside

CANADA GROWTH OF A NATION

ISBN 0 88902 199 6

Here is a key to the images that appear on the cover of this book. Some faces are familiar and famous, others represent the countless ordinary people who have contributed to the growth of Canada as a nation.

1. James Wolfe, 1727-1759, soldier and general
2. Emily Carr, 1871-1945, painter and writer
3. Louis Cochin, 1890s, missionary priest
4. George Etienne Cartier, 1814-1873, Father of Confederation
5. Gold miner, 1860s, British Columbia
6. Jacques Cartier, 1491-1557, navigator and explorer
7. Paul Kane, 1810-1871, travelling painter
8. Joseph Howe, 1804-1873, writer and statesman
9. Scottish highland piper, 1770s, Nova Scotia
10. Inuit boy and dog
11. Immigrant girl, 1905, New Brunswick
12. Ukrainian settler, 1910s, Manitoba
13. Marie de l'Incarnation, 1599-1672, teacher and nun
14. Laura Secord, 1775-1868, Canadian patriot
15. Fisherman, 1900s, Newfoundland
16. Matthew Begbie, 1819-1894, judge
17. Parliament Buildings, Ottawa
18. Plains Indian, 1890s, Alberta
19. Thomas Chandler Haliburton, 1796-1865, writer and judge
20. Louis Riel, 1844-1885, Métis leader
21. Gabriel Dumont, 1838-1906, Métis commander-in-chief
22. Wilfrid Laurier, 1841-1919, prime minister
23. British soldier, War of 1812
24. Isaac Brock, 1769-1812, soldier and general
25. Susanna Moodie, 1803-1885, settler, writer and painter
26. Louis Joseph de Montcalm, 1712-1759, soldier and general
27. Nellie McClung, 1873-1951, writer, teacher, suffragette and politician
28. William Lyon Mackenzie, 1795-1861, shopkeeper, journalist and politician
29. Alexander Graham Bell, 1847-1922, inventor
30. James Cook, 1728-1779, navigator and explorer
31. Farming family, 1890s, Saskatchewan
32. Emily Stowe, 1831-1903, teacher, doctor and feminist
33. Crowfoot, 1830-1890, Blackfoot leader
34. John A. Macdonald, 1815-1891, prime minister
35. Catherine Schubert, 1835-1918, teacher and settler

Picture Gallery

ROYAL ONTARIO MUSEUM

View Combining Signal Hill, The Narrows, Cochrane Street and South Side of St. John's, Newfoundland (1851) by W.R. Best. Signal Hill is where Marconi received the first radio signal sent across the Atlantic.

The One-Room School, Canoe Cove, Prince Edward Island by Robert Harris. This was typical of schools in small communities in the late nineteenth century. Children of all ages shared one teacher. The pot-bellied stove in the centre was the only source of heat.

Gold washing near Lunenburg, Nova Scotia (1865) by C. Williams.
Many of the early explorers in Canada were looking for gold. They
failed to find it. The big strikes were in the Cariboo in British
Columbia and the Klondike in the Yukon. But gold was also found in
other parts of the country.

Meeting of the Sleigh Club at Saint John, New Brunswick (1837) by
Sir Richard Levinge. Sleighing was a popular winter social activity
across Canada. Many of the people shown here would have been
Loyalists. Levinge was an English soldier posted to Saint John from
1835 to 1837. His regiment marched overland to Montreal to help
put down the rebellion in Lower Canada in 1837.

A view of Chateau Richer (1787) by Thomas Davies. Each farm on the seigneury ran back from the river in a long strip. Chateau Richer is on the St. Lawrence about 25 km northeast of Quebec. Ile d'Orléans can be seen across the water.

A Timber Raft on the St. Lawrence (about 1860) by Frances Anne
Hopkins. After timber was cut, it was tied together in huge rafts to
float down the rivers. When the raft reached the port (Quebec, or
Saint John in the Maritimes) the raft would be broken up. The logs it
had been made of were loaded on ships to supply Europe with timber.

Behind Bonsecours Market (1866) by William Raphael. The artist has portrayed his own arrival as an immigrant. He is the man carrying the candlestick and sketch book. He probably came in the sailing ship at the dock, but other immigrants might arrive in the new steamships seen in the background.

Old Fort Erie with the Migration of Wild Pigeons in Spring (12 April 1804) by Edward Walsh. Fort Erie was built to protect Upper Canada from invasion by the Americans. The passenger pigeon of North America, like the buffalo, used to be plentiful. It was wiped out by hunters. The last passenger pigeon died in a Cincinnati zoo in 1914.

The Canada Southern Railway at Niagara (about 1870) by Robert
Whale. The first railway in Canada ran about 25 km from Laprairie
to St. Jean, Quebec. It was opened in 1835. Many lines were built in
eastern Canada before the CPR reached the Pacific.

Fort Garry (1869) by William Armstrong. Fort Garry, where the
Assiniboine River meets the Red, was an important Hudson's Bay
Company trading post. The cities of Winnipeg and St. Boniface later

ROYAL ONTARIO MUSEUM

Buffalo Hunt on the Prairies (1847) by Henry Hine.

ROYAL ONTARIO MUSEUM

Red River Carts on a Prairie Road (1877) by Adrian Neison.

A Logger's Camp on Vancouver Island by E. Sandys. Logging is still a major industry in British Columbia.

Heina (1928) by Emily Carr. Villages like this existed on the Northwest Coast until well into the twentieth century.

First Winter in the Ice at Beachey Island, Sir John Franklin's Last Expedition by an unknown painter. Franklin was an Arctic explorer. On his third expedition, started in 1845 he tried to find the Northwest Passage. His ships became trapped in ice. Franklin died in June 1847. The next April the remaining crew members abandoned ship. They tried to make their way overland. But they did not know how to survive in the North and they all died. Over 40 expeditions were sent to search for Franklin before his fate was discovered.

The First Canadians
ADVANCE ORGANIZER

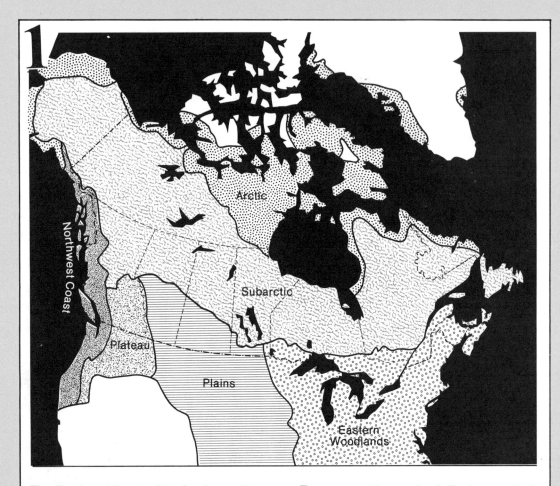

The first inhabitants of the land we call Canada came from Asia many thousands of years ago. Over time, they occupied nearly all of North and South America. We call these firstcomers *native people*. They are also called *Indians,* because early explorers to reach the Americas thought they had found India.

There were many different groups of native people in North America before European settlers arrived. Each group had a distinctive way of life. We call this way of life a *culture.*

Before the Europeans came, there were six main native cultures in what is now Canada. Each group had its own way of obtaining food, its own style of clothing, distinct types of houses, its own language and religion.

The Northwest Coast people lived along the Pacific coast of British Columbia. They were fishermen, catching the salmon that came into the rivers each year to spawn. Their homes and canoes were built from the giant cedar trees that grew on the coastal mountains.

The Plateau people lived between the Coastal and Rocky Mountain ranges of British Columbia. They were hunters and gatherers. Plateau people built pit houses below the surface of the ground.

Word List

confederacy	legend	tradition
council	nomad	trait
culture	permafrost	tundra
Ice Age	potlatch	warrior

4

The Plains people hunted buffalo on the prairies. Their way of life developed after Europeans brought horses to America. Horses made it easier to follow the herds of buffalo over long distances. The Plains people lived in buffalo-hide tipis. The tipis could be moved easily as they followed the buffalo herds.

5

The Arctic region of Canada was home to the Inuit people. These people are sometimes called *Eskimos*. They were skilled hunters and fishermen. Hunting provided not only food but the warm skins and furs needed to keep warm in the cold Arctic climate.

6

The Subarctic people lived in the great evergreen forest zone that stretches across northern Canada from British Columbia to the Maritimes. They were hunters who followed the herds of animals as they moved with the seasons.

7

The Eastern Woodlands people lived around the Great Lakes. Their way of life was different from all other Canadian native groups because they were farmers. They grew corn, squash, beans, and tobacco. Farming meant that these people could live in permanent villages.

8

These were the native people who met the first Europeans who came to Canada. From them the Europeans obtained food and furs in trade. The native people taught the newcomers the skills needed to survive in Canada.
In return, the Europeans gave the natives new tools and weapons. The influence of the new European culture changed the native ways of life.

Introduction

There was a time when Canada was nothing but land and water. There were no plants, no animals and no people. Millions of years passed. Volcanoes erupted and cooled. Mountains rose up. Seas covered the land, then disappeared again. Dinosaurs walked the plains, then vanished in their turn. Rivers formed in the mountains and cut across the land. Trees, grass and flowers grew. Animals thrived everywhere.

Then sheets of ice spread out from the North Pole, covering most of the land. Time passed and the ice melted, leaving new valleys, rivers and lakes. Flowers and trees grew again, and the animals returned.

All of this took millions of years to happen. During these years, there were no people in what is now Canada, or in any other part of the North or South American continents.

Two Moons, a Cheyenne chief.

People Come to North America

About 30 000 to 35 000 years ago, the first people arrived in North America. About this time, ice covered most of the earth. So much water was turned into ice that the level of the oceans dropped. This created a bridge between Siberia and Alaska. It is thought that hunters from Asia followed herds of bison, mammoths, caribou and other animals across this land bridge from Siberia to North America.

Over several thousand years, these people moved south. Much of what is now Canada was then covered by ice. But for a long time there was a large open path that led down the Mackenzie River to the Great Plains. It is known that some of the newcomers reached as far south as Southern California. About 12 000 years ago, men with flint-tipped spears were hunting bison in Arizona and New Mexico.

These first arrivals were wandering hunters. Later, some groups learned to farm, growing corn and other crops. Six thousand years ago, people were growing corn in central Mexico.

Many Tribes and Ways of Life

These first North Americans banded together in families, tribes, kingdoms and even empires. They built villages, towns and cities. Each tribe developed its own language, dress, religion and customs. The tribes fought wars with each other. They wrote poetry, composed music, made tools and some developed a form of writing.

The tribes also traded with each other. Goods from Mexico were carried up the Mississippi to the Ohio area. Goods moved along the Pacific coast from California to Alaska.

Some groups, such as the Maya of Mexico and Central America, were skilled scientists, mathematicians and builders.

These were the people whom early explorers from Europe called *Indians,* because the Europeans thought they had reached India. But the native people had their own names for their tribes and kingdoms, names like Aztec, Maya, Apache, Cree, Mohawk, Navajo and Salish.

Each group was as different from the other as the English are from the French, or the Italians from the Germans. Six of these groups lived in what is now Canada: the peoples of the Northwest Coast, the Plateau, the Plains, the Arctic, the Subarctic and the Eastern Woodlands.

An Inuit wearing snow goggles to protect his eyes from the bright sun reflected off the snow.

A Cree girl.

A Piegan dandy.

The Northwest Coast

The ocean waves roll in on the north Pacific coast, crashing on the rocks and the beaches. The mountains soar up from the coast. There is almost no flat land here.

The west wind drives the clouds from the Pacific up to the mountains. Here, the clouds rise and drop their rain and snow on the western slopes. The heavy rain feeds the plants. The rain forest grows thick here.

Cedar, Douglas fir and spruce crowd together in a green mass.

The rain and snow feed the many rivers and streams that run down from the mountains. The ocean cuts deeply into the coast, forming long inlets that meet the rivers.

In these rivers and streams live the salmon. They begin their lives in the streams, then make their way to

Fish drying on racks along the banks of a
Northwest Coast river.

the ocean. When their lives are complete, they return
to the streams to lay their eggs and die.

The forests support life too. Deer, moose, bear,
mountain goats, eagles and many other birds live along
the coast.

This was the land of the Northwest Coast people.
They developed a way of life that used the riches of the
sea and of the woods.

The Salmon Family

Pink or Humpback Salmon — average length, 90 cm;
mass, 1.5 to 4.5 kg.
Coho or Silver Salmon — average length, 90 cm;
average mass, 4 kg.
Chinook, Spring, King or Tyee Salmon — average
length, 100 cm; 4.5 to 24 kg (record 60 kg).
Chum or Dog Salmon — length, up to 100 cm; mass,
4 to 8 kg.
Sockeye, Red, Blueback, or Kokanee Salmon —
length, up to 90 cm; mass, 1.5 to 4 kg.
BORN: in the spawning grounds of coastal streams
and rivers, often many kilometres from the ocean.
HABITS: As young fish, salmon live in fresh water.
They gradually make their way downstream to the
sea. Their adult lives are spent in salt water. After
spending from two to five years in salt water
(depending on the species), they return to the
streams where they were born. There they lay and
fertilize their eggs (spawn) and then die. Spawning
runs begin in midsummer and continue through the
fall. Salmon of different species spawn at different
times.
HISTORY: the main source of food for the people of the
Northwest Coast. Still the major catch of British
Columbia commercial fishermen, accounting for 80
percent of the value of the industry. Sockeye is the
most important species for commercial fishing.
Overfishing, especially by foreign fleets, has reduced
the number of salmon on the Northwest Coast. A
major conservation program to increase the number
of salmon is now underway.

Village Life

A village in the Queen Charlotte Islands. The carved houseposts show the crest of the family group that live in the house: bear, wolf, eagle, fireweed, frog, raven or killer whale.

The huge dugout canoe slips silently through the drizzle toward the beach. Above the beach is the village, home to the fishermen returning in their canoe. The cedar houses face the waters of the cove. Behind the houses tower the cedars and Douglas firs of the west coast forest. The green blends into the grey of the rain-soaked mountains.

The carved houseposts and painted designs on the housefronts seem to look down on the fishermen as they unload the catch. They fill cedar boxes with fish. The fish are taken to be smoked or dried. There will be food for the people of the village in the winter.

Smoke rises from the vents of the houses where meals are being cooked. The warmth of the fires keeps away the chill of the wet afternoon. Children play in the dim light of the fires as their mothers hang the fish from the rafters to dry.

Village By the Water

Northwest Coast villages such as this were located near good fishing spots. These were found in sheltered coastal coves and bays or along the rivers and streams that the salmon spawned in. Fishing on the Pacific coast was so good that the native people could stay in one place, and the fish would come to them. In the summers, they might move to fishing camps along the streams, but the large village was always home.

A typical village might have a dozen or more houses of different sizes. The largest of the houses could hold 50 to 60 people. These people would be members of several related families, and also slaves. Each house had a leader, or chief, the oldest and wisest member of the group. A chief who was wealthy or successful in war might be looked on as a leader of the village.

 **Picture Gallery page 16**

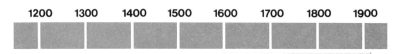

The chiefs and their families owned rights to areas around the village. Fishing grounds, berry-picking spots, even beaches, were their property.

Other forms of wealth included masks, songs, and crests that belonged to the chief or family. A chief also had to make sure that there was peace in the community and that there was enough for everyone to eat.

The village would gather together for important activities such as winter dance ceremonies, celebrations or war against a neighbouring group. Warfare was important. It provided an opportunity for a young man or rising chief to show bravery and cunning. It was also a means of getting slaves, and a way of gaining wealth and importance in the community.

Potlatches

Wealth and importance were at the centre of Northwest Coast life. Events such as weddings, deaths, becoming chief and victories in war were celebrated by large gatherings of villagers and neighbouring people. These celebrations were called *potlatches*. Dances, songs, speeches, feasts and rituals were all part of potlatches. Skins, blankets, canoes and other riches were given away to the guests by the people holding the potlatch.

The more gifts given, and the larger the potlatch, the more likely it was that it would be remembered as a special event. The potlatch was the best way of keeping a record of important events. The Northwest Coast people had no written language. The songs, chants and stories of the potlatch told the story of the event. They were passed on in the family and the village for years afterward.

A summer fishing camp.

A potlatch at Alert Bay, 1910.

Cedar

The mountain slopes and river valleys of Canada's Pacific coast are covered with forests of cedar, spruce and fir. A few centuries ago, the forests were thicker than they are now, and the trees were taller. Every native village was close to the forest. Of all the trees, the great Douglas fir was king, towering 100 m or more above the ground. But to the Northwest Coast peoples, the cedar was the most important tree.

There were many cedar trees then. The wood was strong, yet easy to work with. The grain was straight and the wood split easily into planks and boards. It could be carved into pleasing shapes. The bark was soft and had long strong fibres. Nearly everything the coast peoples used in their daily lives was made of cedar.

Ceremonial mask.

Household Uses for Cedar

Their great houses and ceremonial buildings were built of cedar. Long cedar poles were used for houseposts and beams. Planks split from cedar logs were laid over this frame. The planks for the walls and roof were lashed in place with cord made of cedar bark or spruce roots. Inside the house, the walls of each family apartment were made with cedar planks. Beds were made of cedar. Baby cradles were woven of cedar bark. Soft fluffy inner bark made a bed for the baby.

Cedar bark was also used to make clothing. Women pounded long strips of bark into fibre which could be woven or braided. Raincapes, skirts and hats were all made of cedar bark. The bark could also be used to make cords for rope or fishnets.

The people of the Northwest Coast made long and graceful canoes. Each canoe was shaped from a single cedar tree. The bow and stern were cut in smooth, curving lines that allowed the boat to cut smoothly through the waters of the Pacific Ocean.

The largest canoes were nearly 20 m long. They were the freight canoes of the Nootka and Haida peoples. The Northwest Coast people were great traders. They travelled hundreds of kilometres along the coast to trade shells, hides and fish among the various groups. Every year, the Chinook tribe along the Columbia River held a giant trade gathering. Traders came in canoes from as far away as California and Alaska.

Canoes for Hunting and Fishing

The Nootka tribe built large canoes for whaling. Other types of canoes were used for fishing or for hunting sea otters or seals. There were even tiny cedar canoes that young boys could paddle to learn the skills that were so important on the coast.

Cedar planks could be steamed and bent into boxes. Bent boxes could be made waterproof by having their joints sealed with pitch. These boxes were used for storing food in the winter — or could even be used for cooking. Food and water were placed in the box and then hot rocks were dropped in to boil the water and cook the food.

Cedar was also used for beautiful works of art. The Northwest Coast people decorated their homes with carved poles and panels. Feast dishes were carved in the shape of animals. Masks were carved of cedar or other wood for the winter dances or other potlatch ceremonies. Axes, canoe paddles and other everyday tools were carved in graceful shapes.

Raven rattle.

Bear dish.

Cedar-bark clothing.

Sails were not used until after the arrival of the Europeans.

Life from the Sea

Many large rivers and small streams flow out of the coastal mountains into the Pacific. These streams are the highways along which millions of salmon travel every year. Here, and in the Pacific Ocean, the peoples of the Northwest Coast found their food supply.

The Pacific salmon begin their lives in the small streams of the coast. Every year, millions of eggs are laid in the gravel of the shallow waters of the streams. The young salmon hatch and slowly make their way downstream to the ocean. In the ocean they grow to adult size. After several years, the adult fish return to the same stream where they hatched. There they lay their eggs, called *spawn,* and the life cycle begins again.

Other fish were also important in the diet of the Pacific Coast people. Halibut, large flat fish, were caught with hooks made of wood and bone. Women used large rakes to harvest the herring, small fish that came in close to shore in large schools. Herring eggs were also used as food.

Oolichans, another small fish, were trapped. They were then boiled down to supply a rich oil. Oolichan oil was used with berries and other dishes. It was so popular that it could be traded across the mountains to the Plateau people and Subarctic people for goods like caribou hides.

The ocean also provided shellfish, such as crabs, clams and oysters, and edible seaweed.

Seals, sea otters and whales lived there. These animals were hunted from canoes with spears and harpoons. Only the Nootka of Vancouver Island are known to have been whalers. Other tribes such as the Haida would eat whale meat if one of the great sea mammals washed up on the beach. Seals and sea otters provided skins and furs as well as meat.

Bringing oolichans to shore.

Religion

The sound of a shaman's rattle, a spirit mask, a design carved in the stone wall of a cave. Hearing and seeing these things reminded the Northwest Coast people that they lived in a world filled with spirits. Some of the spirits were good and kind; others were wicked. The spirits had created the world and the people who lived in it. They had created the salmon, the other fish, the birds and the animals on which the people depended.

The Northwest Coast people were thankful for these gifts, and they took care to respect the spirits. The spirits were everywhere, in the streams and in the forests. Garbage must not be thrown into the streams, for if it were, the salmon spirits would be offended and the salmon would come no more. It was believed that the salmon were really people who lived in villages beneath the sea. Every year these people changed magically into salmon to bring food to the coast.

Prayers to the spirits marked the start of each fishing season. The Nootka whalers prayed to the whale and asked forgiveness for killing it. Good hunts and fishing catches were celebrated with prayers and thanks to the spirits.

The spirits of the coast were the subjects of many stories and legends. Some stories were about the creation of the world, the animals and the people. Others were ways of teaching children how to behave properly. Some stories were just funny, for even the spirits liked to laugh. The spirits and their animal forms were common designs in Northwest Coast art. Spirit ancestors were shown in family crests and housepoles. The spirits seemed to be brought to life at ceremonies, when masked dancers represented them.

Masked dancers at a festival.

The Plateau

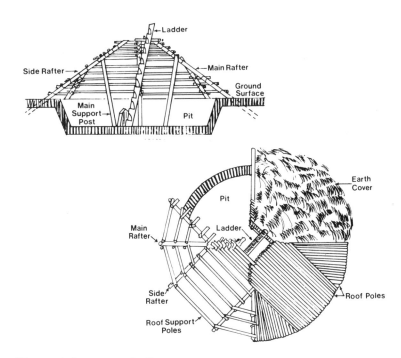

How a pit house was built.

A decorated cooking basket.

Between the Pacific coast mountains and the Rocky Mountains lies a flat area called the Plateau. The Plateau runs from central British Columbia south to Washington and Oregon and east into Montana and Idaho. Here too were found native people, many of whom traded with the Northwest Coast people to the west.

The weather here is different from that of the coast. There is less rain and snow. The land is cooler in winter and warmer in summer. The trees, mostly pine and larch, are smaller. Large forests grow along the mountainsides that drop down to the major rivers. Away from the rivers, however, the land is dry and few trees grow.

Salmon in the Rivers

Several major rivers cut through the Plateau. Among them are the Thompson, Fraser and Columbia. These rivers flow to the Pacific. The spawning salmon travel along these rivers, returning to their birthplaces hundreds of kilometres from the ocean. Salmon were an important part of the diet of the Plateau people, just as they were for the Northwest Coast tribes. Many Plateau villages were built near spawning streams. Salmon were caught with long-handled nets as the fish leapt up the fast-flowing streams.

The forests of the Plateau were home to deer and other wild animals. The Plateau people hunted deer by chasing them with dogs and driving them into the water. There, the deer could be killed with arrows shot from canoes. Other foods included wild berries, water plants and edible roots.

The Way of Life

The Plateau people spent the winter in pit houses. These houses, built by the women, were partly underground and were covered with logs and earth. The largest pit houses could hold as many as 30 people at a time. A fire in the centre heated the house and was used for cooking. There were hammocks for sleeping. Fur blankets and animal hides covered the earth floor. Baskets for storing and cooking food hung from the roof.

Summer homes were tipi-shaped. They were built of pine poles covered with hides, mats or blankets. These summer homes could be quickly moved to fishing, root-gathering or berry-picking places.

The Plateau people made dugout canoes to fish and gather cattails for food in the many lakes on the Plateau. The canoes were each made from a single log. They were not as large as those on the Pacific Coast: the trees in the Plateau area were smaller.

Cattails and bullrushes were woven into baskets. These finely woven baskets could be made watertight. Food was cooked by being placed in the baskets with water and hot rocks.

Plateau people made their clothing from deerskins. For ceremonial purposes, clothing was decorated with moosehair embroidery and porcupine quill designs.

A platform was built near the summer home to store food out of reach of animals.

The Plains

The Great Plains of North America run from southern Alberta, Saskatchewan and Manitoba south to New Mexico and Texas. From the foothills of the Rocky Mountains, the Plains slope gently eastward to the Mississippi River. Great herds of buffalo used to roam here, over two million square kilometres of rolling hills and grasslands. The way of life of the native people of the Plains developed around these buffalo.

Sometime after the last Ice Age, mammoths and giant bison lived on the Plains. Slowly, these huge animals died out. Smaller bison, which we call buffalo, came north from Mexico and took over the prairie grasslands. Small isolated groups of stone-age hunters followed these herds of buffalo, similar to the buffalo that lived later on the Plains. By 1200 A.D., these hunters had left the area. The buffalo were left alone without anyone or anything to harm them. Their herds grew quickly. Soon there were millions of these shaggy brown beasts on the Plains.

People Return to the Plains

As these herds grew, people began to move back onto the Plains. Late in the thirteenth century, people from the Eastern Woodlands moved into what is now Manitoba and Saskatchewan. The Kiowa-Apache, Apache and Navaho started out in the Mackenzie River area of northern Canada and moved south almost to Mexico. These people moved on foot. It was easy to walk the Plains; 500 km could be covered on foot in a month.

When they reached the Plains, these migrants settled down on the rich land. They became farmers. The Pawnees and Mandans grew corn, sunflowers,

An early stone carving of a buffalo.

A Plains Indian chief.

An Assiniboine mother and child.

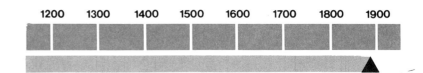
squash and beans. Gardens were found as far north as Manitoba. Farming meant permanent villages. The Pawnee and the Mandan lived in pit houses like those of the Plateau people.

The early Plains people also gathered wild rice, roots and berries. They hunted elk, deer, moose, rabbits and buffalo. But it was difficult to hunt buffalo on foot.

Hunting Buffalo

The movie flashes onto the screen. The people of the Plains gallop by on their horses, riding hard and fast after the buffalo. They look as if they have always ridden like this.

But it was not so. At first, the Plains people hunted on foot. Small hunting parties went out twice a year, in the spring and in the fall. The fall hunt was for animals with thick coats that could be made into winter robes.

The hunters used several methods to kill the buffalo. They stalked lone animals and shot them with bows and arrows. Or, they drove herds of the beasts into corrals or box canyons. Sometimes they lit fires that would sweep across the prairie grass and force the animals over cliffs known as buffalo jumps.

The hunters could carry only a small amount of meat and hides back to the villages. They could not travel far from their homes. They had to dry the meat quickly before it spoiled.

This was the way of life for the Plains people for about 300 years. By this time, the Spanish had arrived in Mexico and New Mexico. The Plains people obtained horses from the Spanish, and by 1750, there were horses in the farthest northern area of the Plains.

Trapping buffalo in a corral, or "buffalo pound."

Changes on the Plains

Horses changed the entire way of life of the Plains people. Now hunters could chase the buffalo for many kilometres. On horseback, they could outrun a fleeing buffalo and shoot it much more easily. They could drag heavy loads of meat back to the village on a horse-drawn travois.

The Plains people stopped being full-time farmers and became full-time buffalo hunters. The people began to follow the buffalo herds across the land. The herds of buffalo would move north into what is now Canada each spring. Plains groups like the Blackfoot and Sioux followed them. Each year the Plains people, following the buffalo, moved south again for the winter.

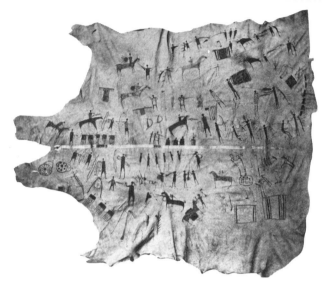

A Blackfoot warrior's robe.

A Blackfoot village in the 1880s. A large village might contain 600 to 700 tipis.

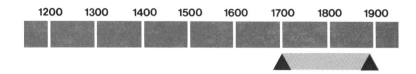

Guns Come to the Plains

The horse was not the only thing the Plains people obtained from the Europeans. The Europeans traded guns to the Eastern Woodlands people and these people traded the guns to the people of the Plains. The arrival of guns had two results. They allowed the Plains people to kill more buffalo more easily. They also made wars between tribes more deadly. In the eighteenth and nineteenth centuries, tribes were often at war. Wars were fought over hunting areas. Raids on neighbouring tribes were common. So important was the horse to the people that raids were usually marked by horse stealing.

The horse and gun brought about a great change in the life of the Plains people. But the new way of life lasted less than 200 years. The Europeans who brought the guns and horses soon killed off the buffalo.

Uses of the Buffalo

The buffalo was almost like a supermarket on hooves for the Plains people. Buffalo meat was their main source of food. Dried in the sun or over a fire, it would keep for a long time. Thick furry hides from animals killed in the fall made warm robes and blankets for the cold prairie winter. Tipis were covered with buffalo hides, carefully cut and sewn together by the women. Moccasins and other clothing were made from buffalo hide. Warriors used shields made from the tough neck-hide of bull buffalos. The Plains people even made boats from buffalo hide stretched over a wooden frame. Sinews were used in sewing and in making bow strings. Bones and horns were used to make tools and utensils.

Movable Villages

The Plains people wanted to stay close to the source of all these riches. They moved north in the spring and south in the fall with the buffalo. The Plains villages were designed to be moved easily when the buffalo moved. The tipis could be taken down and folded up. The poles of the tipis were used to make the travois that carried their goods. Trees were rare on the grasslands of the Plains. Using tipi poles for the travois meant that the precious wood could be moved easily and would be useful at the same time. At migration time, horses, dogs, travois and people would form a long line, moving across the prairie.

The Medicine Pipe Stem Dance. Religious dances were important to the Plains people. Many tribes had special buffalo dances to help the hunters. The dancers would wear buffalo heads and skins. They danced until the buffalo arrived. Sometimes the dancing went on for many days.

The Arctic

Throwing a harpoon from a kayak.

Canada's far north is known as the Arctic. Most of the Arctic is flat, treeless land called *tundra*. Much of the Arctic is made up of islands in the Arctic Ocean. The Arctic is bitterly cold and snow covered for up to nine months a year. In some places, the ground is frozen solid all year round. This ground is known as *permafrost*. Here, the native people of the Arctic developed a rich culture. They used the resources that the area provides very efficiently.

The people of the Arctic are often called Eskimos. *Eskimo* is an Athabaskan word meaning "eaters of raw meat." The natives of the Arctic would rather be called *Inuit*, which means "the people" in their language.

The Inuit were probably the last arrivals from Asia. There are still Inuit peoples living in Siberia today. The Inuit arrived in the western Arctic about 2000 years ago, moving slowly eastward until they reached Greenland. Perhaps the Subarctic people who moved earlier to the south kept the Inuit from moving south.

The Inuit were hunters, whalers and fishermen. They lived in villages through the long winters. In summer, they followed the wandering caribou.

Inuit Culture

The Inuit word for house is *igloo*. All houses are igloos, not just the snow house that is usually called an igloo. The dome-shaped snow house was most often used as a temporary shelter by winter hunting parties. (A snow igloo could be built in one hour, using blocks of snow cut on the spot.) Winter houses were built below the surface of the permafrost. The Inuit used whalebone or wood to support a roof of sod or animal hides. Some Arctic people built their houses of large stone slabs. In summer, hunting parties lived in skin tents.

1200	1300	1400	1500	1600	1700	1800	1900

The Inuit hunted many animals both on land and on the sea. They used bows and arrows to hunt caribou and other land animals. Seals, whales and walrus were hunted with harpoons from skin boats. Seals were also hunted in winter through breathing holes in the ice.

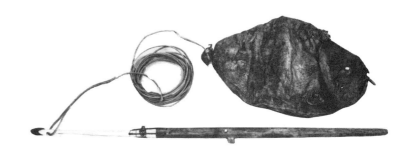

A harpoon.

Inuit Food

Most of the Inuit food came from these animals, from birds and from fish. In summer, the Inuit picked berries, which they preserved in seal oil. Food storage was not difficult, since permafrost makes a natural deepfreeze. Hunters could kill and store enough food during the summer to last the long winter. The Inuit had no vegetables. They got vitamins from the lichen in the stomachs of the caribou they killed.

Despite their "Eskimo" name, the Inuit did not eat all their food raw. Meat was usually cooked over seal-oil lamps or stoves made of stone.

Warm clothing was very important to the Inuit. In the freezing cold, clothing made the difference between life and death. The Inuit wore two layers of clothing. The inner layer was of fur, turned toward the wearer's skin. The outer layer was of caribou hide or fur turned outward. The clothing was loose, but fitted tightly at neck, wrists and ankles, to keep in body heat.

The Inuit were excellent craftspeople. They made fine tools and other articles from wood and bone. Bows, harpoons and other weapons were made of wood and bone lashed together with animal skins. The Inuit travelled by boat or sled. Boats were made of skins stretched over wood frames. Sleds were made of wood or bone, lashed together with rawhide. Dogs pulled the sleds.

An Inuit sled.

Dogs were used to pull sleds. In summer, they were used as pack animals.

The Subarctic

From British Columbia to the Maritimes, a large area of Canada is covered with forests of pine, birch and maple. This region, the Subarctic, covers more than half of Canada, and is home to many native people.

The Subarctic region has long, cold snowy winters. Summers are warm and dry. Moose, elk, deer, caribou, rabbits, beaver and muskrats fill the forests. Most of these animals move with the seasons, travelling north as spring comes. Winter chases them south again. The area is well supplied with lakes and streams. Many fish move into the streams each fall to spawn.

The people of the Subarctic moved with the animals they hunted. They never stayed long in one spot. They would live in a hunting or fishing camp for as long as the catch was good. Then they moved on.

Nomads

People like the natives of Canada's Subarctic are called *nomads*. Nomads must be able to move easily. They have to be able to take their homes and belongings with them. Therefore their houses have to be easy to set up and take down. Nomads have no permanent villages. They do not farm or build cities.

The nomadic people of the Subarctic had to be able to move easily. The Subarctic people had several ways of moving after game. For winter travel, they had snowshoes and toboggans. In summer, birchbark canoes carried them along the many rivers and lakes of the Subarctic.

Nomadic people cannot have many heavy possessions. Heavy wooden boxes or clay pots slow down movement. The peoples of the Subarctic relied on bark instead. The bark of trees like the birch was used to

Some Subarctic tribes

Koturon
Ingalik
Tanaha
Tanana
Ahtena
Kutchin
Tutchone
Kaska
Tahltan
Sekani
Carrier
Hare
Dogrib
Slave
Beaver
Yellowknife
Chipewyan
Cree
Ojibwa
Montagnais
Naskapi
Algonquin
Micmac
Beothuk

A Kutchin hunter.

An encampment on Lake Huron.

cover canoes and houses. Bark pouches made cooking pots and containers in which to store food. These objects were light and easily moved. A birchbark canoe could be carried easily over a long portage.

The Subarctic people lived in a larger area than any other native group in North America. Hunting bands were small. Each had several thousand square kilometres in which to track moose and other game. Bows and arrows were used for hunting.

The lives of the Subarctic people were also shaped by other native groups with whom they came in contact. The great region of the Subarctic touches on the areas in which all other native cultures lived. Because of this, for example, western Subarctic people shared some of the ways of the Plateau and Northwest Coast peoples.

A Micmac birchbark box decorated with porcupine quills and a birchbark cooking pot.

The Ojibwa and the Beothuks

The Ojibwa Way of Life

Not all of the Subarctic groups were few in number. One group, the Ojibwa, may have been the largest single native group in Canada before the Europeans arrived. There may have been as many as 20 000 Ojibwa living between Hudson Bay and the Great Lakes.

The Ojibwa lived in small hunting bands of 300 to 400 people. Each band had its own hunting area. The Ojibwa hunted moose in the winter. Snowshoes were used to follow the moose across the snow. In the summer, they hunted muskrats, beaver and other small animals. Berries were picked. Fall was the time for harvesting wild rice and spearing salmon as they came up the streams to spawn. In the spring, the Ojibwa gathered maple syrup.

Some Ojibwa, living in the south, learned farming from the Huron. These Ojibwa grew maize and beans. But they too followed the wild game and fish.

The Ojibwa lived in wigwams made of birchbark. *Wigwam* is an Ojibwa word. Ojibwa canoes were also made of birchbark. They travelled far along the rivers and lakes of the Canadian Shield following the game they needed for food.

The clothing of the Ojibwa was made from buckskin. The deer, moose and caribou that were used for food also provided clothing. The women would skin the animals the hunters brought back. The skins were made into clothing: loincloths, leggings, shirts, dresses, gloves and moccasins.

Ojibwa Celebrations

The Ojibwa year was marked by many ceremonies. There were feasts and dancing after successful hunts. Feasts were also held to give thanks after the wild rice harvest and after maple syrup gathering. Celebrations were often times for games. The Ojibwa men played lacrosse; Ojibwa women had their own special ball game too.

The Ojibwa believed the world was filled with powerful spirits. There were also shamans, medicine men and women who had special powers. A shaman made a medicine bag for each hunter to protect him. Each medicine bag contained roots, herbs and feathers to help the hunter and protect him from evil spirits.

An Ojibwa snowshoe dance.

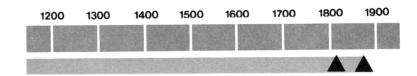

| 1200 | 1300 | 1400 | 1500 | 1600 | 1700 | 1800 | 1900 |

The Extinction of the Beothuks

In Newfoundland lived a tribe of Subarctic native people called the Beothuks. They were a small tribe, probably fewer than 1000 people. They painted their bodies with red ochre. Thus, early European visitors to Newfoundland called them "Red Indians."

The Beothuks were nomadic hunters who lived in bark tipis. They made birchbark canoes. They were a very simple people. Their tools were primitive. They had no dogs to help them when they hunted caribou and seals. The seals were hunted with harpoons like those of the Inuit.

Then European fishermen arrived in Newfoundland. They were angry when the Beothuks stole from them. They shot the Beothuks whenever they could. Some even hunted them for sport. The French gave a cash reward to anyone who killed a Beothuk. The Micmacs hunted the Beothuks too, with guns given to them by their French allies. The Beothuks, armed only with bows and arrows, could not defend themselves.

The Europeans brought new diseases, like TB. The Beothuks had no resistance to these diseases. Slowly but surely the tribe began to die out. By the beginning of the nineteenth century, there were very few Beothuks left alive. They were always on the run, always afraid of the newcomers. The last known Beothuk, Shanawdithit, died of TB in 1829. She ended her life as a household servant.

Most of what we know about Beothuk life comes from Shanawdithit. William Epps Cormack, a Newfoundland explorer, asked her to tell him about her people. She drew these pictures to help describe their way of life.

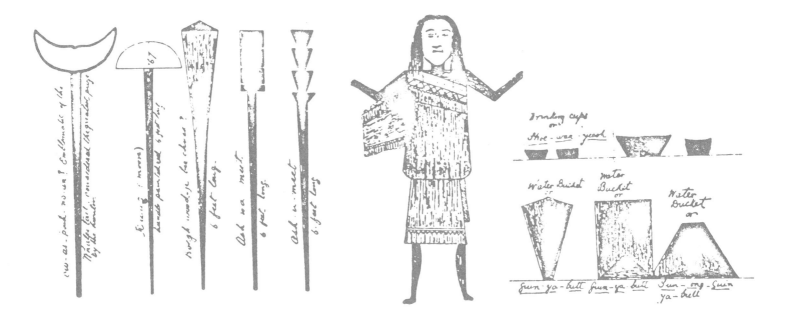

The Eastern Woodlands

From the Mississippi River in the west to the Atlantic in the east, there are rolling hills and valleys, covered with forests of maple, birch and elm. Thousands of lakes, rivers and streams, left behind after the last Ice Age, dot the land. The area is warm in summer and cold in winter. In the northern part of the area, winters are very cold. Snow is common from October to March, so the growing season is short.

The land around the Great Lakes and the St. Lawrence and Ohio rivers was home to the Eastern Woodlands people. They were Canada's first farmers. They grew corn, beans and squash. The Iroquois called these crops "the three sisters" because they were important sources of food. Farming set the people of the Eastern Woodlands apart from the hunters, gatherers and fishermen of the rest of Canada.

Villages in the Eastern Woodlands were built for defence. They were surrounded by a wall of logs.

C.W. JEFFERYS

Creek ↓

Entrance Gate

Corn Fields

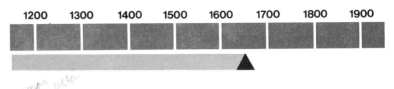

| 1200 | 1300 | 1400 | 1500 | 1600 | 1700 | 1800 | 1900 |

Eastern Woodlands Tribes

The people of the Eastern Woodlands shared a common way of life. They spoke similar languages. Their culture and language are called *Iroquoian,* named for the largest and most powerful tribe. Other important groups of Eastern Woodlands people were the Hurons and the Algonquins. Major groups in what is now the United States were the Sauk-Fox, the Abenaki and members of the Iroquois Confederacy.

At their northern limit, the Eastern Woodlands become part of the Subarctic forest. People living in this area share traits of both the Eastern woodlands and the Subarctic tribes. Some tribes, like the Ojibwa and the Algonquins, had members in both groups.

The Village

Seen from below, the village seems to tower over the lake. It is set high on a hilltop, overlooking the surrounding countryside. Cleared fields run down the hillside to the water's edge. It is a safe place to return to after a day working in the fields or hunting.

In the fields, the women of the village are working. They are carefully weeding and tending the young corn plants. The women working in the fields never stray far from the safety of the walled village above.

Several birchbark canoes are drawn up on the shore of the lake. One man is working on a canoe, patching a hole in its hull. It is summer; most of the men of the village are away, fighting an enemy tribe. Only the old men and young boys stay behind with the women.

Beyond the cleared fields near the village is a thick forest of birch and maple trees. In the fall, the men of the village hunt the deer and other game that live in the woods. But there is danger in the woods too. The trees may hide a raiding party, waiting to attack the people remaining in the village.

The Longhouses

Huron and Iroquois villages were surrounded by a sturdy wall of logs. These walls, five metres or more in height, kept out raiders from enemy tribes. Inside the wall were 20 to 30 longhouses. The longhouses were about 20 m long and 6 m wide. Long poles bent inward formed a barrel-shaped roof. Smaller branches and bark, usually from elm trees, covered the poles. These longhouses were larger versions of the bark wigwam of the people of the Subarctic.

Inside each longhouse was a long hallway running the length of the house. The cooking fires burned here, each shared by two families. Longhouses held from eight to twenty-four families. Each family had about five members. On a winter evening a longhouse was a crowded, smoky, warm place. Children and dogs played along the hallways; songs and hunting stories added to the noise.

Booths and apartments led off both sides of the hallway. Each family had two booths: a small one for storage and a larger one for sleeping. Beds stood on a platform about one metre off the floor. In winter, the family slept on skins or mats closer to the fire.

Farming

Keeping the birds from the crop

Corn, beans and squash were the main crops of all Indian farmers in North America before the Europeans arrived. These three crops were grown from Mexico to the Great Lakes.

The natives of the Eastern Woodlands grew two other crops as well: tobacco and sunflowers. Tobacco was used for religious and ceremonial purposes. Sunflowers were grown for their seeds and the oil that could be produced from them.

The farmers had to clear the fields for several kilometres around each village. With only stone tools, this was no easy task. Trees were ringed (a cut made through their bark all the way around) to kill them. They were then burned. The ashes from the burnt trees helped fertilize the soil.

The farm fields could only be used for about 15 years. After that time, crops would not grow well in that soil. When that happened, the whole village had to be moved to a new site.

The women of the Eastern Woodlands tribes usually did the farming. Huron men helped during harvest and other busy times. But most men of the Eastern Woodlands thought it was disgraceful for men to farm.

Farming shaped the lives of the Eastern Woodlands people. It allowed them to build more permanent settlements. Farming required fewer people working to feed the village than did hunting or gathering. Men were free to go trading, wage war or go hunting. More food was grown on the farms than the people needed. Extra corn or tobacco was traded to the Subarctic tribes for birchbark canoes and furs.

Changing Seasons

The scene in the village changed from season to season. In winter, people bundled up. Men wore buckskin shirts, loincloths, leggings, moccasins and mittens. Women wore buckskin dresses and moccasins. On a snowy winter day, a hunting party might return on snowshoes, carrying a load of fresh-killed moose meat.

The spring was the time for planting crops. This was a busy time for the village women. Not only did they have to plant the fields, they also had to do all the other work in the village. They gathered firewood, picked berries, made clothing and did all the household chores. The men used this time to get ready for trading and war. They busied themselves making weapons and practising the skills of warriors.

The men of the village were gone from June to September. During the summer, they traded with the

Lacrosse.

people of the Subarctic forest or made war with other tribes in the area. While the men were away, no one remained to protect the village. During the summer, the Iroquois raided Huron villages, and the Huron raided Iroquois villages. The Micmacs and other Subarctic tribes also attacked. The raiders killed the villagers or took them as prisoners to become slaves. The raiders burnt the houses to the ground.

Harvest was the high point of the fall. The corn was picked, and then poured into a hollowed-out tree or stump. With a shorter heavy piece of wood, the women pounded the grain into flour. The ground corn was stored in woven baskets or pottery containers for use during the winter. Wild rice was also harvested in the fall. A great celebration, with dancing and games, followed the harvests.

Leisure Activities

Because these people had free time, they developed a rich ceremonial and religious life. In winter, when the Subarctic tribes were out hunting game, the Eastern Woodlands people could enjoy themselves. They played games; lacrosse was invented by these people. It was a popular game, often involving several tribes and hundreds of players. Dancing, gambling and religious festivals were common. Religious ceremonies were held to give thanks for good harvests.

The people of the Eastern Woodlands also hunted for moose, deer and other game, and fished in the lakes and streams. They gathered wild rice, berries and other edible plants. The Iroquois tapped the maple trees for their sap.

The Iroquois Confederacy

The Iroquois were the most powerful and aggressive of the Eastern Woodlands people. Their way of life was similar in some ways to that of the other woodlands tribes. What made them different was the way they were organized to defend themselves and attack other tribes. The name of the Iroquois was enough to bring terror to all those who knew of them in the sixteenth and seventeenth centuries.

The people we call Iroquois were a confederacy of five Indian Nations: the Mohawk, the Oneida, the Onondaga, the Seneca and the Cayuga. They were also known as the League of Five Nations. (Later a sixth tribe, the Tuscarora, joined the Iroquois Confederacy after English settlers forced them out of their homeland. When the Tuscarora joined, the Iroquois Confederacy became known as the Six Nations.)

At one time, each of these nations attacked each other as well as the Hurons and other tribes. Then they decided to band together, fight together and protect each other.

A white man's impression of an Iroquois warrior.

Members of the False Face Society and the Husk Face Society wore masks in ceremonies to heal the sick.

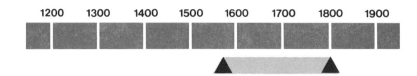

1200 1300 1400 1500 1600 1700 1800 1900

The Sachem

The Iroquois Confederacy was governed by a council of leaders called sachem. The sachem met whenever decisions about war or defence had to be made. They met at a place in Onondaga country. There, they planted a tree called The Tree of the Great Peace.

There were 50 sachem. The power of the sachem was limited. They were there to keep the confederacy tribes from fighting each other. The council had the power to order war chiefs to put armies together to protect Iroquois groups from a common enemy. But Iroquois war chiefs did not have to get permission to start a war on the Huron or other tribes. Wars were started often, even by individual warriors. Success in war was important to the Iroquois men.

The sachem were not always strong. The council met for only a few days each year. In an emergency, it might take several weeks to get messages to all the members of the council. Sachem were chosen by their family positions, not because they were good leaders.

Wampum belts of shell beads were made to remind the people of the laws of the confederacy. They were also used as money.

The Power of Women

A sachem was chosen by the women of the tribe. An older woman ruled each clan or family. She led the longhouse and lived in the apartment nearest the entrance. When the time came to name a new sachem, the head woman consulted with the other women of her family before naming the sachem.

Women ruled the family life of the Iroquois. Names and family traditions were passed down through the mother's side of the family. A young man's mother chose a wife for him. The mothers of the two met and arranged the marriage. The young couple were then told that they were man and wife. Fathers were not consulted in these matters. Yet the Iroquois men felt that women and women's work were inferior to men and men's work.

Hiawatha and Deganawidah

Hiawatha was a Mohawk chief. He wanted to end the wars that were weakening the tribes of the Eastern Woodlands. He was helped by a Huron prophet named Deganawidah. This means "double tongue," because he was a stutterer. Deganawidah had a dream about a great tree with five strong roots. The roots fed on three ideals: soundness of mind, justice for all, and military power for self-defence. Hiawatha told the tribes about his friend's dream. In about 1570, the Iroquois Confederacy of Five Nations was formed. The Hurons were invited, but they did not join. Later, the confederacy which the Huron Deganawidah had helped set up was to destroy his people.

Summary and Questions

The native people of Canada formed many tribes before the first Europeans arrived.

Contact with Europeans brought rapid change to the native cultures. Some groups, like the Plains people, flourished at first, as they acquired guns and horses from the newcomers. Others, like the Beothuks, were wiped out entirely. Different groups were affected at different rates, depending on where they lived. The Inuit of Canada's Arctic were the last to feel the full effect of European contact.

After contact with the Europeans, native people continued to be participants in the development of the country. They played important roles in the early exploration and settlement of Canada, the fur trade, the wars between the French and English, the American Revolution, the Northwest Rebellion and many other events in Canadian history.

Lessons for the Newcomers

The first European settlers in Canada learned a great deal from the native people. Without their assistance the Europeans might never have survived in Canada. The Hurons showed the French how to make spruce beer, which contained the vitamin C needed to prevent scurvy. Native people taught the newcomers about many other medicinal plants.

Native people also taught the settlers how to make light-weight bark canoes, and snowshoes, toboggans and dog sleds. The settlers learned the native skills of tracking animals and of trapping them.

From the native farmers of North America, Europeans learned to grow corn, beans, squash and tobacco. None of these was grown in Europe before the exploration of the Americas.

Native crews manned and guided the canoes of early explorers. Native guides led the Europeans across the Canadian shield, over the Great Plains, and through the Rocky Mountains. Today many of our highways and railroads follow the older trails along which the explorers were led.

Problems

In return, native peoples received guns, metal knives, and other products of European technology. The Europeans also brought with them diseases such as smallpox. The native people had had no contact with such diseases and had no resistance to them. Many died as disease spread quickly through native villages. Traders gave the native people brandy and other alcoholic drinks. Unused to alcohol and its effects, the native peoples suffered greatly. As European settlement spread, the native people lost their traditional hunting and farming lands. Many were placed on small areas of land called reserves. By the late nineteenth century the numbers of native peoples in Canada had dropped sharply.

Today, Canada's native peoples are growing in number again. They have kept their cultures alive, despite the pressures on them. Land claims, native rights and equal opportunities have become important goals for Canada's native peoples.

Can You Recall?

1. a) List at least four types of food that the people of the Northwest Coast obtained from the sea.
    b) How was each type cooked or preserved?
2. a) What is the name of the wood that the people of the Northwest Coast used so much of in their daily lives?
    b) List at least five things that they made from this wood.
3. What did the people of the Plateau live in during winter?
4. From whom did the people of the Plains get their first horses?
5. How did horses and guns change the way the Plains people hunted buffalo?
6. How did the Inuit find food in the harsh Arctic environment?
7. a) Define the word *nomad*.
    b) Why are the people of the Subarctic referred to as nomads?
8. Explain how the Beothuks of Newfoundland came to be wiped out.
9. What three crops were the main sources of food for the people of the Eastern Woodlands?
10. Describe the differences between jobs done by Iroquois men and women.

Ideas for Discussion

1. The natives of the Northwest Coast are often called "people of the sea." Discuss the importance of the sea to these people.
2. Describe the environment of the Plateau people. Discuss the ways in which it was different from that of the Northwest Coast.
3. The buffalo was like a supermarket on hooves to the people of the Plains. Discuss the various ways in which they used the buffalo.
4. Look at a map of Canada. Discuss reasons why the Inuit way of life was one of the last to be affected by the arrival of Europeans in Canada.

5. Discuss the reasons why the Northwest Coast and Eastern Woodlands peoples had large populations living in permanent villages. Why did the other native groups not do so?

Do Some Research

1. Many of the native peoples of Canada were very active traders. One of the most active groups was the Huron. Find out about the Huron fur trade. Using your atlas, find routes along which the Huron might have traded for furs with the Ojibwa, Algonquins or other people of the Subarctic. Make a map showing those routes and include it with your research report.
2. Make a research report describing the Ojibwa way of life. In your report use the following headings:
    a) Hunting bands
    b) Wigwams
    c) Clothing
    d) Games, Dances, and Celebrations
    e) "A World of Powerful Spirits."
3. Make a research report on the Iroquois Confederacy. Try to compare it to similar political organizations that exist today such as NATO.
4. Prepare a research report on Northwest Coast art. Include examples of various designs used in Northwest Coast art.

Be Creative

1. Make a display, poster or diorama showing the way of life of one of the native groups you have just studied. Include the following aspects of their culture: food, clothing, shelter, tools, transportation, art and religion.
2. Make models or draw pictures comparing the various types of houses made by the native peoples of Canada.
3. Make or draw examples of Northwest Coast or Iroquois masks. Display them in your classroom.

Exploration
ADVANCE ORGANIZER

1 What makes an explorer set out to find new and distant lands? Curiosity? The promise of fame? The lure of unknown riches? National pride? For all of these reasons men set out on voyages of discovery that led them to Canada.

Beginning in the tenth century, ships sailed west from Europe across the vast Atlantic ocean. These ships were made of wood. They were tiny compared to modern ships.

2 When they set out, the first explorers did not know what dangers lay ahead. They had none of the maps or navigation and communication systems that modern seafarers have.

3 The first Europeans known to have reached Canada were the Vikings. They sailed west from Iceland and Greenland into the Arctic and along the coast of Canada. The Vikings had settlements in Newfoundland, but did not stay long. We do not know why they left.

4 It is thought that Basque fishermen and whalers came to Newfoundland in the early 1400s. Fishermen from Portugal came to the rich cod-fishing grounds.

5 In the late 1400s, Europeans wanted to find a quick route to the riches of Asia. In 1492, Christopher Columbus sailed west. He found land he claimed for Spain. But it was not Asia: it was an island in the Caribbean.

6

John Cabot was next to sail west. In 1497, Cabot reached an island off the coast of Canada. He named his landfall Newfoundland and claimed it for the king of England.

7

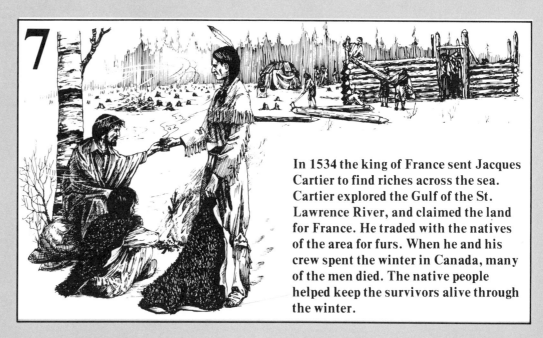

In 1534 the king of France sent Jacques Cartier to find riches across the sea. Cartier explored the Gulf of the St. Lawrence River, and claimed the land for France. He traded with the natives of the area for furs. When he and his crew spent the winter in Canada, many of the men died. The native people helped keep the survivors alive through the winter.

8

North America was in the way of ships trying to sail west to Asia. Some explorers tried to find a northern route around North America. Martin Frobisher, Henry Hudson and others sailed into Canada's northern waters in search of the Northwest Passage. The ice and cold defeated them.

9

The early attempts to reach Asia had failed. Explorers lost interest in Canada for a time. Then, in 1604, Samuel de Champlain sailed from France to Canada. On the shores of the Bay of Fundy, he founded a small colony. France had begun to settle Canada.

Introduction

What lies beyond the world that human beings have travelled? Today, we can make guesses about that distant world of space. We know about planets and galaxies and stars. Space probes and satellites and radar scans have let us travel with our minds and our eyes to regions where our feet could not take us.

For people living in Europe in the tenth century, things were very different. They knew the world that they themselves lived in, but very little more. What was out there beyond the horizon? Did anything exist there at all? Did monsters lurk, waiting for a chance to destroy anyone who ventured out of sight of land? Some people suggested that the world was round. If it was, you would eventually return home if you continued in the same direction. But how could you be sure of that?

Yet, in the tenth and eleventh centuries, explorers did begin to sail out across the Atlantic, away from known shores.

Sailing Into the Unknown

Back then, there was no way of finding out except by sailing into that unknown world. Explorers had none of the support that today's explorers rely on. There were no radio communications, no huge telescopes, no airplanes. Once you left home, you were on your own, in frail and fragile ships far smaller than ocean-going ships today.

The ships were powered by sail. There were no engines to move you out of danger if wind and waves threatened to smash you on the rocks. There were no canned foods to keep you alive if you could not find food on your journey. No one would send out a search party if you did not return when you were expected.

Why did they go? For some, it was a search for new and empty land. For some, it was a search for riches. And for some, surely, it was curiosity, the same curiosity that makes you wonder what is around the next corner or where a road leads.

These were the first explorers from Europe. They brought about the first meetings between the cultures of Europe and the cultures of Canada's native people.

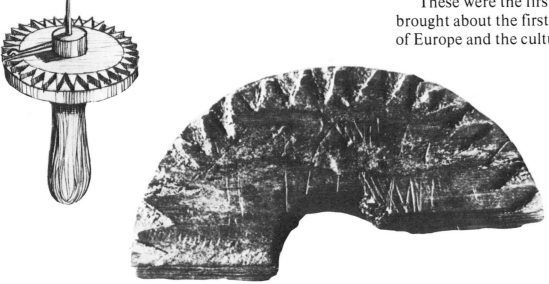

Wooden bearing dials were a type of sundial used by the Vikings for navigation one thousand years ago. This piece of bearing dial was found in Greenland. A whole bearing dial might have looked like the one on the left. At noon, the shadow of the centre pin would point north.

Some ideas about sea monsters were based on reports of real animals. Others were purely imaginary.

The Vikings

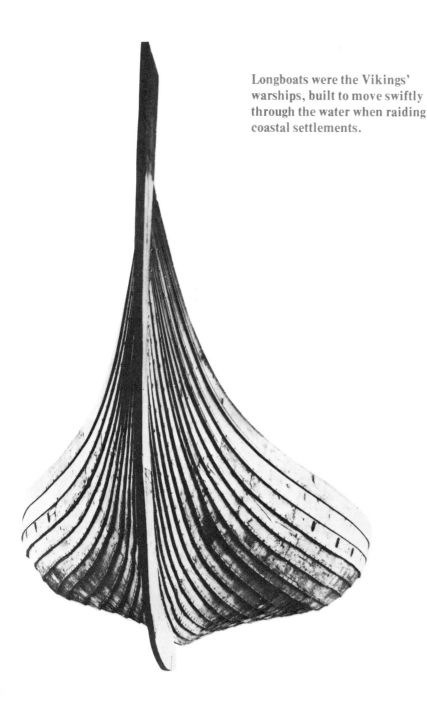

Longboats were the Vikings' warships, built to move swiftly through the water when raiding coastal settlements.

From the fury of the Northmen, deliver us O Lord! The people who cried out this prayer lived in terror of the Norsemen who might sweep down on European coastal settlements at any time. Who were the Norsemen and why were they so feared?

The Norse settlements perched by the edges of the fjords that cut deeply into the coast of what we now know as Scandinavia. There is little land here for farming. Yet there was enough to keep these settlements alive until the eighth century. Then their population began to increase until there were too many people for the land to support. Raiders, known as Vikings, swept out of the north, looking for other settlements to raid and plunder. They took their booty home with them. The Vikings brought terror to many of the people of Britain and northern Europe.

The Settlement of Iceland

Seeking new land for themselves, the Vikings started a settlement in Iceland. In 982, a Viking named Eric the Red was found guilty of murdering three of his neighbours and banished from Iceland for three years. He gathered other colonists and sailed westward to establish a settlement on what we know as Greenland.

Four years later, the Viking Bjarni sailed west from Iceland, but was blown off course. He sighted land before he turned north and east again, but he did not go ashore. It is thought that this was Newfoundland, and that Bjarni was the first European to glimpse the coast of North America.

In the year 1000, Leif the Lucky, son of Eric the Red, sailed west from Greenland and sighted two new lands. One was probably Baffin Island, the other

Labrador. He and his crew landed again further south. They called this place Vineland, because of the wild grapes that grew there. This may have been as far south as present-day New England or as far north as Newfoundland.

The Settlement in Vineland

The Vikings established settlements along the coast and traded with the native people, whom they called *Skraelings*. These were probably Inuit people. At first relations between the two groups were friendly. But then battles broke out as the native people realized that the newcomers intended to stay on their land.

Eventually, the Vikings abandoned their North American settlements. Perhaps the Skraelings drove them away. Perhaps the settlements were too far from their homes in Greenland and Iceland. Even though their stay was brief, they are acknowledged as the first Europeans to explore and settle on the coast of what is now Canada.

L'Anse aux Meadows

For many years archeologists have been looking for proof that the Vikings established a settlement in North America. In 1962, two Norwegians, Helge and Anne Ingstad, discovered the foundations of a Viking settlement at L'Anse aux Meadows in northern Newfoundland.

They found the remains of seven longhouses, a smithy, a steambath, two cooking pots and four boat sheds. One of the longhouses was 21 m by 17 m. It was very like the long Viking halls found in Greenland.

The settlement at L'Anse aux Meadows did not last long. But it does show that the Vikings lived in North America 500 years before Columbus.

Leif Ericson (Leif the Lucky)
BORN — about 975
DIED — about 1020
The son of Eric the Red, founder of the Viking colony in Greenland.
999 — sailed to Norway and was converted to Christianity. Returned to Greenland and converted many people. His father, Eric, was very angry about the new religion and separated from his wife because she became a Christian.
1002 — explored the east coast of North America. Saw lands he named Helluland (Land of Flat Stone — probably Baffin Island), Markland (Woodland — probably Labrador), and Vineland (Wineland — probably Newfoundland).
Leif's brothers later tried to establish a colony in Vineland.

Snorri

The sagas (Viking histories) record that a woman named Gudred was in the first Viking settlement. She gave birth to a child who was named Snorri. Snorri was the first European born in North America.

"Cattle die, kinsfolk die and we ourselves die. One thing lives on — a man's reputation."
from a Viking saga

Europe in the Age of Exploration

War and hunger, work and taxes, illness and death: these were the realities of life for most of the people of Europe. The kings, the queens, the lords and their ladies lived well, for they owned the land. They let the rest of the people — the peasants — work on the land. The peasants had to work for their lord and provide him with most of the crops they produced. The peasants had only a few vegetables, some barley and oats, and a few scrawny animals to keep them from starvation.

Europe at the end of the fourteenth century was not divided into countries as it is today. There was no France, no Spain, no Germany. Instead, there were many kings, princes and dukes. Each ruled a small area of Europe. Each had his own army. Wars were fought between neighbouring lords. In the fifteenth century this began to change. Some of the kings, stronger than the others, began to control larger and larger areas. Nations such as Spain, Portugal and France were created. The kings of these countries went to war against each other. All tried to gain control of more and more territory.

Trade with Asia

People began to explore outward from the lands of Europe. For centuries the people of the Mediterranean had traded with their Arab neighbours to the east. The Arabs in turn had traded with the Indians and the Chinese. Long caravan routes stretched from India through the mountains and deserts to the Mediterranean.

In 1275, a Venetian, Marco Polo, travelled eastward along the caravan routes across Asia and into China.

His trip took nearly 20 years. When he returned he wrote a book about his travels. In it he told stories of jewels, silks, perfumes and spices. The book Marco Polo wrote was read by many important people all across Europe. Interest in the riches of Asia increased. The kings and queens, princes and princesses of Europe were eager to buy them.

The rulers of Europe dressed in fine silks. Jewels sparkled in the crowns of kings and queens. Spices gave flavour to foods at feasts in noble homes and palaces. Food spoiled quickly in those days before refrigerators; spices hid the taste. They also made the taste of ordinary foods more exciting.

In the 1400s, Venice dominated shipping on the Mediterranean Sea. This meant Venice controlled the spice trade in Europe.

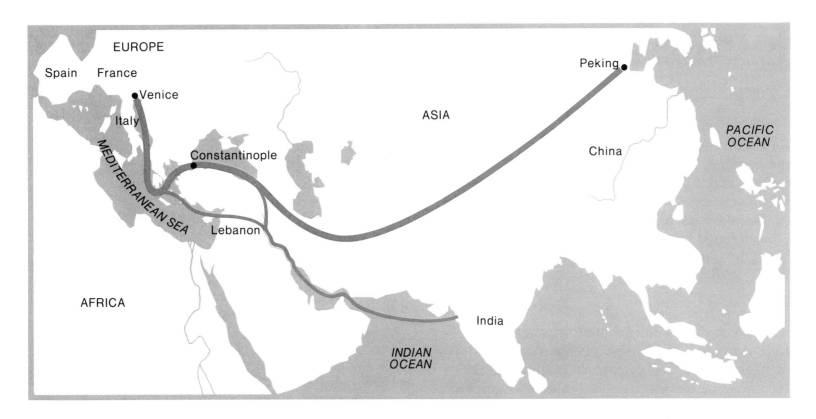

The Caravans

Merchants became rich because of the trade with the East. The merchants of Venice built large fleets of trading ships. Camel caravans would carry the fine goods across Asia to Constantinople or Lebanon. There the caravans were met by the ships. The ships carried the goods across the Mediterranean Sea to Europe.

The trip from Asia to Europe could take as long as three years. Bandits often attacked the caravans on their route through the mountains. Then, in the fifteenth century, the caravan routes were blocked completely. The armies of the Ottoman Empire captured Constantinople, driving out all foreigners. The trade with the East was barred to European traders. No longer could the caravans come overland, carrying the riches desired by the ruling families of Europe.

Loading a camel in Persia on the caravan route.

European Explorers

Europeans began to look for a cheaper, safer route to the Far East. The Portuguese were the first to seek a route by sea. Throughout the fifteenth century Portuguese ships tried to find a route around Africa to India and China. In 1497, Vasco da Gama rounded the Cape of Good Hope at the southern tip of Africa. He sailed on to India, returning in 1498.

Christopher Columbus

Before Vasco da Gama made his trip, another European sailor thought he and his crew were the first to reach India by sea. Christopher Columbus, an Italian sailing for Spain, sailed west from Europe in 1492. He was sure that he could reach India by sailing west. He reached land in October of that year. The land that Columbus had reached was an island in the Caribbean.

Columbus is often given credit for discovering America. But in the fifteenth century, many sailors knew that the world was round. Fishermen and whalers had sailed west for years, perhaps following the Viking routes. They sailed to Newfoundland where the waters were crowded with cod.

John Cabot

John Cabot (Giovanni Caboto) was a trader from Venice who knew of the route the fishermen followed to the west. He thought it might lead to Asia if he went further in the same direction. He wanted to be the first to find a new trade route to the riches of the Orient.

At first he approached the Venetian merchants, but they gave him no help. His next stop was Bristol, England. There he persuaded the merchants to finance his trip to the west. On May 2, 1497, Cabot and his crew of 18 men left Bristol. Their ship was the *Matthew*, just 40 m long.

Fifty-two days later, the sailors sighted land. But it was not China. Cabot called this unknown land on which he landed Newfoundland. He planted the flag of the English King, Henry VII and claimed the land for England. Then he sailed north, looking for settlements. Finally, he sailed for home and, pushed by westerly winds, reached Bristol 15 days later.

John Cabot's ship, the *Matthew*.

Cod Fish

Cabot did not find a new route to the east. We think now that he may have landed on Cape Breton Island. But he did bring news of something that other sailors had known for some time. He told the merchants of Bristol and the court of England about the great schools of cod that swam off the banks of the coast he had ''discovered.''

Cabot reported that fish in the new waters were so plentiful that at times they slowed his boat. Cabot's reports led to the growth of a fishing fleet. The ships made the trip to Newfoundland's Grand Banks for the cod fishing every year for centuries.

Cabot set out the next year with five ships, to make a new search for a route to the riches of the east. What happened to him? No one knows. A storm came up and he landed for a short time in Ireland. Then he set sail once more — and he and his ships disappeared forever. However, he had made the first English claim in North America.

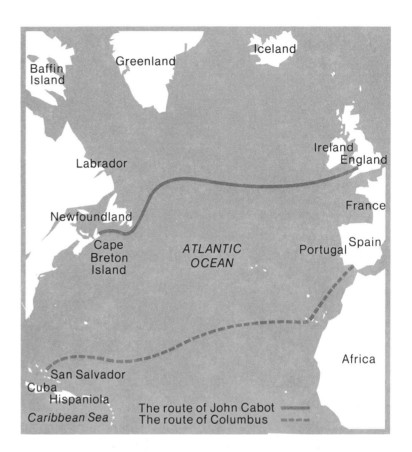

The route of John Cabot ——
The route of Columbus - - - -

Newfoundland
John Cabot gave the name ''New Found Land'' to the land he discovered. Historians now think he probably reached Cape Breton Island. But in the early 1500s, sailors and fishermen thought he meant the island we now call Newfoundland.

Cod (Gadus morhua)
DESCRIPTION: Dark spotted fish, ranging in colour from green-grey to black — some are even red. Average length, 75 to 100 cm; average mass, 11.5 kg.
BORN: In the cold waters of the north Atlantic Ocean.
HABITS: Found in large numbers off the east coast of Canada. Follows set migration routes from spawning grounds in shallow waters out to deeper water. A female may lay millions of eggs each season.
HISTORY: Codfish were so abundant off the mouth of the Saint Lawrence River in the 16th century that they appeared to fill the waters. As early as the 15th century, English, French and Portuguese fishermen were crossing the Atlantic to catch cod. An important part of the diet in Europe. The church decreed that no one could eat meat on Fridays.

Jacques Cartier

In the early 1500s, Spain and Portugal had started colonies in Central and South America. The Spanish were bringing back shiploads of gold from their new empire. In 1522, Ferdinand Magellan and his Spanish ship and crew sailed around the world. They proved that the riches of the east could be reached by sailing to the west.

The king of France was determined that France would join in this search for riches. In 1534, he sent Jacques Cartier to find a route to the east — or to find riches in America. Twenty days after Cartier left St. Malo, on the French coast, he sighted Newfoundland. He entered what is now called the Gulf of St. Lawrence. Then he turned south, exploring every bay or sound that might lead further west. Finding nothing promising, he turned north again. On the Gaspé peninsula, he and his crew built a cross 10 m high. Mounted on it was a shield with the words ''Vive le Roi de France'' and three fleurs-de-lis.

A party of Iroquois from a village called Stadacona was hunting on the Gaspé. Some of them paddled out to meet Cartier. Cartier kept on board two sons of the chief, Donnacona. He took the two boys back with him to France, promising to return them home the following year.

Cartier Reports to the King

Cartier did not bring gold or silver home with him. Nor had he discovered a way through America to China and Japan. But he did bring the two young Indians. And he also brought stories of the fish in the waters and the forested land he had seen. These were enough to persuade the king of France to send him west again.

On this second voyage, Cartier took three ships and 110 men. He reached the native village at Stadacona and returned the young Indians to their father. The Indians told Cartier about a village further up the river, at Hochelaga. They also told him the river he was following "goes so far no man has ever been to the end."

Cartier knew that this freshwater route would probably not lead to an ocean. But he wanted to see where the river would lead. He led an expedition to the large Indian village at Hochelaga. He climbed to the top of a hill he named Mont Réal (Royal Mountain). From here he could see the rapids upstream. He realized he could not follow this river, and returned to Stadacona where he and his men prepared for winter.

Winter Suffering at Stadacona

It was a horrifying winter. Snow drifted ever higher. The winds swept in from the north. The cold crept into every corner and chilled the men as they had never been chilled before. Illness came over them. Men suffered with bleeding gums, swellings in their legs and arms, and high fever.

The natives showed Cartier the cure for this strange disease, called scurvy. Still, many died. The natives began to be less friendly now that it looked as if the French might want to stay permanently.

The next spring, Cartier and what was left of his crew sailed for home. First, they invited the Indians to a feast. At the feast, they kidnapped Chief Donnacona, and took him back to the French king. Donnacona told the king of the mysterious "Kingdom of the Saguenay," rich in gold and rubies and all that a man might desire. Here, he said, white men like the French lived. He probably told these tales in the hope that the French would make another voyage and take him home. But he died in France.

The king of France determined that there must be a third voyage to test these stories. In 1541, Cartier set out again, this time with five ships and a large crew. Again, winter swept in and again the men suffered from the bitter cold and from the strange disease they could not cure. And the Indians were now not friendly at all. In the spring, Cartier and his men, discouraged and no longer believing the stories, went home. France would not try again to establish a settlement for another 60 years.

Canada
The origin of the name Canada is believed to be an Iroquois word meaning a collection of houses. In 1535, the Iroquois described the land to Cartier. They pointed to the land on the north shore of the St. Lawrence and said "Kanata." They probably meant the village at that place. But the French applied the word to the entire area. Later the name was extended to the whole country.

When Columbus reached the West Indies in 1492, he thought he was in India. He called the natives *Indians*. This mistaken name came to be used for all the native peoples of the Americas. The natives themselves never used this term. They had names only for their own people, such as *Iroquois* or *Haida*.

The Search for the Northwest Passage

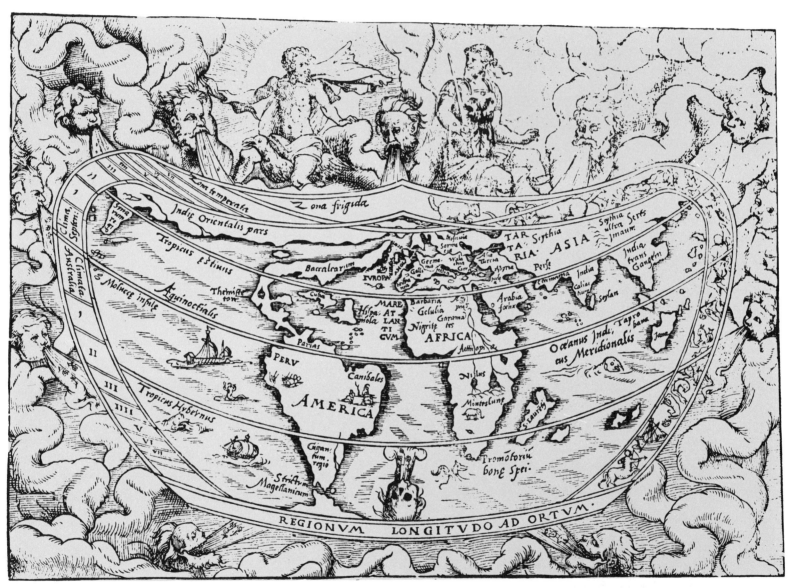

This map of the world was published in 1544. By then, Europeans knew a lot about South America. They knew how big it was. They knew that the route to Asia round Cape Horn through the Straits of Magellan was long and dangerous. But they knew little about North America. They thought it was much smaller than it really was. People were still hoping to find an easy way across the north to get to Asia.

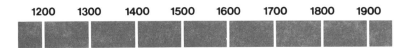

America was definitely in the way. You couldn't go over it to reach China and Japan. You couldn't go through it — at least, no one had found a water route to the west. Yet there must be some way of getting past this bulky continent that barred the way to the Orient.

The first explorers tried to find a route to the south. Spanish sailors rounded Cape Horn and sailed into the Pacific. But the English and French dared not try this route, since the powerful Spanish fleet would attack if they did. And it was a very long way from England and France to South America. They decided instead that they would try to find a route to the north of the Americas.

They knew very little about this northern route. How long was it? How cold was it? How much ice barred the way? They were determined to find out.

Henry Hudson

One explorer to tackle the north was Henry Hudson. An Englishman who sailed for Holland, Hudson explored Hudson strait and Hudson Bay in 1610. But Arctic ice is cruel to men at sea. The nights are long and lonely and the weather freezing cold. Soon Hudson's men demanded that the ships return home. Hudson refused. The crew threw Hudson, his son and the loyal crew members into a small open boat and set them adrift. They were never seen again. The mutineers set off for home. Four stood trial for piracy. Robert Bylot, who had joined the mutineers, was not tried. He went on to an honoured career as an Arctic explorer himself.

The Passage is Found

In the following years, more ships came to the bay. These ships and the men aboard were more interested in the furs that might be found on land than they were in breaking through the ice to the west. The search for the passage continued, however. Finally, at the beginning of the twentieth century, a Norwegian, Roald Amundsen, made the trip through the Northwest passage in the *Gjoa*. The *Gjoa* was so small that she only held a crew of six. The ship took three years to make the trip from 1903 to 1906. In 1942 an RCMP ship, the *St. Roch,* captained by Sergeant Henry Larsen, made an uninterrupted journey through the Northwest Passage from the west to the east. In 1944 the voyage was repeated from the east to the west.

By the 1960s, oil was discovered in the Arctic. This again raised the question of ships in northern seas.

Martin Frobisher
BORN — Doncaster, England, date not known
DIED — Brest, France, 1594
1576 — Queen Elizabeth I invested in an attempt to find a Northwest Passage to be led by Frobisher. He sailed into Frobisher Bay. Brought back a chunk of black rock. "Experts" in London said it was gold ore.
1577 — returned for more ore. Brought back nearly 200 t. But it was iron pyrites — "fool's gold".
1578 — on third voyage, turned back just before discovering Hudson Bay.
1588 — fought under Sir Francis Drake against Spanish Armada. Knighted for his bravery.
1594 — died of bullet wound received in naval attack on Brest, France.

Samuel de Champlain

For 60 years, memories of bitter winters and ugly deaths kept France from trying to settle in America. Some traders came to the St. Lawrence to seek furs. Some fishermen made the yearly trip to load their ships with cod. But no French people came to live in Canada.

Other countries continued to explore. To the north, English explorers sought a northwest passage to China. The English claimed Newfoundland as an English colony. The French began to worry. They wanted a base from which they could seek a passage to the East. They also wanted a share of the riches, whether furs or gold, to be found in the new land.

In 1604, a new French expedition, headed by the Sieur de Monts, with Samuel de Champlain as one of the ships' captains and map-maker for the trip, set out from France. They dropped anchor in what is now called the Bay of Fundy. They decided to winter on an island near the mouth of the St. Croix River.

Champlain's drawing of the habitation at Port Royal.

The Founding of Port Royal

Cold, hunger and scurvy again took a fearsome toll. By spring, 35 of the 79 would-be settlers were dead. The settlement could not survive in this unpleasant and marshy place. When spring came, the survivors moved across the bay, to a place they called Port Royal.

This settlement became the first successful French settlement in Canada. The French became friends with the Micmac Indians and were able to trade for furs and other goods. The Micmacs taught the new arrivals much about how to survive in this land. It seemed that, at last, the French had found their place in the new world.

Yet the location of Port Royal frustrated the French. There was little country surrounding the fort where furs could be obtained. From Port Royal it was not easy to explore inland and to seek out a western passage. De Monts and Champlain decided that they must establish another settlement.

Quebec

The location they chose carried bad memories for the French. It was Stadacona, where Cartier's men had suffered and starved and died. But this time, the French thought they had learned enough about Canada to build a successful settlement. Champlain and his men built a habitation where they spent the winter. Again, it was a difficult winter. But the settlement slowly, very slowly prospered and grew. By 1650, there were still only 70 people living at Quebec — but the colony had lasted long enough to prove France's claim to New France.

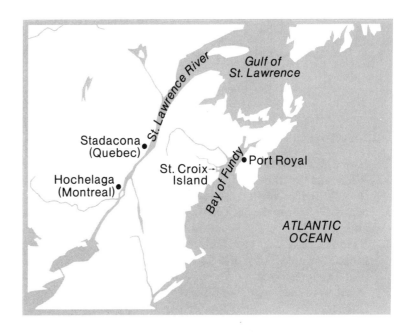

Marguerite de Roberval
BORN — about 1520
DIED — about 1570
When Cartier made his third trip to the New World in 1541, the king sent the Sieur de Roberval to establish a colony. Roberval brought along his niece, Marguerite. On the voyage, she fell in love with a young sailor. Roberval was furious. To punish her, he left Marguerite, her lover and an elderly servant on an uninhabited island. Marguerite called it the Isle of Demons. It was probably Fogo Island, off the coast of Newfoundland. The small group lived like Robinson Crusoe. They built a cabin, hunted, caught fish and collected berries. Marguerite became pregnant. Before the baby was born, her lover died. She had to take care of the baby and the elderly servant. One day she killed three bears. One was "as white as an egg."

Within a year, both the servant and the baby died. Marguerite was left all alone. For two years and five months she survived on the island. Finally she saw a ship. She lit a fire and was rescued by some fishermen from Brittany. They took her back to France.

Sixty years later, Champlain heard the story of Marguerite de Roberval. If she could survive, a colony could do so too.

Questions

Can You Recall?

1. How did the Vikings travel to North America?
2. What was the name the Vikings gave to the place where they settled in North America?
3. Marco Polo brought back news of _____, _____ and _____ to the people of Europe.
4. Basque _____ and fishermen from _____ probably were sailing into Canadian waters before explorers like Cartier arrived.
5. What were explorers like Christopher Columbus trying to find?
6. Who claimed Newfoundland for England (1497)?
7. In what year did Jacques Cartier first come to Canada?
8. For what country did Cartier claim the lands along the St. Lawrence River?
9. Name the two settlements founded by Champlain.

Ideas for Discussion

1. Discuss the reasons why Europeans began to explore west across the Atlantic in the fifteenth and sixteenth centuries.
2. What was the importance of the voyages of Jacques Cartier?
3. Discuss the importance of the search for the Northwest Passage.
4. Explain the ways in which Champlain differed from other early explorers.
5. Compare the early exploration of North America in the time of Cabot, Cartier and Champlain with space exploration today. In what ways are they similar? In what ways are they different?

Do Some Research

1. Native people provided "the first prescription" in North America to help Cartier and his crew survive the winter at Stadacona. Cartier's crew were suffering from *scurvy*. Scurvy is caused by a lack of vitamin C. What foods were available for sailors and explorers to take on long journeys? Find out how people learned to prevent scurvy. Why were British sailors called *limeys*?

The first prescription.

2. Write a brief report on the Northwest Passage. Your report should include:
   a) What we mean by the term *Northwest Passage.*
   b) Why explorers sought this passage.
   c) The *difficulties* in finding the passage.
   d) The importance of one of the following in the search for the passage:
   Martin Frobisher
   Henry Hudson
   John Franklin
   Roald Amundsen
   Henry Larsen

3. A group activity — after studying about the Northwest Passage, your group should prepare a folder about this adventurous search. Your folder should include:
   a) a *map* showing the voyages of several explorers.
   b) a *letter* to your family describing the problems of sailing in the Arctic.
   c) a *drawing* of one ship engaged in the search for the Northwest Passage.
   d) a *newspaper report* describing any event in this search.

4. On a map of eastern Canada, show the routes sailed or explored by Champlain.

5. On 7 June 1613, Champlain lost his *astrolabe* while exploring near the Ottawa River. More than 250 years later in 1867, this astrolabe was found near Pembroke, Ontario by a farmer ploughing his field. It is almost certainly the one Champlain lost. What is an astrolabe? How is it used to plot one's position? Compare the astrolabe with the bearing dial used by the Vikings. What instruments do modern explorers, sailors and airplane pilots use today to work out exactly where they are?

Be Creative

1. Draw a picture or write a poem describing a Viking raid.
2. Make a picture gallery showing the types of ships that the Vikings and other early European explorers used to cross the Atlantic.
3. Write a letter home from either:
   a) a member of Jacques Cartier's crew,
      or
   b) a colonist at Port Royal in 1605.
4. Make a gallery using pictures you have drawn of Columbus, Cabot, Cartier, Frobisher, Hudson, and Champlain. Include a brief biocard on each.

Champlain's astrolabe.

Eastern Settlement
ADVANCE ORGANIZER

1

The early explorers were followed by other Europeans who came to settle the New World across the sea. Some people cleared land and started farms. Others went out in search of furs, gold and other valuable goods. Soon there were villages and towns in many parts of the New World.

2

The colonists came to lands that were already occupied by native peoples. Most colonists did not understand the native peoples' ways of life, but the new settlers learned important skills from them. Without their help, many of the pioneers in the New World would not have survived. Native peoples were sometimes forced to help the colonists. Some turned against the settlers.

3

The first colony in Canada was established by the French. Located along the Bay of Fundy, it was called Acadia. The first settlement in Acadia was Port Royal, founded in 1605 by Samuel de Champlain. Other settlers followed, and the colony slowly grew.

Word List

charter	deport	*habitation*
colonist	dyke	missionary
continent	expand	*seigneur*
convert	*habitant*	strategy

4

The French settled along the St. Lawrence soon after Acadia was founded. The St. Lawrence colony grew quickly. The French had a rich fur trade with the native peoples. Towns grew up at Quebec, Montreal and Trois Rivières. Missionaries were sent to convert the native people to Christianity. Some French settlers came to farm the lands along the St. Lawrence.

5

At the same time that the French were building Port Royal, England was quickly building colonies along the Atlantic coast south of Acadia. The first English colony in North America was Virginia, established in 1607. Soon more colonies followed.

6

There was no peace between the English and French colonies. France and England were enemies in Europe. Some of their battles were fought in North America. Each country fought to take over the other country's colonies. By 1760, Britain controlled almost all of eastern North America.

Acadia

Players in a Game

The game was about to begin. The players were France and England. The board was Canada. The stakes were the fisheries, the fur trade and the land we call Canada. The pawns — moved across the board and sacrificed by the main players — were the people who came to Canada to make new lives in the forests of the new land.

For 150 years, France and England would start their settlements, fight their wars and battle for this land. The game would begin in Acadia, the area we now know as Nova Scotia.

When Champlain and his settlers came to Port Royal, they chose a carefully protected place for their settlement. The land along the eastern shore of the Bay of Fundy was good farming land. It was protected from the bad weather and cold winters that the French had found along the St. Lawrence to the north.

But the bay was not a good place to be in the war between French and English. It would be too easy for the settlers in New England to attack Acadia. It would be too difficult for the French to defend the settlement. Thus, the Acadians and the Micmac Indians with whom they shared Acadia would become the victims in the struggle.

In 1605, the French colonists moved to the mouth of the Annapolis River. They built a habitation of logs, a fortlike building with a wall of logs around it. It contained kitchens, storerooms, sleeping rooms and a chapel. This was Port Royal, the first permanent settlement. The settlers called the land Acadia.

The Acadian colonists were well prepared for the cold of winter. But their leader, Samuel de Champlain, realized that boredom and illness might destroy more men than the cold.

The Order of Good Cheer

Champlain decided to fight both enemies through the Order of Good Cheer (in French, *l'Ordre de Bon Temps*). The order provided good food to fight illness and theatrical performances to prevent boredom. Each week, a banquet was organized by a member of the company; each dinner began with a parade and a ceremony.

Duck, goose, grouse, venison, caribou, rabbit, fresh fish, bread and wine might all be part of the dinner. After dinner, there were songs, dancing and plays. The Micmacs often helped provide game and on several occasions Champlain invited their chief to join the banquet. Not a man died that second winter in Acadia.

The next spring, crops were planted, the habitation was improved and trade with the Micmacs increased. All seemed to be going well — but only for a short while.

The Sieur de Monts had been given an exclusive licence to trade with the Indians in Acadia. In 1606, the

Then, one day in 1613, foreign ships sailed into the bay. Men swarmed ashore and set fire to the settlers' homes and the crops in the fields. The raid, led by Samuel Argall of the Virginia colony to the south, was intended to drive away the settlers.

It did not succeed. Once the raiders sailed away, the settlers emerged from the forests where they had hidden and set about rebuilding their homes.

This picture of Argall's raid appeared in a book on America published in France in 1619.

Louis Hébert sows his first crop at Quebec.

Louis Hébert
BORN: **Paris, France, date unknown**
DIED: **Quebec, 1627**
Hébert was an apothecary (druggist) at French court.
1604 — joined the colonists headed for Acadia. At Port Royal, experimented with farming. Was particularly interested in growing herbs for medicine.
1614 — returned to France.
1617 — persuaded by Champlain to settle in Quebec.
1623 — granted land for a farm on the site of what is now the Upper Town of Quebec.
1627 — died on his farm as a result of a fall.
Hébert was the first Canadian farmer. Many French Canadian families trace their descent to him.

king of France changed his mind and opened trade to others. The Sieur de Monts decided he could not afford the colony if there were other traders taking the furs from him. He decided to give up the Port Royal colony.

The Settlers Return

For four years, no one lived at Port Royal. Then, in 1610, one of the original settlers at the habitation, Biencourt, returned with a small group of settlers. Again, crops were planted and trade began.

Growth of Settlement

The real settlement of Acadia by the French began about 25 years after Argall's attack on Port Royal. Even then, settlement was slow, with only a few dozen people arriving from France each year.

Half the settlers who came to Acadia were poor people from the cities of France. Others were soldiers who had left the army. Fewer than one-quarter had any farming experience.

The new settlers usually came to Acadia as *engagés* — that is, they promised to work for a seigneur who owned the land. In fact, they rarely had to do much work for the seigneur.

At first, the settlers depended on the Micmac Indians for help. The Micmacs taught them the skills of hunting and fishing and of building birch bark canoes.

The Settlers Thrive

But the soil of Acadia was fertile. Farming quickly became the centre of Acadian life. The life the settlers built for themselves in Acadia was better than their life in France. They were better fed and healthier than French families. Many of the children born in France at that time died soon after birth. In Acadia, the death rate for children was very low.

The population of Acadia began to grow quickly after 1650, when there were about 200 people living there. By 1670, there were more than 370 colonists.

Micmac Indians.

New settlements grew up at Les Mines, Beaubassin and other places along the Bay of Fundy. By 1750, there were nearly 10 000 Acadians.

The Acadians led simple lives. Most were illiterate, unable to read or write. Priests and government officials were the only ones who could read or write. Some of the priests were missionaries sent to convert the Indians to Christianity.

The settlers lived in small houses made of rough planks laid over log frames. Some homes were built of squared logs pegged into log uprights at each corner.

The Acadians had to depend on their own skills or on those they learned from the Indians. They had to make their own furniture and tools, their own clothing, medicines and food. They received little help from France. It seemed that France did not think that Acadia was important.

Farming the Marshes

The tides along the Bay of Fundy surge 12 m up the land that rings the bay. They carry with them the silt and soil dredged from the coasts of the bay. As they roll over the land, they drop the soil, then slide slowly back to low tide and the sea. The soil that they leave behind is excellent for farming. The Acadian settlers who came from Brittany remembered the Breton way of dyking the tidal marshes in Brittany. They decided to copy those dykes in Acadia. They built dykes around the tidal marshlands to keep the salt water out. These log and sod dykes had to be high enough and strong enough to keep the high tides from flooding the marshes.

Once the dykes were built, the fields had to be left alone for at least a year. In that time, rain and the streams that ran through them could wash out the salt that would keep crops from growing.

Gates were built into the dykes to let out the water as it washed away the salt. At high tide, these gates kept the sea water from coming back in.

Once the salt was washed out, the land could be used for farming. Because the soil was very fertile, grain crops grew well. The Acadians also grew peas and, in smaller vegetable plots, cabbage and turnips.

The Acadians used the natural grass that grew along the marshes as hay fodder for farm animals. The Acadians raised sheep, hogs and cattle. Cattle were important, especially in the Beaubassin area. Horses came late and in small numbers to Acadia.

Nicolas Denys
BORN: Tours, France, 1598
DIED: Nepisiguit (Bathurst, N.B.), 1688
1632 — came to Acadia. Set up Canada's first lumber business. Built fishing and trading posts at various places in Acadia.
1653 — thrown in prison by a merchant who claimed his lands at Nepisiguit and Saint-Pierre.
1654 — appointed governor of the coasts and islands in the Gulf of St Lawrence, including Newfoundland.
1669 — Fire destroyed Denys's trading post at Saint-Pierre. He returned to France.
1671 — wrote *The Description and Natural History of the Coasts of North America,* an entertaining book about Acadia.
1685 — came back to Acadia at age of 87.
Nicknamed "la Grande Barbe" for his full beard.

The French and the English

While the French were beginning to build settlements in Acadia and Quebec, the English were starting their own colonies to the south. These were known as the New England colonies.

The New England colonies grew more quickly than Acadia. More people came to live in New England. Industries such as shipbuilding and tool making were growing in New England. Trading ships from England and the Caribbean arrived regularly in ports such as Boston.

The things that the Acadians could not grow or make themselves, they had to buy from somewhere else. Traders from New England were able to bring these goods to Acadia. They sailed to Acadia more often than the French, and they offered a better price than the French.

Each spring, three or four ships from New England would visit the Acadian settlements. By foot or by canoe, the Acadians would come down to the ships from their farms. They would bring their livestock, wheat, fur and feathers. These were traded for the molasses, brandy, sugar and manufactured goods offered by the New Englanders.

The French did not like the Acadians to trade with the New Englanders. But the French could do little to stop the trade. The Acadians thought they had been neglected by France. They felt that they no longer had to do what France told them to do. They thought of themselves as Acadians, not as French people.

French-English Clashes

The name *Acadia* was given to a large area of land that included what we now know as Nova Scotia, Prince Edward Island and New Brunswick. The French claimed all this land, but their settlements were small and clustered around the Bay of Fundy.

The English also claimed this land. In 1621, King James I of England gave Acadia to Sir William Alexander. Alexander, a Scot, named the country Nova Scotia (New Scotland). His son tried to start a colony there, but the settlement soon failed.

The Attraction of Acadia

Why did England and France both want Acadia? England had settlements in Newfoundland and controlled the cod fishing off the Grand Banks there. France had settlements along the St. Lawrence and controlled the fur trade with the Indians. Whoever could control Acadia would control the approaches to the St. Lawrence and the fur trade. They would also have control over the cod fishing off Cape Cod.

Acadia Changes Hands

1604 — French set up colony on St. Croix Island.
1605 — Move to Port Royal.
1613 — Captain Argall raids Port Royal, but the colony remains French.
1628 — Scots drive French out of Port Royal and attempt to set up colony.
1632 — Acadia returned to France by treaty.
1654 — Port Royal captured by New England troops.
1668 — Treaty of Breda gives Acadia back to France.
1690 — Port Royal captured again by New England troops under Sir William Phips.
1697 — Acadia returned to France. Raids continue.
1710 — English recapture Acadia for final time.

Boston in 1722.

For the next 100 years, Acadia was handed back and forth as the two countries fought over the fisheries and the fur trade. But Acadia was not the only battlefield for the French and English. The two countries were struggling for all of North America.

The Indians Become Involved

Much of the fighting was done by Indian allies. The Iroquois fought for the English. The Huron and, in Acadia, the Micmacs, fought for the French.

The struggles between the two countries ended for a while after the Peace of Utrecht, signed in 1713. This treaty gave the English control over Hudson Bay, Newfoundland and Acadia.

The colony at Acadia was richer in natural resources than France's other settlements in North America. There were furs available from the Indians. There were excellent harbours, access to the world's best cod-fishing grounds, good farming lands, huge stands of timber, coal and even a mild climate.

Yet France failed to defend her colony. She let the colonists fall under the influence of New England traders and left them defenceless against attack.

British Rule and Deportation

Once the Peace of Utrecht was signed, the Acadians became British subjects. They were given one year to leave Acadia if they wished to remain French. The French wanted them to do so. The French still owned Cape Breton Island and Ile St. Jean. The Acadians were asked to move to these two islands.

Louisbourg is Built

But most of the Acadians remained where they were along the Bay of Fundy. On Cape Breton Island (called Ile Royale by the French), the French began to build a fortified military port. The town was solidly built of stone and was thought to be safe from attack. It was named Louisbourg, for the king of France.

French settlers from Placentia in Newfoundland were brought to settle Louisbourg. Learning from their experiences in Acadia, the French stationed a large number of soldiers at Louisbourg.

The Acadians under British rule were asked to take an oath of loyalty. They refused. They did promise not to fight on either side if the wars between France and England started again. The British were doubtful — but they let the Acadians stay on their farms. They were known as the "Neutral French."

Halifax is Built

The British decided to make themselves strong in Acadia so that they would not lose the region again. They brought a strong army to Nova Scotia. They also brought in settlers. Halifax, now the capital of Nova Scotia, was built in 1749 as a military and naval base. The British thought that if they could build a strong

Louisbourg.

base of their own, they might be able to drive the French out of Acadia altogether.

During the summer of 1749, naval transports brought more than 2500 people to Halifax. Slowly a town took shape; 300 houses were put up, but there was still not enough room for all the settlers. Some of them spent the winter aboard ships; others lived in cold and draughty tents.

The Micmacs, aroused by French missionaries who also worked for the French government, attacked Halifax. A party of men, building a sawmill at Dartmouth across the harbour from Halifax, was ambushed and killed. A wall was built to protect Halifax. The British offered a reward of 10 guineas for each Micmac or Acadian scalp.

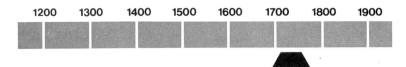
New Settlers Arrive

The British decided to bring in more settlers. They decided to send "foreign Protestants" — mostly Germans and Swiss — to Nova Scotia to offset the Catholic Acadians. Other colonists were recruited in Holland. French Protestants came from Normandy and Brittany.

Several thousand foreign Protestants arrived in Nova Scotia between 1750 and 1753, most of them German speaking. They settled mainly in the area around Lunenburg. German was the chief language in this area until well into the nineteenth century.

A look at the map shows that the settlers at Halifax and Lunenburg formed a pocket of settlement well removed from the Acadian settlements around the Bay of Fundy. The two groups of settlers were suspicious of each other.

Even though Halifax guarded Acadia, the Nova Scotia colony felt insecure. The French Acadians outnumbered the British and their settlers nearly three to one. The British were not sure that the Acadians would stay neutral. They thought that the missionaries might persuade the Acadians to rebel.

In 1755, British fears grew. Word was received that 4000 French soldiers were to be stationed at Louisbourg. The British governor demanded again that the Acadians take an oath of loyalty. The Acadians refused.

The British were also unhappy about the religion of the Acadians. The Protestant settlers did not like Acadian Catholics. When the missionaries persuaded the Micmacs to attack the British settlements, this unhappiness became even stronger.

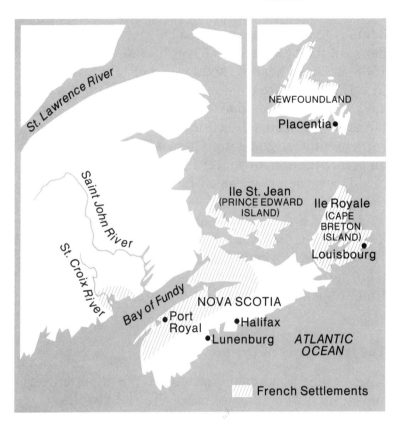

Deportation of the Acadians

Finally, in 1755, the British ordered the Acadians to leave Acadia. More than 8000 of the 10 000 French Acadians were driven off their land and herded like cattle aboard British ships. Families were broken up, never to see each other again. Many died at sea. Those who survived were sent to English colonies to the south. Some went as far as Louisiana, where their decendants still live.

English, Scottish and German settlers took over the fertile lands along the Bay of Fundy, and England took firm control of her section of Acadia.

Champlain's Dream

Samuel de Champlain watched his men working by the banks of the St. Lawrence River. In this summer of 1608, he could hear the sounds of axes biting into wood as trees were cut down. The ring of shovels and axes as they struck stones echoed through the forest. Under Champlain's direction, the walls of a fortified settlement were going up. There would be rooms for all before the cold of winter came. The ditches would be dug and the drawbridge would be ready to protect the settlement.

Champlain could draw upon the experience and knowledge he had gained at Port Royal in Acadia, five years earlier. His knowledge would prevent his men from suffering the same fate as Cartier's, who had tried to spend the winter at the very same spot.

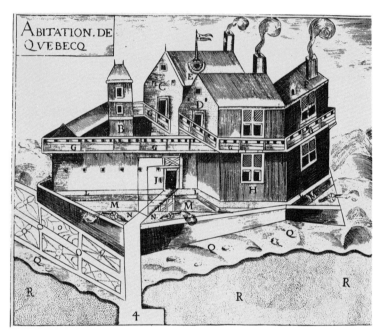

Champlain's drawing of the habitation at Quebec.

The Importance of Quebec

Like Cartier, Champlain recognized the importance of the location where the waters of the St. Lawrence suddenly narrowed. Once it had been the site of the Iroquois village of Stadacona, where Cartier spent the winter. Now it was to become the site of Quebec, the capital of the colony of New France.

From Champlain's fortress several cannons would point over the river. Let any enemy try to pass up river and a shot across the bow would turn him for home as fast as sails could carry him. With Quebec as its capital and its protection, New France could flourish on the shores of the St. Lawrence.

Champlain had a magnificent dream for this colony. He saw towns and farms, soldiers and settlers, furs that could be traded home to France and tall straight trees for ship building. He thought that here, along the St. Lawrence, a true "new" France could be created.

How New France Developed

Some parts of Champlain's dream came true. People came from France to live in the town of Quebec and to start farms along the river banks. Missionaries, priests and nuns came to New France to teach the French and the Indians. Fur traders went inland to gather the rich furs of the region. Explorers struggled overland to within sight of the Rocky Mountains. Bustling towns grew up along the river.

But some of Champlain's hopes did not come to pass. The first French colony and the first English colony in North America were founded at about the same time. Yet, 150 years later, more than 2 000 000 people lived in the English colonies. Only 60 000 people lived in the French colonies. The French colonies would always need help and support from France. The English colonies could survive on their own.

And when the time came for war between France and Britain, it would be the British who would win. Champlain's dream of French colonies would be over.

Champlain's dream for New France was strong and clear. As the land he had come to love began to grow, he might have written a letter like this to the the king of France.

Summer, 1618

Farms along the St. Lawrence River today.

New France is a beautiful land. It has great rivers and lakes, full of fish. The forests run for hundreds of miles. There is endless lumber for shipbuilding and homes in France. Much land near the St. Lawrence River is suitable for farming. From the river, you can paddle by rivers and lakes to huge open waters which have never been explored. I believe that they will lead to China.

But the key to it all is Quebec. We must build a strong fort and large settlement here. We should bring over the Recollet friars to convert the Indians. We need families to settle here permanently. We must bring over domestic animals for their farms. We must provide soldiers to protect the community. We must develop the fisheries. The waters are full of cod, salmon and whale. We must establish shipbuilding. We must mine the minerals here. Farms will provide us with our meat and food. Vineyards can provide us with our wine. The fur trade can be encouraged even more.

If we do not do this, the colony will fail. The English and Dutch are establishing settlements to the south. If Quebec does not grow, it will fall to them.

Hélène Boulle Champlain
BORN: France, 1598
DIED: Ursuline Convent, Meaux, France, 1654
1610 — daughter of a secretary to the French king, at age of 12 married Samuel de Champlain (then 43). It was agreed they would not live together until she was 15.
1611 — Champlain named St. Helen's Island, near Montreal, after his wife.
1620 — Hélène came to Quebec. Taught the Indians, who loved her for her beauty and kindness. But she found life too lonely in Quebec.
1624 — because of homesickness, returned to France forever.
1635 — Champlain died.
1645 — entered a convent as a nun.

Explorers

Quebec became the capital of New France. For some of the 50 men who came to live at Quebec, however, it was only a stop along the way.

The real lure for these men was the river and the way west. Was it the search for furs and riches that led them west? Was it the desire to find a passage to the other side of the continent? Or was it just the desire to know what lay over the next hill, the need for excitement? Perhaps a combination of all these things led the French explorers west into the unknown land.

Champlain's Exploration

Champlain was the first to feel the lure of this land. The Huron Indians made a bargain with him. They would take him west if he would help them against their enemies, the Iroquois. Champlain agreed. He set out with his Indian allies in 1615 and, at Lake Champlain, he and the Hurons met the Iroquois. A few shots from the noisy, smoky guns of the French sent the Iroquois fleeing into the woods. And the Iroquois became the everlasting enemies of the French.

Champlain returned to Quebec — but a few years later, he was on his way west again. On these later trips, he wandered as far west as Georgian Bay.

Over the next 15 years, other Frenchmen ventured into the land of the Indians. Men like Etienne Brulé and Jean Nicolet lived with the Indians, ate their food and spoke their language, travelled with them and learned about the land that lay beyond the St. Lawrence.

The Search for China

French explorers were still hoping to find a new way to the riches of Asia. Jean Nicolet even took Chinese robes on his journey. He planned to wear them when he met the king of China. The Sieur de La Salle was sure he could find a way to China.

La Salle lived near the rapids on the St. Lawrence above Montreal. He spoke to fur traders when they came down the river. He was so convinced the river led to China that as a joke, the traders called his home "Lachine" (China in French).

In 1678, La Salle set out. He reached the Mississippi River and followed it to its mouth. He realized he had reached the Gulf of Mexico and not China. He claimed all the land drained by the river for Louis XIV, the King of France. He called it Louisiana.

The explorers had many difficulties. The rivers and lakes were the only means of moving through the dense forests. The Indians were used to paddling for up to 16 hours a day. The French explorers at first found this exhausting. Canoes and supplies often had to be portaged (carried) for as much as 5 km, often through forests where no trails existed. At night, the explorers would sleep by the river shore with no protection from mosquitoes and flies. The bites often led to infections, with lumps the size of lemons.

It was small wonder that many explorers wished to return to the relative peace of France.

Etienne Brulé

BORN: France, about 1592

DIED: near Penetanguishene, Ontario, 1633

1608 — came to Quebec with Champlain's colonists

1610 — asked to be allowed to live among Indians. Champlain, in need of interpreters, sent him to live with Algonquins for a year.

1611 — returned after a trip that took him 400 km up the Ottawa River and to Huronia, south of Georgian Bay.

1615 — accompanied Champlain to Huronia.

1618 — went south to present-day Pennsylvania and Chesapeake Bay.

1622 — first European to reach Lake Superior.

1629 — English captured Quebec. Brulé worked for them.

1633 — tortured and killed by Hurons, probably for betraying their friend Champlain.

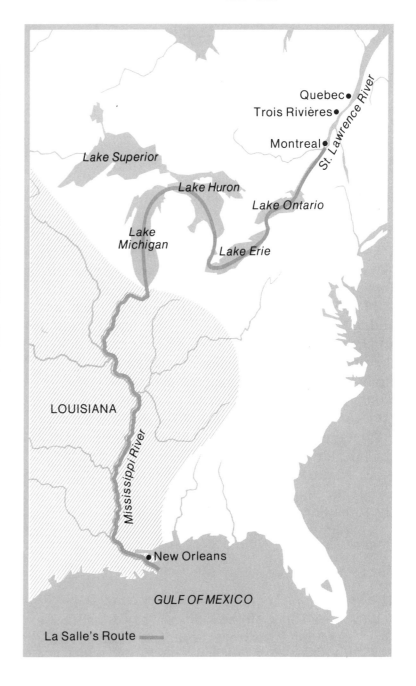

Fur Traders

Most of the explorers who pushed west were seeking furs. The greatest riches of New France appeared to be furs. Furs for beaver hats, furs for robes and coats, furs to clothe the people of Europe: these could come only from North America.

The Coureurs de Bois

After the explorers came the *coureurs de bois*. These "runners of the woods" were the traders who did the work of the fur trade. They travelled long distances in their bark canoes. Usually, they lived like the Indians. They carried trade goods to the Indians and brought furs back to the St. Lawrence.

The life of the coureurs de bois appealed to many young Frenchmen. They left the towns and their farms and headed into the woods, seeking the excitement of the fur trade. This alarmed the governor of New France. If all the young men left the settled areas, who would be left to defend the colony if the English attacked? He forbade the men to go into the woods.

But the life of a coureur de bois was more exciting than the life of a farmer or a town dweller. And there was a chance to make much money in the fur trade. Even though the governor forbade it, men still took to the forests to trade for furs.

Fur Forts

The French built fur forts, where they could stay and trade for furs with the Indians. They established a chain of trading posts from the St. Lawrence west to Lake Winnipeg and south along the Mississippi. Each year, the fur brigade would leave the St. Lawrence for these forts, carrying trade goods with it. Each year, the Indians would come to the forts with their furs. Each year, the brigade would return to the St. Lawrence, bringing back furs.

But the English explorers were also seeking furs. It became necessary to move further and further west to get the furs. Pierre Gaultier de La Vérendrye and his sons extended the chain of fur forts as far as Lake Manitoba.

In 1743, they explored as far west as the foothills of the Rockies. They were the first Europeans to see the Rockies. They succeeded in establishing French fur trading with the Indians of the region.

A 1908 postage stamp in honour of the 300th anniversary of the founding of Quebec.

Champlain was very sympathetic to the Indians. He tried to help them by encouraging trade and treating them fairly. However, one result of the establishment of his colony was a great change in the Indians' way of life. The Indians had always lived in harmony with nature. They had hunted only to meet their own needs for food and clothing. They did very little trading for goods from other areas. Each tribe or group had lived independently.

The arrival of the white man, and the fur trade changed this balanced way of life. Indians now hunted as many furs as they could get. They gradually came to need the white man's guns, knives and other tools — even some clothing and food. They trapped or hunted animals now to meet the white man's needs. They moved far from their home area to hunt for more and more furs. As a result, they stopped being as independent.

Do you think that the Indians were better off by trading furs with the French and English traders?

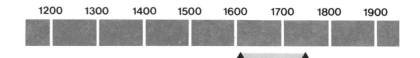

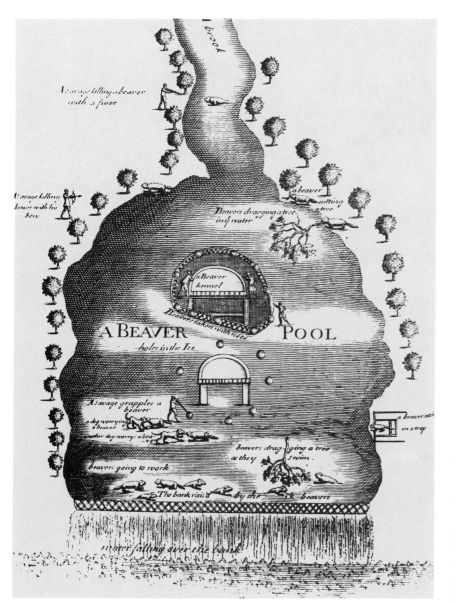

Europeans were fascinated by stories of beavers and their dams. Here is one early impression of how beavers lived and how they were trapped.

A beaver from a book published in the 1600s.

Beaver (Castor Canadensis, The Dam Builder)

BORN: once almost anywhere in North America, though now limited to areas less affected by man.

DESCRIPTION: brown furry creature of the rodent family (next of kin include rats.) Up to one metre long; mass 25 kg. Broad, flat, scaly tail that acts as rudder in water; also used to slap loudly on water as warning to family members. Long yellowish teeth that keep growing.

HABITS: cutting down saplings and small trees to make lodges up to 2 m high; building dams to make ponds; eating bark, buds and sometimes wood.

HISTORY: greatly prized by fur traders. The pelt, with long glossy guard hairs attached, was used for a variety of clothing. The underhair, combed out, was matted and used to make felt for beaver hats.

New France Grows

"Send me 400 families and 300 soldiers," Champlain pleaded with the king of France. Champlain knew that New France must have families to grow crops and work in the towns if it were to survive. And it must have soldiers to protect these people against the English and against hostile Indians.

But the king had other problems. He was fighting with the lords in France. He had no money and no men to spare to send to New France. By 1628, there were still only 80 people in New France.

The Company of One Hundred Associates

That year, the king granted the land of New France to the Company of One Hundred Associates. This company promised to send settlers to New France. In return, they had the right to the rich fur trade of the colony. The first group of 400 settlers left France in 1628. They never arrived at Quebec. Just after the ship carrying them entered the St. Lawrence River, raiders flying the flag of England captured the ship and the settlers.

David Kirke, the captain of the raider ship, wanted more than just this one French ship. The following spring, he and his brother sailed up to Quebec and demanded that the town surrender. With so few people to help defend the town, the French had little choice. Quebec was turned over to the Kirkes.

Quebec remained in English hands for three years, until a treaty turned it back to the French. During the next 30 years, the fur trading company brought some settlers to New France and rented land to them. These people began farming along the St. Lawrence.

Jean Talon often visited habitant homes. In his position as intendant, he wanted to find out what living conditions were really like for the people.

The King Takes Over

In 1663, the king of France decided to take over the colony of New France himself. He sent out 1000 soldiers to defend the colony against the Iroquois and the English. He appointed three people to look after the affairs of the colony.

The governor represented the king, and carried out the king's orders in the colony. He was responsible for the defence of the colony, and for enforcing the laws. The bishop represented the church, and was in charge of missionaries, the churches, hospitals and schools. The intendant looked after the day-to-day running of the colony. He was in charge of the fur trade, the importing and exporting of goods, and obtaining new settlers. He was responsible for the prosperity of the colony.

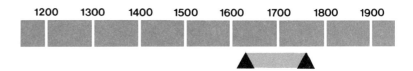

The first governor under this system was Louis de Buade, the Comte de Frontenac; the first intendant was Jean Talon; the first bishop was François de Laval. All three had a great deal of influence on the way in which New France grew over the rest of the century.

The Influence of Jean Talon

Talon saw that New France needed to increase its population. In the 1660s and 1670s he arranged for young women to be sent to New France as wives for the soldiers and unmarried settlers. He also offered free passage to people who wished to settle and gave them cheap land. For the first time, it was possible for families to settle and prosper in New France. In just seven years, the population of New France doubled. By 1675, there were 8000 people in the colony.

Over the next 100 years, New France continued to grow. Farms were established along the banks of the St. Lawrence and the other major rivers. Ships were built in New France. The colony traded with the West Indies, sending lumber, fish, furs, peas and corn in return for molasses and spices. Explorers went out into the country to the west, expanding the fur trade for the French. The future of New France seemed bright.

Quebec
The name Quebec comes from an Indian word meaning "where the river narrows." Quebec city was built at the first narrow point on the St. Lawrence River. The French called their colony New France. Only later was the name Quebec extended from the city to the entire province.

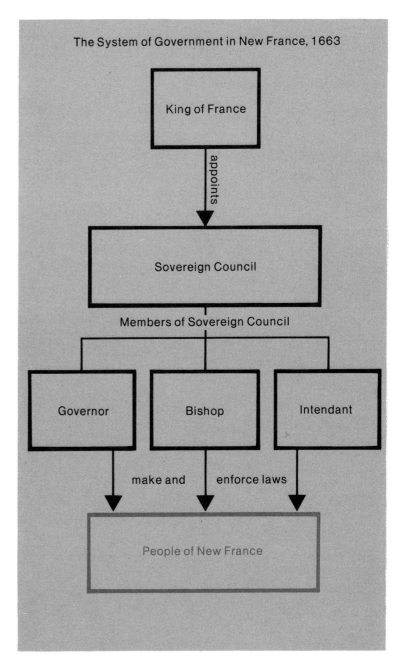

The System of Government in New France, 1663

King of France

appoints

Sovereign Council

Members of Sovereign Council

Governor — Bishop — Intendant

make and enforce laws

People of New France

The Seigneurial System

In 1663, the king of France took New France back from the Company of One Hundred Associates and granted it to lords called *seigneurs.* The seigneurs were to divide it among the habitants, who would farm it. This was the seigneurial system, and was also the way land was divided in France.

In New France, the rivers were the main roads. People travelled along the St. Lawrence and other rivers to reach towns or to visit neighbours. For this reason, most of the land was divided into long narrow strips. Each strip fronted on the river. Usually, each farmer had some good farmland along the river, land behind that for hay, and land behind that for wood-cutting.

Each seigneur had to do certain things for the king in order to keep his seigneury. He had to build and operate a flour mill and provide a chapel and a priest for his tenants.

The Habitants

The tenants, known as *habitants,* owed certain dues to their seigneur. Each habitant family had to pay a rent — usually, a very small one — and give the seigneur some of their farm produce every year. They had to work for the seigneur a few days in each year. They had to use the seigneur's mill — and pay him a small fee to do so. They also had to promise the seigneur that they would farm their land.

Most seigneurs gave the habitants land in long strips. Jean Talon thought it might be more efficient to have the habitants' lots go outward from a central village.

1200	1300	1400	1500	1600	1700	1800	1900

Under the seigneurial system, large amounts of land were divided and farms were begun along the main rivers. By 1750, a map of New France showed the long farms stretching back from most of the rivers near the St. Lawrence.

Advantages and Disadvantages of the System

The system worked fairly well for both seigneurs and habitants. The seigneurs had the honour of "owning" large amounts of land. But, because they had difficulty getting settlers to come from France, they could not ask for too much work from their tenants. Thus, the habitants were better off than they would have been in France. Almost all of their crops were used to feed their families or to trade in town for goods they needed.

There were some problems. Because the farms were in a thin line along the river, very few villages developed. This made it very difficult for the habitants to defend themselves against the raids by the Iroquois. Habitants in the areas far from Quebec were often killed in these raids.

Marie de l'Incarnation, one of the first French nuns to live in New France, wrote this of Jean Talon:

Since he has been here as intendant, the country has developed and business has progressed more than since the French first came.

Jean Talon
BORN: Chalons-sur-Marne, France, 1626.
DIED: France, 1694.
Position: Intendant, New France, 1665-68; 1670-72.
Major Accomplishments: brought Bride Ships from France, with brides for soldiers and settlers in New France. Increased other immigration. Passed laws ordering bachelors to marry and giving grants to families with more than 10 children. Set up round seigneuries. Tried to get habitants to grow flax, hemp, and hops for cloth and beer so these things would not have to be imported. Started shipyard, lumber industry, trade with West Indies. Encouraged mining.
Main Problems: fought with Governor Frontenac and Bishop Laval. Tried to do their jobs for them. Did not stay long enough to see many of his ideas work.

The Indians and the French

The first thing a Frenchman built on the shores of North America was a huge cross. Jacques Cartier and his men set up this cross on the Gaspé in 1534.

The cross showed how important religion was to the people who founded New France. The king wanted them to collect furs and riches. But he also wanted them to tell the Indians about the Christian God and the Catholic religion. Missionaries came to New France to convert the Indians. They thought it was important to save their souls so they could go to Heaven.

The Recollets and the Jesuits

It was so important to convert the Indians that missionaries were sent to New France. A group called the Recollets were the first religious group to arrive in New France. They were followed by the Jesuits. The Jesuits, priests of the Catholic church, were determined to convert as many Indians as possible. They decided that they must travel away from Quebec and the St. Lawrence communities, to the Indian settlements. They wanted to live with the Indians.

The Jesuits built a mission far inland, near Georgian Bay. The mission, called Ste. Marie among the Hurons, had a chapel, a hospital, a forge, a mill, stables and places for the priests to live. Some of the Hurons also came to live at the mission. Some of them became Christians. But many did not want to give up their own religion and customs.

Other religious people also came to work in New France. Some were priests or nuns who were sent by their orders — the groups they belonged to — to work in New France. Others, like Jeanne Mance, who founded the hospital at Montreal, came because they felt they had a mission to work in the New World.

The Role of the Nuns

The nuns who came to New France were responsible for looking after the sick and working in the hospitals run by their orders. They also looked after the education of the young French girls and the young Indian girls of the area.

Iroquois Warfare

When Champlain agreed to help the Hurons by fighting the Iroquois, he started a war that would almost destroy New France. The Iroquois did not accept their defeat by the French and Hurons. Instead, they decided that they needed allies — and the guns

Champlain's drawing of himself and the Hurons fighting the Iroquois in a battle near Lake Champlain.

that allies could give them. They became the allies of the Dutch and the English, who were starting colonies along the Atlantic coast south of Acadia. The Iroquois received guns from these allies and the Hurons, in turn, received guns from the French. War among the Indians changed completely.

Before the Europeans arrived, the Indians had raided each other's villages and camps. Each raid was swift. Sometimes a prisoner or two would be taken. Rarely were people killed. But now, with each side using guns, more people were killed. The wars became more serious.

Then, in the 1640s, a great illness swept through the Huron tribe. Almost half the Hurons died of it. Not long after, the Iroquois invaded the Huron land, killing as many as they could and scattering those who were left. In 1649, they destroyed Ste. Marie among the Hurons. The mission was burned to the ground and the priests were killed. A decade later, the Iroquois attacked the heart of New France.

In 1660, the Iroquois set out to capture Montreal, the town furthest west in New France. They were stopped by Dollard des Ormeaux and a small party of Frenchmen and Indians at Long Sault, on the Ottawa River. The defenders were all killed, but the Iroquois had lost the advantage of surprise. They turned back without attacking Montreal.

The Iroquois never attacked the city of Quebec. But, over the next few decades, they made swift and fierce raids on the farms furthest from the towns. Many French people became afraid to go out into the fields alone. No one knew where the Iroquois would be or when they would strike. Many farmers were killed by the Iroquois after the defeat of the Hurons.

Madeleine de Verchères
BORN: Verchères seigneury, 1678
DIED: Quebec, 1747
The Verchères family had a seigneury about 35 km from Montreal.

One day when Madeleine was 14, her parents were away. She was out in the fields when she heard guns. She ran into the fort, just ahead of 45 Iroquois.

When she had barred the gate, she realized that the only other people in the fort were her two younger brothers, two soldiers, an old man of 80 and some women and children. Madeleine quickly took charge. She put on a soldier's helmet, seized a gun, and said to her brothers, "Let us remember our father's words: Gentlemen are born to shed their blood in the service of their God and king."

Madeleine ordered her "troops" to keep guard on the walls of the fort. She told them to fire the cannon and to call out military orders. She made the women and children march about to sound like soldiers. She wanted to make the Iroquois believe the fort was strongly defended.

For eight days they kept it up. The Iroquois believed they could not succeed in attacking the fort. Finally soldiers arrived from Montreal. The siege was over. Madeleine had saved not only the fort, but the lives of the inhabitants.

The City of Quebec in 1700

The small settlement that Champlain started at Quebec had become an important town by 1690. Quebec was the home of the governor of the colony of New France. All the important political leaders of the colony lived in Quebec. So did all the religious leaders. There were also many soldiers, merchants, craftsmen and working people living in the city. In all, there were more than 2000 people living in Quebec by 1700.

Visitors from France arrived at Quebec by ship. Sailing up the St. Lawrence, the ships rounded the Ile d'Orléans. As they came round the island, passengers on the ships could see the town on a high bluff overlooking the river. They could see the spires of the churches and fine government buildings of the upper town. Above the town was a fort, the Citadel.

The Docks at Quebec

As the ships approached the many docks along the river's edge, the passengers could see the warehouses, shops and stone houses of the lower town. Ships of the French navy stood at anchor in a protected bay. Small fishing boats and canoes moved through the water.

Wagons and push-carts came and went from the docks and storehouses. Men loaded bundles of furs onto ships bound for France. Cargos unloaded included trade goods to be exchanged for furs: steel knives and axes, cooking pots, guns, cloth and brandy. Once these goods would have been traded to native trappers at a fur fair in Quebec itself. By 1700 they were being shipped up-river to Montreal. As French explorers moved further west in search of furs, the great fur fair moved west too. First it was held in Quebec, then Trois Rivières, and later Montreal.

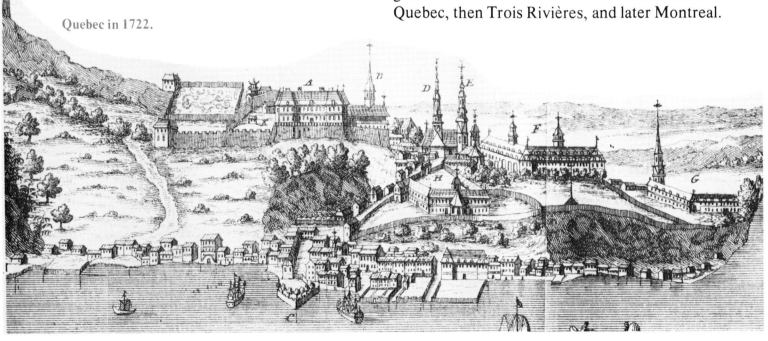

Quebec in 1722.

Every year a great fair was held when the coureurs de bois and native people would bring in their furs. The French merchants would trade the guns, tools and brandy to the natives for their furs. The streets of the town would be crowded with people. Native men and women in colourful costumes, coureurs de bois in buckskins, and French traders in fancy European clothes could be seen at the fur fair. The governor would start the fair by smoking the peace-pipe with the native traders. Then the trading began.

Horse-drawn carriages took the visitor from the docks to the upper town. On the way the carriage passed along narrow streets that wound their way through rows of stone houses. The streets had interesting names: the Street Beneath the Fort, Sailor's Leap, the Street of Ducks, the Street of Canoes, and the Street at the Side of the Mountain.

A street in the lower town. This drawing was made after the English had conquered Quebec.

A fish seller in the lower town.

The Lower Town

The houses of the lower town were the homes of the workers and craftspeople of Quebec. Here the carpenters, stonemasons, toolmakers, the shopkeepers, the seamstresses and the domestic servants lived with their families. Their houses were made of a type of black stone found near the town. The roofs were thatched with straw. Because of this, fire was always a danger in the crowded lower town. A law ordered that all chimneys of the lower town had to be swept regularly. Another law required homes to be kept very clean. Hay and other dried animal food could not be kept in the houses. Many families had small vegetable gardens and kept animals for food and milk.

Often the homes of the craftsmen were also their shops. A person's trade could be told by the sign that hung over the door. Words or pictures on the sign would let passersby know that a weaver or a shoemaker lived there.

Quebec: the Upper Town

A ballroom dance. Note the black musicians. Black slaves were first brought to New France in the 1620s. Slaves were used as domestic servants and as field hands. By 1750, there were about 4000 black slaves in New France.

Driving up the hill to the upper town, the visitor would see many fine buildings. These buildings, built of stone by the masons from the lower town, were the places where the political and religious leaders of the colony lived and worked. Nearby were the fine homes of wealthy merchants and landowners.

The Cathedral with its tall spire stood at the heart of the upper town. The home of the Bishop of Quebec stood across the square from the Cathedral. The bishop was a very wealthy man. The first Bishop of Quebec, Monseigneur Laval, owned the seigneuries of Beaupré and Ile d'Orléans. Close by were the Seminary and the Jesuit monastery where priests and missionaries were trained.

Further up the bluff, overlooking the river and the town, was the governor's manor. His home was called Chateau Saint-Louis.

Life was very pleasant for the wealthy people of the upper town. They dressed in fine silk clothes brought from France. Visitors said that they lived just as well as they could have in Paris. There were many parties with good food and fine wines. Musicians played the latest music from France at dances and other festive events. There were servants to wait on the guests. Many of the wealthy families owned black slaves brought to New France from Africa or the West Indies.

Soldiers of God and of the King

Perhaps as many as half the people of Quebec at this time were either members of the various religious groups or in the army. Religious orders played an important part in the life of the town. The children of Quebec attended schools run by the religious orders. The hospital in Quebec was operated by nuns.

The religious orders of the upper town lived a very simple life. They wore plain black or grey homespun woolen robes. Their meals were simple. Many worked long hours, broken only by prayers and religious services. They had dedicated their lives to serving God in the New World. As missionaries in remote areas of the colony, many would die or suffer hardships. Their lives were in sharp contrast to the wealth and comfort of the bishop and his priests.

The soldiers were stationed at Quebec to protect the colony. English ships and soldiers attacked the town several times in the seventeenth century. There was also the ever-present possibility of attack by the Iroquois. The soldiers were brought to Quebec for short periods of service. Many stayed on as settlers after they left the army.

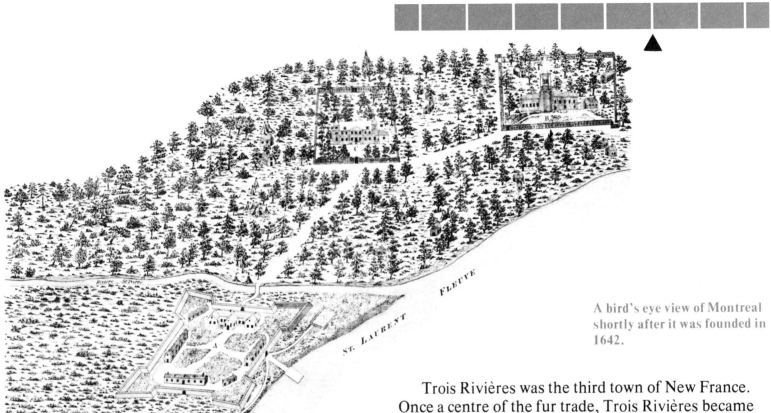

A bird's eye view of Montreal shortly after it was founded in 1642.

Trois Rivières was the third town of New France. Once a centre of the fur trade, Trois Rivières became important for the making of canoes. There the birchbark canoes used by the coureurs de bois were made. Like Montreal, Trois Rivières was surrounded by a wall, made of logs, to protect it from attack.

Trois Rivières in 1709.

Montreal and Trois Rivières

Quebec was the most important town in New France during the seventeenth century. But it was losing out in importance to Montreal by the end of the century. Montreal was started as a mission to bring the Catholic religion to the native peoples. In its early years, Montreal was often attacked by the Iroquois. A wall was built around the city to protect it. Later, as the fur trade spread westward around the Great Lakes, it became the most important trading centre.

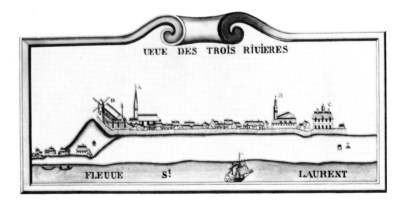

Country Life in New France

The people who farmed in New France lived a life much different from that of the people in the towns. Their lives were centred around the farms in their area, with the occasional trip to town.

A typical day in the life of a habitant began early in the morning. The men in the family would go out to the fields, to work at seeding or caring for the crops or harvestings. They would take their midday meal with them. Usually, this was a loaf of bread made by the women of the family: reports from that time say that the average habitant would eat a kilogram of bread a day.

The women worked at home during the day. There was cooking to do for the evening meal. There was sewing and caring for the house and sometimes weaving. The vegetable garden had to be tended, the washing done and the children cared for.

A church on Ile d'Orléans, opposite Quebec city. Less than 20 m long, it was built in 1695. This photograph was taken in 1864, just before the church was torn down.

Habitants baked their bread in outdoor ovens. The seigneur provided the oven for the use of all the people in the village.

Food came mainly from the products grown on the farm and whatever could be caught in the river. Eels from the river were salted and barrelled and eaten throughout the winter. The habitants ate beef, pork, poultry, bread made from the grains they grew and many vegetables — but not potatoes. Potatoes were considered to be fit food only for the pigs.

In the evenings, the habitants might play cards or visit the next farm along the river.Sometimes, there would be celebrations with fiddle music and dancing.

Each small area — called a parish — had a parish priest, who looked after church services, weddings, christenings, funerals and other important events in life. On Sundays and on the many saints' days, the family would go to the parish church.

In the early days of the colony, all travel was by water: by boat in the summer, by sled in the winter. Later, some roads were built, so that families could travel on land.

The habitants grew most of the things they needed. Some items, however, such as sugar and spices, had to be bought in town. They sold some of their farm produce to earn money for these items.

The habitants owed their seigneur some days of work every year, and had to give him some of their crops. These payments however, did not amount to much. Often the payment of a few hens or a bushel of wheat was an excuse for the people on the seigneury to get together, talk and have a good time.

Habitants paying their yearly rent to the seigneur.

The English at the Bay

When Radisson and Groseilliers returned to England from Hudson Bay in the *Nonsuch*, the ship was loaded with furs. The next year the king granted a charter founding the Hudson's Bay Company. This is a modern replica of the *Nonsuch*.

Henry Hudson's voyage to the north had ended in death and tragedy. For 50 years, the search for the Northwest Passage was abandoned. The next Europeans to set out for Hudson Bay did so by land. Pierre Esprit Radisson and Médard Chouart, Sieur des Groseilliers, left from the St. Lawrence to try to go overland to the bay. They did not complete their journey. They did, however, bring back many furs.

But the governor of New France was angry because Radisson and Groseilliers had travelled and traded for furs without his permission. He took away their furs and threw them in jail. Once out of jail, the two decided to go to England for help with their next trip.

The Hudson's Bay Company

The king of England and a number of wealthy Englishmen paid for their sea voyage to Hudson Bay from England. Radisson and Groseilliers reached the bay and returned with furs. The wealthy Englishmen decided to establish posts and trade for furs. They started a company — called the Hudson's Bay Company — to do this trading.

In 1670, the king of England gave this company the right to trade in a huge area that stretched far to the south and west. It included all of the land drained by the rivers flowing into Hudson Bay. Over the next 50 years, the Hudson's Bay Company built posts at the bay and sent men to run them.

They did not want their men to travel inland to trade. They feared that the traders would begin to live like Indians and that this would be bad for the fur trade. But the French were sending fur traders west.

The Indians would rather trade with the French inland than travel all the way to Hudson Bay. The English realized that they would have to explore inland and build their own posts. Henry Kelsey, Anthony Henday and other men from the Hudson's Bay Company travelled inland. They established fur-trading posts to compete with the posts built by La Vérendrye and other French traders.

Indians at a Hudson's Bay Company trading post.

Pierre Esprit Radisson
BORN: France, 1636
DIED: England, 1710

Médard Chouart des Groseilliers
BORN: France, 1618
DIED: New France, about 1696

Pierre Radisson came to New France at the age of 15. A year later he was captured and adopted by the Iroquois. He spent two years with them and came to love their way of live.

Médard Chouart des Groseilliers was Radisson's brother-in-law. When Radisson returned to New France, the two decided to go west and trade for furs. The Iroquois had stopped the Hurons from bringing furs to New France. Radisson and Groseilliers went to Lake Superior and opened up the trade again. When they returned, their canoes were piled high with furs. The people greeted them as heroes. Without the fur trade, the colony would fail. But the governor punished them because they had traded without a permit.

Radisson and Groseilliers thought the governor wanted their riches for himself. They were so angry they went to England. They hoped to be more fairly treated there. They persuaded the English king to sponsor a voyage to Hudson Bay. The Hudson Bay route opened up a whole new fur trading area for England.

Thus the Hudson's Bay Company was begun. As a result of the work of two French coureurs de bois, England gained control of the northern part of what is now Canada. How differently the history of Canada might have turned out if the French had treated Radisson and Groseilliers fairly and kept their loyalty.

English Colonies on the Atlantic Coast

By the 1600s several European countries had obtained empires in the Americas. Spain and Portugal had established colonies in Mexico, Central America and South America. These colonies were rich in gold, silver and precious jewels. France was establishing colonies on the St. Lawrence, in Acadia and in the Caribbean.

England's efforts began as early as 1585, with the Virginia Colony. Like the French colonists further north, Walter Raleigh and the settlers he took with him suffered from winter weather, disease and battles with the Indians. The colony failed.

Many English merchants still wanted to develop colonies in the Americas. They hoped to claim the land north of the Spanish colonies. They expected that they would also find gold and silver. The king of England did not invest in these colonies. He granted a charter to companies. They had the right to establish colonies. In return, the king hoped to get power and some of the riches from the colonies.

The Earliest Colonies

The first successful English colony was Jamestown, Virginia in 1607. The colony was named after King James I. Although they hoped to find rich minerals, they found only fool's gold (pyrite). The colonists had great difficulty getting established. The winters were severe, and they almost ran out of food and supplies.

Finally, Captain John Smith took control of the colony. He established friendly relations with the Indians. From them he learned how to grow tobacco, which the settlers could sell in England for money to buy the necessities of life. This became the first permanent English colony in America.

In 1620, a group of English colonists sailed on the *Mayflower,* and landed near Plymouth, Massachussets. They called themselves the Puritans. They wanted to follow their own religion without control from the Church of England. Upon arrival, they drew

up an agreement called the *Mayflower Compact.* By this, they agreed to obey all of the rules and laws which they drew up for the good of the colony. The first winter was a most difficult time, because the Puritans had not had time to build homes or prepare crops before the cold weather arrived. Many died over the winter. However, the colony survived and became the second English settlement in the Americas.

Events in Virginia, 1619
Representatives were elected from each district to the "House of Burgesses." This was the first elected government in the Americas.
Ninety women arrived from England to be wives for the settlers. Each settler had to pay 120 pounds of tobacco for his future wife's journey.
A Dutch ship stopped and sold 20 black slaves to local farmers. This was the beginning of slavery in the colonies.

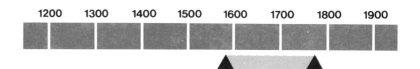

| 1200 | 1300 | 1400 | 1500 | 1600 | 1700 | 1800 | 1900 |

The Settlement of the Thirteen Colonies

Over the next 150 years colonies were settled from Georgia to Massachusetts. Most of the settlers were English. Others came from Ireland, Scotland, Germany and Holland. The population grew rapidly. These colonies could be divided into three groups: New England, the Middle Colonies, and the Southern Colonies.

The New England colonies (Massachusetts, New Hampshire, Rhode Island and Connecticut) were in the north. Most of the colonists lived in towns along the coast. Many were fishermen or shipbuilders or traders and merchants. Boston was the biggest city. The Middle Colonies (New York, Pennsylvania, New Jersey, Delaware) were flatter and more fertile areas. Most of the people were farmers. They pushed westward into unsettled areas to find new farmland. This often led them to fight with the Indians. Although these were English colonies, many of the people in them came from Germany, Holland, Sweden, Scotland and Ireland. The Southern Colonies (Maryland, Virginia, North Carolina, South Carolina, Georgia) were in a flat coastal plain. The temperature was quite warm. The land and climate were suited for growing crops such as rice, tobacco and indigo. Later, this would be the area to grow cotton. In 1619, the first slaves were brought from Africa. Gradually, the large southern cotton plantations became dependent on black slaves to do the work.

By 1770, the population of the Thirteen Colonies was about 2 100 000. Of these, 400 000 were black slaves. Most slaves lived in the south. The presence of blacks affected the course of American history.

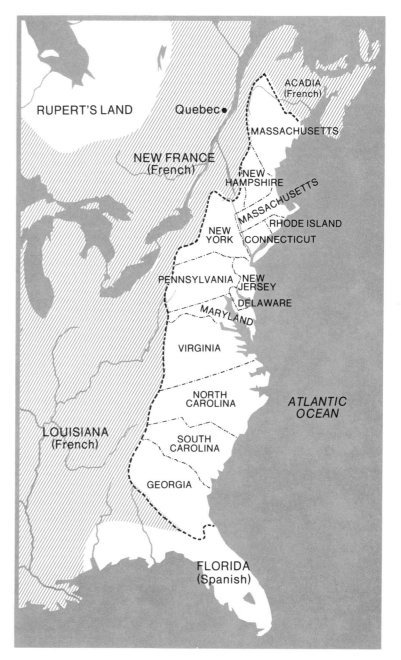

Nova Scotia and St. John Island to 1783

The Acadians were deported from their homeland in 1755. The British wanted to be sure that Acadia was a completely British colony. To do this, they needed more British settlers.

Between 1760 and 1776, more than 7000 New Englanders were encouraged to move into Nova Scotia. The New Englanders knew about the rich Acadian farms along the Bay of Fundy. They quickly took over the best of these farms. However, the New Englanders did not know how to keep the dykes in good repair. Much fertile farmland was lost to the sea when the dykes failed.

Soon after the conquest of Acadia by the British, Nova Scotia became a self-governing British colony. In 1758, a legislative assembly was established in Halifax. The wealthy merchants and officers of Halifax held most of the power in this government.

This picture of Halifax was published in 1750, one year after the city was founded. The artist wrote in the location of the gallows and the stocks. What are stocks?

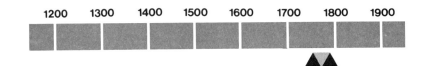

| 1200 | 1300 | 1400 | 1500 | 1600 | 1700 | 1800 | 1900 |

Scottish Settlement in Nova Scotia

The Pennsylvania Land Company brought more new settlers to Nova Scotia. The company got a large grant of land near Pictou in 1769. It could not persuade many New Englanders to settle there. It began to advertise in Scotland for settlers.

Between 1763 and 1776, 25 000 Scots left Scotland for North America. They moved because the Scottish landowners were turning them off their land at home. Some 2000 of these Scots came to the area around Pictou and Antigonish. Most were poor farmers, who grew mostly potatoes and wheat. Some were part-time fishermen. Most of the early Scots settlers had a difficult time making a living in their new homes.

Britain's main interest in Nova Scotia was the tall trees that grew there. The Maritime colonies were covered with thick stands of white pine and spruce. The trees were needed for masts, for the ships of the Royal Navy. These trees were straight and free from knots. A mast 35 m high could be made from a single white pine tree.

Trees were cut along the coasts of Nova Scotia, along the Saint John and Miramichi Rivers, and on Ile St. Jean. Ile St. Jean was renamed St. John Island by the British. Later again, it would be renamed Prince Edward Island. These forests along the coasts were owned by British officers or by land companies that held large land grants. So many trees were cut down that all the trees were gone from the coast by 1800.

St. John Island

On Ile St. Jean, renamed St. John Island by the British, the population was growing very slowly. The British government wanted to reserve the riches of both this and Cape Breton Island for itself. The people who would be allowed to settle on these islands were chosen very carefully. St. John Island was divided into 67 lots. Each lot was given to a British nobleman or officer. A few of these landowners brought in settlers, but by 1784, there were still only about 1000 people living on the island. Even the Scots who had emigrated to this island had abandoned it in favour of the cheaper land and easier life in Nova Scotia.

Charlottetown in 1779.

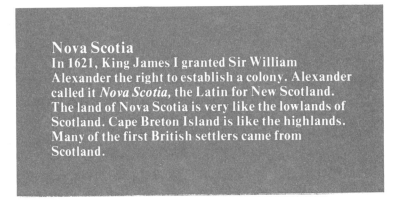

Nova Scotia
In 1621, King James I granted Sir William Alexander the right to establish a colony. Alexander called it *Nova Scotia,* the Latin for New Scotland. The land of Nova Scotia is very like the lowlands of Scotland. Cape Breton Island is like the highlands. Many of the first British settlers came from Scotland.

Newfoundland in the Eighteenth Century

The cod fishing along the Grand Banks off Newfoundland had been of great importance to Britain and France for over 200 years. Both countries claimed the island as their own property. Both had settlements there at the same time. The French settled near Port aux Basques and the English near Placentia harbour and along the east coast. But few people lived on the island. The soil was too poor to support good farming and the weather was cold and wet.

The English did not want people to settle in Newfoundland. They wanted the cod fishermen to come to the Grand Banks from England each year, not to live there year round. The boats travelling across the Atlantic every year provided an excellent training ground for future sailors for the Royal Navy. They could also provide sailors for the merchant ships that traded with India, China and the West Indies. The English also wanted to keep control of the cod fisheries. The few resident fishermen usually sold their catch to merchants from Boston who sailed north to buy the catch. This way, the profits from the fishery stayed in North America instead of going back to England.

Fishing for Cod

In the eighteenth century, cod were caught with hook and line, just as they had been when the first English fishermen crossed the Atlantic in the fifteenth century.

At first, the fish were salted aboard ship, and then carried back to Europe in barrels of brine. In the late seventeenth century, the fishermen began to dry the fish before returning to England. The fish were first cleaned on board ship. Then they were taken ashore where they were cleaned again, salted lightly and placed on racks to dry. Drying resulted in less spoilage than did salting. This meant better prices for the fish.

But drying the fish required more people. Workers had to be available on shore to carry out the drying. This meant permanent settlers in Newfoundland.

The Growth of Settlement

The British government had passed a law saying that no property on the island could be owned for any reason not directly related to the fishery. At first, the only full-time residents were watchmen who guarded the fishery docks and buildings during the stormy Newfoundland winter. However, the English law was not strictly enforced. The permanent population of Newfoundland grew slowly but steadily during the eighteenth century. In 1713, there were about 3000 people living on the island. In 1749, about 6000 people lived there and in 1765, about 12 000 people.

Many of these people came from the west country of England, and were poor sailors and fishermen.

Placentia in 1758.

Some Irish people came over as labourers, picked up by the English ships when they stopped at Irish ports for provisions on their way to Newfoundland. When the ships stopped at Placentia, many of the Irish left ship. Often, they would work during the winter as woodcutters, to supply the island's shipyards.

Other early arrivals in Newfoundland included Basques, French and a few Portuguese fishermen. These people usually spent only the summer months in Newfoundland. Many of the early French settlers left Port aux Basques in the 1750s when Britain took over Acadia.

This picture appeared on a map of North America published in 1714. It shows "ye manner of fishing for, Curing & Drying Cod at New Found Land." The artist also explained what was going on by referring to the letters on the picture.

A. What the fishermen wear.
B. The fishing line.
C. The way they fish.
D. Dressing the fish.
E. A trough to receive the dressed cod.
F. Salt boxes.
G. How the cod was carried.
H. Cleaning the cod.
I. A press to extract oil from the cod livers.
K. Casks to receive water and blood from the livers.
L. Another cask to receive the oil.
M. How the cod are dried.

Questions

Can You Recall?

1. What did Champlain set up to prevent boredom among the colonists at Port Royal?
2. What was the name of the native group that helped the Acadians survive during the early years of the colony?
3. Merchants from the _____ colonies traded with the Acadians.
4. Most of the settlements in Acadia were clustered around the Bay of _____.
5. What treaty, signed in 1713, gave the English control over Acadia?
6. In what year was Halifax built?
7. When were the Acadians deported, and why?
8. Who were the *coureurs de bois?*
9. Who were
   a) Jean Talon;
   b) Bishop Laval;
   c) the Comte de Frontenac?
10. What did the habitants have to do in order to pay their seigneurs?
11. Why did so many nuns and priests come to New France?
12. What was the name of the fur trading company set up by the English in 1670 to compete with the French?
13. What was England's main interest in the Nova Scotia colony?
14. Today Ile St. Jean is called _____.
15. What change took place in the Newfoundland cod fishing industry in the late seventeenth century?

Ideas for Discussion

1. Champlain has been called "the father of New France." Do you agree or disagree with this description? Discuss your position.
2. Discuss the role of missionaries in New France. How did their activities affect the native people of the area?
3. Champlain was a map-maker by profession. He drew this map for the king of France in 1613. Compare it to a modern map of eastern Canada. Look for the following places on

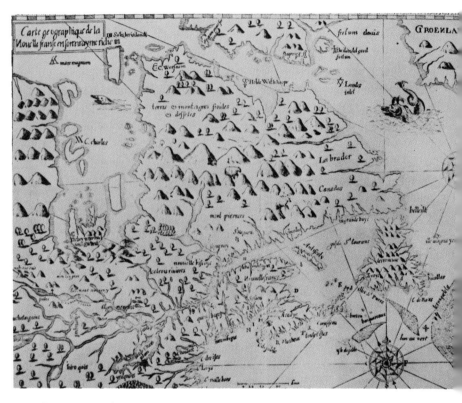

both maps. (Remember that Champlain wrote in French. Also, he may have used different spellings from the ones we are used to.)
a) Montreal (Hochelaga)
b) Lake Champlain
c) Trois Rivières
d) Hudson Bay
e) Greenland
f) Labrador
g) The Gulf of St. Lawrence
h) Cape Breton Island
i) Nova Scotia (Acadia)
j) Newfoundland
k) The Grand Banks
Discuss why Champlain may have made some mistakes when he drew his map.

4. Discuss the reasons for the British expulsion of the Acadians. Do you feel the expulsion was necessary? Was it fair? Explain your reasons.
5. French settlement in New France was based on the fur trade. English settlement along the Atlantic coast was based on farming, fishing, lumbering and trade. Discuss the difference in these two approaches to settlement. How might they have affected the outcome of the clashes between England and France over control of North America?
6. Much of the fighting between French and English in this period was done by the Huron and the Iroquois, their native allies. Do you feel this was fair? How did this role as fighters for the two colonial powers affect the native peoples?

Do Some Research

1. Find out about the history of Montreal. Explain how it came to be more important than Quebec City. Draw a map to show why Montreal's location played an important part in its growth during the fur trade period.
2. Find out about the lives of the *coureurs de bois*. Discuss why their way of life might have been attractive to the young people of New France. Make a map showing the routes along which the coureurs de bois travelled in search of furs.
3. England and France were not the only European countries to have colonies along the eastern coast of North America in the seventeenth century. Find out about the countries that founded the colonies of New York, New Jersey, and Delaware. What happened to these colonies?
4. Do a research report on one of the following:
   a) the Mayflower Compact and the Pilgrims;
   b) the Jamestown Colony in Virginia;
   c) the Salem witch trials;
   d) the introduction of black slaves into the French and English colonies.

5. Make a visual display showing the steps from a beaver in its lodge on a Canadian lake to the purchase of a beaver hat in Paris in 1700. Your display should show:
   a) the natural environment of the beaver;
   b) the skinning and preparing of the pelt;
   c) the roles of the native trapper, the trader, the shipper, the hat maker, the hat seller, and the wearer;
   d) all the forms of transportation used in getting the pelt to Paris;
   e) a scene showing the well-dressed fashions of Paris in 1700.

Be Creative

1. Put on a celebration of the Order of Good Cheer for the class. Dress in appropriate costumes, perform songs and skits. Find some recipes and cook some dishes that the colonists at Port Royal might have eaten.
2. Make a model showing how the Acadians built dykes to extend their fields.
3. Write an imaginary letter home to a friend or relative in France from *either:*
   a) a nun who has just spent her first winter in Quebec City;
   or
   b) a *coureur de bois* who has just returned from his first fur trading expedition.
   Describe both your positive and negative feelings about life in New France.
4. Write an account of the activities of Radisson and Groseilliers and the founding of the Hudson's Bay Company as it might have appeared in a London newspaper of the time. Include appropriate maps and pictures with your stories.
5. Write brief biographies of the following:
   a) Bishop Laval;
   b) Jeanne Mance;
   c) Pierre Gaultier de la Vérendrye;
   d) William Penn, founder of Pennsylvania;
   e) John Winthrop, governor of Massachusetts.

Struggle for a Continent
ADVANCE ORGANIZER

1

2

For almost 100 years, British and French forces fought to control Acadian settlements. When the Acadians refused to take an oath of loyalty to the English king, they were punished. Their homes were burned and they were loaded onto ships. They were to be scattered in the different English colonies.

By the 1700s the French had lived in Acadia and the St. Lawrence valley for over 100 years. Quebec was the oldest city in North America.

For a time, France did not pay much attention to the colony of Acadia. Nevertheless, Acadia grew prosperous. The French settlers wished to live in peace, following their own way of life. But the British colonies along the Atlantic Coast grew stronger. The French colony at Quebec expanded. The Acadians were caught in the middle of the resulting war.

3

The colony of New France remained on the St. Lawrence. The heart of the French colony was Quebec City. Here the fortress on the heights looked out over the river. Whoever controlled Quebec controlled the St. Lawrence. Whoever controlled the St. Lawrence controlled New France.

Word List

conquer	oath	revolution
invasion	oppose	siege
loyalty	prosperous	tax
militia	resist	united

4

The most important battle in Canadian history was fought in 1759. The British climbed up to the heights of Quebec. Here, on a field called the Plains of Abraham, they met the French. The battle was over in ten minutes. The British had won. New France was conquered.

5

To the south, British colonies stretched from Massachusetts to Florida. The British had exercised little control over their colonists. Many colonies had their own governments.

In the 1760s, the British began to tighten control over the colonists. They imposed new taxes on the American colonies. The colonists opposed many of these taxes. When the British tightened the laws, the colonists resisted.

6

In 1775, the British sent troops to Massachusetts. The resulting battle began a war by the colonists to gain their independence. It was called the American Revolution. The colonists won, after a bitter struggle. The former British colonies became the United States of America.

The Struggle for North America

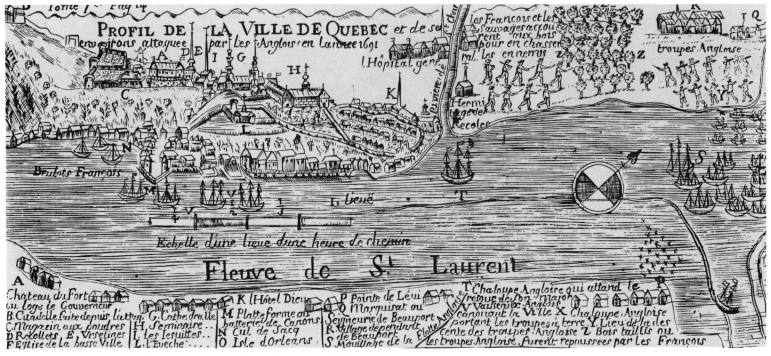

A picture-map showing the English attack on Quebec in 1690.

In the seventeenth century, England and France had colonies spread throughout the world. Each country wanted to keep its own colonies and take some from its rival. From 1689 to 1815, the two fought battles in Europe and around the world.

Late in the seventeenth century, France and England began to fight over control of the fur trade in North America. The Hudson's Bay Company was beginning to cut into the French fur trade. In 1689, war was declared. The French attacked settlements in New England. The English attacked Acadia.

A shaky peace in 1697 seemed to end the struggle. But the French fur traders continued to attack the posts of the Hudson's Bay Company along the bay.

The peace did not last long. The English and French and their Indian allies made savage attacks on each other's settlements. New England forces captured Port Royal in Acadia. The English and New Englanders tried to launch a naval attack on the city of Quebec. But bad weather and lack of co-operation between English and New Englanders saved the French town.

Peace came again in 1713. The Treaty of Utrecht gave Acadia and Newfoundland to England. France also had to give up the forts and territories of the Hudson's Bay Company that had been captured over the past thirty years. Now, France realized she would have to defend her remaining colonies better. Acadia no longer could guard the entrance to the St. Lawrence River, the only route to New France. In 1719, the French began to build the great stone fortress of Louisbourg on Cape Breton Island. French naval ships in the Louisbourg harbour could protect French fishermen off Newfoundland and could guard the mouth of the St. Lawrence.

The Hudson Bay fur area was controlled by the English. The French moved to protect their fur trade in the area south of the Great Lakes along the Ohio and Mississippi rivers. New forts were built along the Mississippi. Forts along the Great Lakes, including Fort Frontenac (now Kingston), were strengthened. The French built a fort at New Orleans, at the Mississippi mouth, to protect New France from attack from the south.

After the Treaty of Utrecht

In 1713 New France was caught in the middle of areas controlled by the English. To the north lay the territory controlled by the Hudson's Bay Company. To the south lay the English colonies.

The treaty made England much stronger in North America. England controlled a great deal of territory, including the rich cod fisheries of Newfoundland. She also had many more people in her colonies.

France was not completely weak. The French had well trained soldiers ready to fight in New France. The English had only poorly trained colonial militia men for defence or attack. New France was a united colony. The English colonies were not. The colonies argued among themselves and with England.

Both the English and the French raided each other's territory. One night in February 1704, 50 Frenchmen and 200 Indians attacked the village of Deerfield, Massachusetts. They killed 53 people. They took 111 prisoners back to Canada, a march of 500 km. It was more than two years before prisoner exchanges were made and the survivors returned to Boston. Some of the children never went back. Eunice Williams was seven when she was captured. A young Indian carried her most of the way. When she grew up she married him and they had children. Several times she visited Deerfield with her new family. But they always returned north.

This picture of the attack on Deerfield is from a book by Eunice's father, John Williams. He was minister of the church in Deerfield. He wrote about his experiences as a captive.

The Fighting Begins Again

These strengths and weaknesses were soon tested again. The borders between French and English areas were not clearly defined. Both sides and their Indian allies continued to fight and raid along these borders.

Then, in 1745, war broke out again in Europe. In North America, the border skirmishes developed into full-scale raids. An army of New Englanders attacked and captured the fortress at Louisbourg. The French navy tried to take back the fort, but failed.

In India, the French were doing better. The French captured the key trading town of Madras. In 1748, the English traded Louisbourg back to the French for Madras.

France then decided to strengthen her North American defences. New forts were built in the Ohio River basin. French traders and explorers pushed westward to the upper reaches of the Saskatchewan River. France still controlled a rich and large area of North America.

But, where it counted, New France was weak; 60 000 settlers now to New England's 2 500 000. The people in New England wanted to move westward, out of the overcrowded coastal colonies. They eyed hungrily the French territory across the Appalachian mountains, along the Ohio River. The English were willing to fight for this land.

Colonial troops from New England capture Louisbourg, 1745.

The Battle at Fort Duquesne

George Washington, later to become first president of the United States, began the battle. With a ragtag group of militia, he was sent to drive the French out of Fort Duquesne in the Ohio Valley.

Washington's party arrived at Fort Duquesne. The French sent out a small party to ask the New Englanders to leave. Washington and his men ambushed the French, killing nine French soldiers and taking 21 prisoners. This was the first battle in a war that would spread around the world and last seven years.

The French reacted swiftly. Five hundred soldiers descended on Washington's motley army and sent them fleeing, leaving guns and baggage behind. The angry English colonists demanded that Britain declare war on France.

Stalemate in North America

War was not declared. The British and French began to fight anyway. British ships attacked French vessels off the coast of Newfoundland and at the mouth of the St. Lawrence. Major General Edward Braddock marched nearly 2000 soldiers over the mountains to attack Fort Duquesne. Only 250 French soldiers and 600 Indians defended the fort. But the British, loaded down with heavy cannons and slowed by their vast wagon train, were easy targets for the French.

The battle was a slaughter. Two-thirds of the British were killed or captured. Braddock was killed. The rest of the British force fled in panic, leaving their guns and supplies behind.

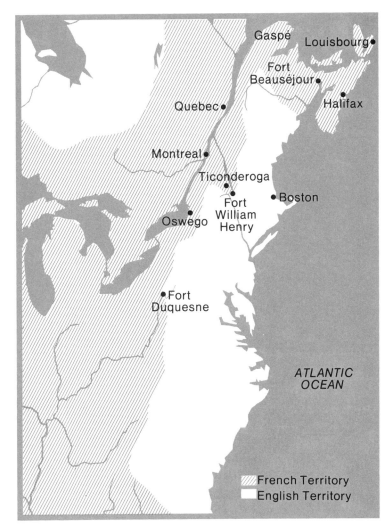

French and British Victories

In other battles near the Great Lakes, the French did well. But in Acadia, the English were winning. In 1755, Fort Beauséjour, at the head of the Bay of Fundy, was captured. This removed the last major threat to the British in Nova Scotia. The same year, the British ordered the Acadians deported.

By 1756, it seemed as though the two sides in the war could not move against each other. Britain and its powerful Royal Navy controlled the seas, but could not stop ships going up the St. Lawrence. On land, the French and their Indian allies held the British at bay.

The Fall of New France

The Seven Years' War, lasting from 1756 to 1763, was the first modern war fought by Britain. It involved the whole of Britain's national resources. Banks, industry, farmers, merchants, the army and the navy joined in the war effort. Careful plans of attack were drawn up by the British generals. But, in the end, it was luck and a series of French errors that led to the fall of New France to the British.

The Fall of Louisbourg

By 1758, the tide of the war for Canada had begun to turn in favour of the British. The fortress of Louisbourg fell first. Defended by 6000 French sailors, soldiers, and militia, the fortress stood against 28 000 British attackers for seven weeks. On July 26, 1758, the French surrendered Louisbourg. With the fall of Louisbourg, the British controlled the approach to the St. Lawrence River, the lifeline of New France. Their next target: Quebec, the capital of New France.

In 1758, New France was weakening rapidly. There was famine; food was in short supply. Farmers ate their horses. Bread was rationed — 60 g per person each day. The great distances in New France made it difficult to supply far-off forts like Niagara and Duquesne. The French army in North America was short of men. Many French soldiers were being used to transport supplies, taking them from battle duties.

France could not provide enough supplies from Europe to help New France. The biggest problem was the Royal Navy. Britain's navy controlled the Atlantic, attacking French ships on their way to America. The British even attacked French ships in their home ports along the coast of France.

Louisbourg falls to the British again, 1758.

Louis Joseph Montcalm

Perhaps New France's great weakness was in the area of leadership. There was a lack of able and informed leadership in both France and the colony. In 1756, Louis Joseph Montcalm was made commander of all the French forces fighting the British in Canada.

Montcalm at once came into conflict with the Governor of New France over strategy. The governor, Vaudreuil, recognized that France's greatest strength lay in the militia and their Indian allies. These forces, using lightning guerilla tactics, had been very successful against the British. Montcalm disliked these irregular forces. He was a French officer; he thought that wars should be fought in a formal and organized way, as they were in Europe.

The French never lost a battle at Fort Duquesne. But by 1758, they could no longer get supplies to the fort. So they burned and abandoned it. The next British expedition against the fort found it empty and in ruins.

Montcalm lies wounded at the battle of the Plains of Abraham.

Louis Joseph Montcalm
BORN: France, 1712
DIED: Quebec, 1759
1721 — entered French army as an ensign (aged 9).
1756 — sent to Canada as army commander-in-chief. Captured and burned Fort Oswego on Lake Ontario.
1757 — captured Fort William Henry. Promised to let the English garrison go. But his Indian allies did not understand and tried to kill the English as they left. Montcalm had to use his own soldiers against the Indians to help save the English.
1758 — defeated the English again at Ticonderoga.
1759 — in command of French troops at Quebec. Wounded in the battle of the Plains of Abraham and taken back to the city. When told he was going to die, he said, "Good. Then I shall not see the surrender of Quebec."

Montcalm believed that France could not win the war in America. His hope was to minimize France's losses. Montcalm decided that the most important thing was to avoid the capture of Quebec. He ordered the French armies to Quebec to fortify and defend the capital.

When Louisbourg fell in the summer of 1758, the seven weeks that it held out delayed the British plans to attack Quebec. The British could not get enough men and materials into the St. Lawrence before it froze. They did not want to be trapped in the ice, cut off from supplies brought by ship.

The British Attack Begins

One of the British generals who commanded the attack on Louisbourg was James Wolfe. Wolfe would have the responsibility of leading the attack on Quebec. To prepare for the attack that would come the following year, Wolfe began a series of raids along the Gaspé coast. The British forces attacked and burned all the French fishing villages along the Gulf of St. Lawrence. This took away from New France one of its most important food supplies. Wolfe wanted to terrorize the civilian population of New France. He had a bitter hatred of the French.

Attitudes in France

By late 1758, Montcalm's defeatist attitude had reached France. Members of the French government began to question the value of the colony in Canada. The feeling was strengthened by the British Navy's control of the seas. France could send few ships or supplies to the colony.

France decided that the war with Britain could not be won in Canada. It could only be won in Europe. With that idea in mind, France attempted to launch a sea-borne invasion of England. The ill-fated invasion force was met by ships of the Royal Navy. The English ships wiped out the French fleet, putting an end to the French Navy. Without the navy, France's ability to defend Quebec was weakened.

The summer of 1759 saw the final stage of the war for control of Canada. Montcalm had organized a line of defence at Quebec. Vaudreuil had called on the people of the villages to assemble their militia forces at Quebec. Remembering Wolfe's acts of terror in the villages of Gaspé, the militiamen came in the

Gaspé Bay at the time of Wolfe's raids along the coast.

thousands. Soon 15 000 soldiers and militia were assembled to defend Quebec.

In June of 1759, a British force of some 164 ships and more than 28 000 men sailed past the Ile d'Orléans and into sight of Quebec. The British forces were commanded by General Wolfe. Wolfe made several landings on the Ile d'Orléans and along both sides of the St. Lawrence. British artillery was set up on the heights at Pointe Lévis, directly across from the city. Montcalm had time to attack these invasion forces before they were fully prepared for battle. Instead he kept to his single line of defence at Beauport, below the city.

The Siege of Quebec

Wolfe had over a month to prepare for his attack on Quebec. On July 31 Wolfe launched his first attack. The British troops were driven back by General Lévis with heavy losses. Throughout July, the British bombarded Quebec with cannon and mortar fire. The siege went on through the month of August. By September, there was not a house in the city that had not been damaged. Wolfe's campaign of terror against the civilian population of New France continued. Villages and farms were put to the torch. These acts only increased French resistance to the British invasion.

Wolfe's activities during the summer accomplished little. His plans of attack were poor and his fellow officers rejected them all. Finally, his officers convinced Wolfe that he should attack Quebec from above the town.

The church of the Recollets was one of many buildings hit during the British bombardment of Quebec.

Attitudes to Canada in France

"Canada is a few acres of snow and not worth a soldier's bones."
Voltaire, a French philosopher

"Nothing ever came from New France except my fur coat."
Madame du Barry, the French king's mistress

The death of Wolfe on the Plains of Abraham.

James Wolfe
BORN: Westerham, Kent, England, 1727
DIED: Quebec, 1759
1741 — entered his father's regiment of Marines as second lieutenant (aged 14). Knew no life but the army: "I would rather listen to the drum and the trumpet than to any softer sound."
1742-1757 — served in the Netherlands, Germany and Scotland.
1758 — led the first assault on Louisbourg. Due to his brilliant tactics, appointed to command the expedition against Quebec.
1759 — shot in lung during battle of the Plains of Abraham. Told that the enemy were fleeing, whispered, "Now God be praised. Since I have conquered, I will die in peace."

The Plains of Abraham and After

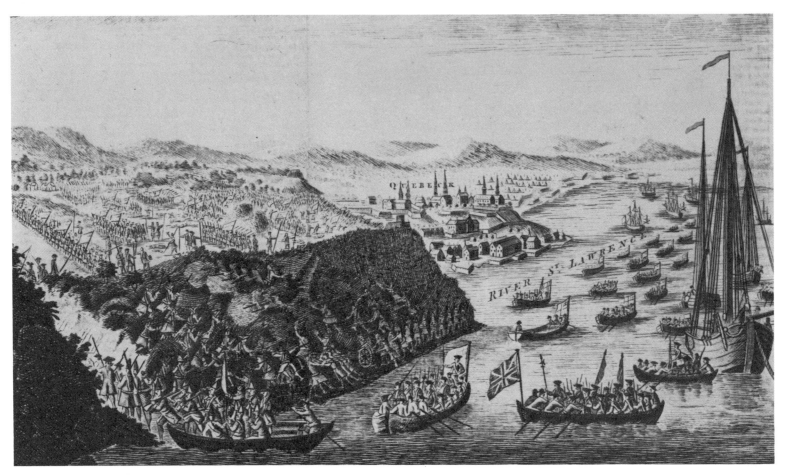

The battle of the Plains of Abraham.

In the early morning darkness of September 13, 1759, Wolfe's forces landed. They began a long and hard climb up the steep and dangerous rock face to the Plains of Abraham above. Montcalm refused to believe that the British would attempt this invasion route. He had defended the area with only 100 men. He was shocked, therefore, to discover that 5000 British soldiers had arrived on the heights.

Montcalm quickly assembled a force of 3500 men to face the British. Had he waited two or three more hours, the French general could have assembled 10 000 troops with strong artillery support. Instead, at 10 o'clock that morning, he appeared before his troops on horseback, sword in hand. Montcalm gave the order to charge.

The Deaths of Wolfe and Montcalm

Montcalm's army rushed at the British in a blind, unruly charge. The British waited with mechanical precision, firing at the French as they rushed forward. In fifteen minutes the struggle was over. In the brief battle, both generals — Montcalm and Wolfe — were killed.

At this point, the French army could have counterattacked and driven the British off. They still had more than 10 000 fresh troops. Vaudreuil proposed a counterattack. But the French officers decided to flee instead. The French army retreated to

The French won the battle of Ste. Foy, but could not retake Quebec.

Montreal. On September 18, Quebec, the largest city in New France, was surrendered to the British. But the British had not yet won a decisive victory. Most of the French army was still intact and the war was not yet over.

Shortly before the fall of Quebec, the French lost Fort Niagara to the British. With the loss of their last major post in the west, the French feared the loss of Montreal as well. When Quebec fell, all that was left of New France was the area around Montreal. Here the remaining armies gathered. But the back of New France had been broken.

The Battle of Ste. Foy

In the spring of 1760, the French forces made one last attempt to drive the British out of Quebec. General Lévis led an army to the old capital, now controlled by General James Murray. Lévis beseiged the city. At the battle of Ste. Foy, just outside the gates of the city, Lévis defeated the British troops. But the French lacked the strength to follow up on their success and retake the city.

After the ice had cleared on the St. Lawrence that spring, the British brought in reinforcements. The French again retreated to Montreal. The French in Canada were surrounded, cut off from any help from France. On September 8, 1760, Montreal surrendered. New France had fallen entirely into British hands. The dream of French Empire in North America had ended. However, French Canadians would never forget their heritage, their language, and their dreams of a French-speaking state on the shores of the St. Lawrence.

The American Revolution

Fights, Wars and Revolutions

Do you ever have a disagreement with your brother or sister? Do you ever feel that your parents are out of touch? Have you ever thought that your teachers were unfair?

Well, it is normal for people to have differences of opinion. In most cases we do not have to *fight* to solve the problem. Usually, we can settle these *conflicts* by discussion. Sometimes one person will change his or her opinion. Sometimes one person has more power and will force the other person to change. Often both sides will give in a little, resulting in a *compromise.*

The same kind of differences can occur between countries. Usually, the countries *negotiate.* If this does not work, the countries may go to *war.*

Sometimes differences of opinion occur between groups within one country or *empire.* When one group or region is dissatisfied, they usually try to get the other group or groups to change their policies. Often, this kind of discussion and compromise is successful. However, if one group continues to be unhappy, as a last resort they may try to obtain control of the government by armed force. This is called a *revolution.*

In England, people looked with pride on the growing empire. They expected all of North America would soon be filled with people who called Britain their mother country.

George III

With control now assured, Britain turned its attention to ruling its North American subjects. Governing the varied peoples of the colonies would require wise and careful leadership. But the new king of England, George III, was in constant conflict with the British parliament. He wanted to run things his own way. He kept on changing the ministers in charge of the colonies. A heavy and inconsistent hand ruled the colonies.

The first test came in 1763. American colonists were moving into the rich farmlands along the Ohio River won from the French in the Seven Years' War. This angered the Ottawa Indians who lived there. Led by their chief, Pontiac, they attacked settlers from Detroit to western Pennsylvania. The attacks killed many settlers before they were stopped by British troops.

In response to Pontiac's Rebellion, the British forbade the American colonists to settle the western lands. Instead, the British suggested that the settlers move to the new colonies of Nova Scotia and Florida. This angered the colonists.

More important, the British government began to try to take more direct control over the American colonies. By the early 1760s, 15 British colonies in North America had their own elected assemblies. All but Florida and Nova Scotia had been running their own affairs for a hundred years or more. The government in England had interfered very little in the activities of the 13 long-established colonies.

Taxes on the Colonies

The British government wanted the colonies to help pay for the Seven Years' War. Since the colonies had wanted to drive the French out of North America, the British thought that they should share the costs.

After the war, the British Parliament passed a number of laws that directly affected the colonies and began to collect taxes from them. This angered the colonists because they did not elect members of the British parliament. They felt that only their own assemblies should make laws and raise taxes for colonies.

The British collected duties on sugar, molasses and other imported goods. They began to prevent smuggling by New England merchants.

Next came the Stamp Act. It required a stamp to be placed on all legal documents, newspapers and playing cards showing that a tax had been paid. The colonists refused to pay the tax. Newspapers in New York, Boston, Halifax, Montreal and other cities were published without displaying the required stamp.

The Sons of Liberty

A group called The Sons of Liberty was formed. They led the merchants of New England in refusing to do any business that required the stamps. The boycott worked. The Stamp Act was repealed by the British Parliament. The colonists learned that they had the strength to defy England.

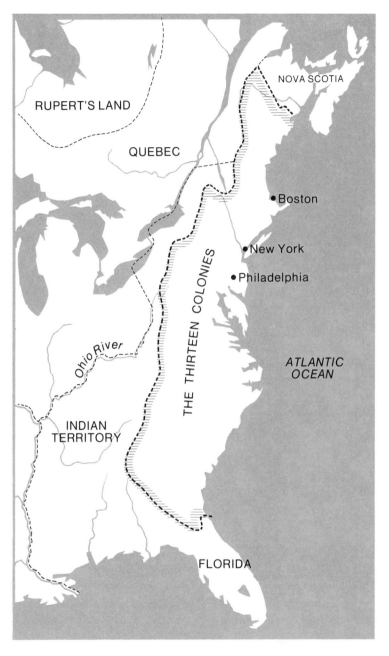

But the British Parliament did not learn the lesson of the Stamp Act. They passed even more laws affecting the colonies. These laws came to be known as the "intolerable acts." The first was the Tea Act, passed in May 1773, placing a tax on tea.

Opposition to Britain Grows

One group of colonists, led by Samuel Adams — one of the Sons of Liberty — was opposed to the taxes that England had imposed. When the Tea Act was passed, they chose to show their anger by throwing a cargo of tea into Boston harbour. This has gone down in history as the Boston Tea Party.

Boston harbour was, as usual, the scene of bustling activity that day in early summer 1773: ships loading, ships arriving, ships leaving, people walking along the quay. Horse-drawn wagons clattered along the cobblestone streets that led to the warehouses and docks.

One ship loaded with tea lay quietly at anchor. A strange party of men appeared in canoes. They were dressed as Indians — but what Indians would come to Boston harbour in their tribal dress? They swarmed aboard the ship.

Once on board, the men began to heave chests of tea over the side. Before they left, 342 chests of tea were floating in Boston harbour.

If the colonists thought that the tea party would change the attitude of the British, they were wrong. Three more "intolerable acts" followed. One act took away many of the political rights of the people of Massachusetts. Another allowed British government employees accused of murder to be tried in England, out of reach of local juries. The last required the townsfolk of the colonies to provide quarters for British troops.

The Quebec Act

These four "intolerable acts" were followed by a fifth, the Quebec Act. This act created the colony of Quebec out of conquered New France. Included in the new colony was the Ohio River area.

The Quebec Act angered the Americans for several reasons. First, it did not give the new colony an elected assembly. Colonists moving to settle in the Ohio territory would lose the right to elect an assembly to govern them. Second, it protected the rights of the Roman Catholic church in Quebec. This angered the Protestants in the Thirteen Colonies. Above all, the Quebec Act upset those colonies which had wanted to expand into the Ohio area. Those lands were now lost to them.

These acts united many of the American colonists in their anger. Before, the Thirteen Colonies had often been in conflict among themselves. Now they felt that it was time for them to act together. They would show the British they were determined to see things changed.

The First Continental Congress

In 1774 the First Continental Congress was held. Representatives of all the colonies except Georgia, Quebec, Florida, Nova Scotia and Prince Edward Island met in Philadelphia. The colonists made a list of their grievances against Britain. They called for a boycott of British goods to back their demands. But they stopped short of calling for an end to all ties with Britain. Instead, they wanted things to return to the way they had been before 1763. If Britain had agreed, the American Revolution might never have taken place.

The delegates invited the people of the new Quebec colony to join the Congress. Many of the merchants in Quebec had come from New England. The delegates expected that the French-speaking Canadians would have little loyalty to their new British masters. But a bitter anti-Catholic speech against the Quebec Act at the Congress left the Canadians suspicious. The French Canadians also feared that they would lose their language rights if they joined with the English-speaking Americans.

Sayings from
Poor Richard's Almanack:

God helps those who help themselves.

Early to bed, early to rise
makes a man healthy, wealthy and wise.

Poor Richard is a forerunner of Sam Slick, the clockmaker with "horse sense" created by Thomas Haliburton of Nova Scotia in the 1800s.

Benjamin Franklin
BORN: Boston, Massachusetts, 1706
DIED: Philadelphia, Pennsylvania, 1790
Printer, publisher, author, inventor, scientist, diplomat.
The 10th of 17 children, left school at age 10.
Apprenticed at age 12 to his brother, a printer.
1723-1748 — worked as a printer in London, England, and Philadelphia. Published and wrote *Poor Richard's Almanack*. Worked to set up a police force, volunteer fire department, public library and university in Philadelphia.
1748 — gave up publishing to devote himself to science. Experimented with electricity and invented lightning rod. Also invented the box stove (giving more heat than a fireplace) and bifocal glasses.
1755 — backed Braddock's attack on Fort Duquesne. Nearly lost 20 000 pounds, but government paid in the end.
1757 — urged British government to take over Canada.
1764-1775 — agent for Pennsylvania in London. Argued against Stamp Act before House of Commons. Also represented the colonies of Georgia, New Jersey, and Massachussetts.
1775 — aware that war might come, returned to America. Day after arrival in Philadelphia, was a delegate to second Continental Congress. Served on committees on postal system, on drafting the Declaration of Independence, and trying to bring Canada into the war on the side of the colonies.
1776 — went to Montreal which had been taken by the Americans to make sure the army was treating the people properly.
1776-1785 — negotiated financial support for the war in France. While in Paris, watched the first balloon ascension.

The War of Independence

The battle of Lexington.

The American Revolution began with a minor skirmish on April 19, 1775. Members of the colonial militia had been hiding arms and ammunition. A detachment of British troops was sent out from Boston to find arms hidden near Concord, Massachusetts. At Lexington, on the way to Concord, the British troops met a company of colonial militia assembled on the village green. The British commander ordered the militia to leave. As they began to do so a shot rang out. No one knows if the shot was fired by a British or American gun. This came to be known as "the shot heard 'round the world." One of the most important political revolutions in modern times had begun.

When they heard the shot, the British troops fired at the departing militiamen. Their shots killed eight colonists and wounded ten. The British were delayed 15 minutes on their march to Concord. At Concord there was another brief clash between the British troops and colonial militia. On the march back to Boston, the British were attacked all along the road by groups of militia.

British authority in the colonies had collapsed. Minor skirmishes gave way to major battles. The Thirteen Colonies co-operated to form a Continental Army under the command of George Washington. But the Thirteen Colonies had not yet declared their independence from Britain. In July of 1775 the colonists sent a petition to the king asking for the return of their rights as Englishmen. George III and the British parliament replied by sending 25 000 more troops to the colonies.

The Declaration of Independence

The first break with England came in March of 1776 when the Congress of South Carolina declared itself a republic. Rhode Island followed in May. On July 4, 1776, the Declaration of Independence was signed.

The war went on for eight years. Sometimes the British had the upper hand, sometimes the colonists. France joined the war on the American side in 1780. With French help, the Americans won a major victory at the Battle of Yorktown in 1781.

It was clear that Britain could not maintain her control. The war ended with the signing of the Treaty of Paris in September 1783. Two months later, British troops left New York, the last major centre to remain in British hands.

The Invasion of Canada

Despite the Americans' best efforts, the Canadian colonies — Quebec, Nova Scotia, Prince Edward Island and Newfoundland — had remained neutral or loyal to Britain. In November of 1775, an American

The revolution was fought on sea as well as on land. This "brig o'war," the *Fair America,* was part of South Carolina's navy. The American flag she is flying has 13 stars. This flag was in use from 1777 to 1794.

force captured Montreal. The government of the colony was forced to flee to Quebec.

A second American army came up to attack Quebec in the winter of 1775–76. Led by Benedict Arnold, the Americans surrounded the city. The siege continued through the long cold winter. In May of 1776, a British fleet arrived to reinforce the garrison at Quebec, and the Americans were driven off. The Americans had expected the French Canadian habitants to support them against the British. They were disappointed.

There was a brief rebellion in 1776 among New England settlers in Cumberland county in Nova Scotia. However, the uprising was quickly put down by the British.

Benedict Arnold (The Turncoat)
BORN: Norwich, Connecticut, 1741
DIED: London, England, 1801
In 1770s was a prosperous businessman and captain in Connecticut militia.
1775 — volunteered for service in Continental Army. Appointed by George Washington to lead expedition through Maine wilderness to Quebec. Joined there by Montgomery, but their attack failed.
1776 — made a brigadier general. Built a "navy" on Lake Champlain and did great damage to British fleet.
1777 — passed over for promotion owing to jealousy of other officers. Only personal appeal from Washington kept him from resigning. Continued to fight brilliantly against British until wounded at Saratoga.
1778 — crippled by his wounds, placed in command of Philadelphia, where he met many Loyalists socially.
1779 — married a Loyalist. Offered to spy for the British.
1780 — told British of a proposed invasion of Canada and offered to sell them West Point. Escaped on a British ship, leaving his British contact to be captured and hanged as a spy.
1781 — led a British raid on New London, Connecticut. After war, hated by both Americans and Loyalists (for abandoning his contact), settled in Saint John, but Loyalists boycotted his business and burned him in effigy. Lived in England till his death. Received a small pension, but never felt properly rewarded for his services to Britain.

Summary and Questions

The victory by the British over the French in 1763 marked the end of the French Empire in North America. The French population continued their way of life, but they did so within a British colony.

Revolution in all the British colonies on the Atlantic Coast could have ended the British Empire in the Americas. Thirteen of the colonies chose to join the revolution: the rest did not.

The future of Canada was greatly affected by these two events. The Conquest of New France determined that for the rest of its history, Canada would be a combination of French and English people.

The fact that Nova Scotia, Prince Edward Island, Newfoundland and Quebec chose not to support the American Revolution determined that there would be a separate British colony or nation sharing North America with the United States.

Can You Recall?

1. Name three things England received under the terms of the Treaty of Utrecht.
2. In 1748, the English traded the fortress of _____ for the town of _____ in India.
3. What were the approximate populations of New France and the English colonies in 1745?
4. Who was named commander of the French forces in Canada in 1756?
5. How did Wolfe, the British commander, terrorize the people of New France?
6. How, in 1759, did France try to defeat Britain in Europe?
7. Where are the Plains of Abraham and why are they important?
8. What happened to Wolfe and Montcalm?
9. When did the French actually surrender New France to Britain?
10. Who were the Sons of Liberty?
11. What were the "intolerable acts" and why were they important?
12. State two provisions of the Quebec Act that annoyed the American colonists.
13. Where and when did the American Revolution start?
14. Did any part of the American Revolution take part in Canada? If so, where?
15. What treaty ended the American Revolution? When was it signed?

Ideas for Discussion

1. Compare the picture below with the pictures of the deaths of Montcalm and Wolfe on pages 113 and 115. Do you think these pictures are realistic? Were they actually drawn at the time of the battles? Discuss the reasons why artists would draw pictures like these.

The death of General Montgomery in the American attack on Quebec, 1775.

2. Discuss the following statement. In the end, New France was lost to Britain because of bad luck and a series of errors.
3. Compare the views of Montcalm and Vaudreuil on how the war against the British should have been fought. Which do you think had the better approach to the problem, given the conditions in New France at the time? Explain your reasons.
4. The motto of Quebec is "Je me souviens" (I remember). Suggest ways in which the events of the British conquest of New France might have contributed to the choice of this motto.
5. The first shot in the American Revolution is often called "the shot heard 'round the world." Suggest some reasons why the description is an appropriate one.
6. Is revolution a legitimate way to end political oppression? If someone took away your rights as a Canadian citizen, would you fight in a revolution? If you had lived in the American colonies in 1775, would you have joined the revolution or supported the British? Answer these questions and then discuss your answers with your classmates.
7. Suggest some things the British might have done to prevent the American Revolution. Discuss the ways in which your suggestions differ from what the British actually did in the years just before the American Revolution.

Do Some Research

1. Make a report on European approaches to warfare in the eighteenth century. Include descriptions of uniforms, weapons and the everyday life of ordinary soldiers.
2. Prepare a research report on the Quebec Act. Examine its role in keeping the French Canadians from joining the American Revolution.

3. Make a brief report on the role of each of the following in the American Revolution:
   a) Benedict Arnold;
   b) Thomas Jefferson;
   c) George Washington;
   d) General Cornwallis;
   e) Chief Pontiac;
   f) Betsy Ross;
   g) George III;
   h) Governor Carleton.
4. Read the American Declaration of Independence. Prepare a report on the reasons it gives for the revolution.
5. Find out about American attitudes toward revolutions other than their own. Have the Americans always supported the principles stated in the Declaration of Independence?

Be Creative

1. Make a series of life-size posters showing French, British and American soldier's uniforms of the eighteenth century.
2. Write a letter from one of the following:
   a) a parish priest in one of the towns along the Gaspé terrorized by Wolfe;
   b) a housewife in Quebec City during the siege of the city;
   c) a British soldier after the Battle of the Plains of Abraham.
   In your letter tell of your experiences during the War of the Conquest of New France. Describe your feelings about those events.
3. Make a series of large wall maps showing the important places, battles, and events of:
   a) The conquest of New France;
   b) The American Revolution.
4. Write newspaper editorials as they might have appeared in a Boston paper and a London paper after the Americans had won the revolution against Britain.

Life in a New Land
ADVANCE ORGANIZER

1

Not all the American colonists supported the revolution. Many chose to remain loyal to Britain. They were called Loyalists. Loyalists established settlements in Nova Scotia and Quebec. They spread out and created new colonies in New Brunswick and Upper Canada (Ontario). They were the pioneers in these two provinces. Together husbands and wives struggled to establish new homes — small log cabins in the clearings. Together, they planted the first crops.

2

Gradually farms were established and pioneer families prepared for a new life in their new country.

World List

agricultural	community	grant	rebel
assembly	economic	loyal	rural
bee	emerge	Loyalist	support
clearing	government	pioneer	title

3

Families depended on each other for help. Houses and barns were built at pioneer bees. New communities of friends and neighbours developed.

4

In Lower Canada, the French-Canadian population increased rapidly. Farm settlements increased in size. But, though most of the population was French, the English controlled the government and business. The French Canadians held fast to their language, their religion and their customs.

5

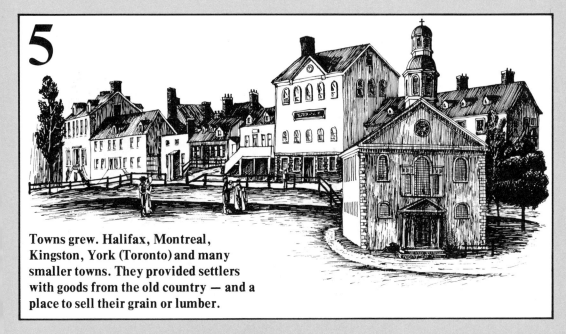

Towns grew. Halifax, Montreal, Kingston, York (Toronto) and many smaller towns. They provided settlers with goods from the old country — and a place to sell their grain or lumber.

6

Gradually a new people emerged. They were no longer British, no longer pioneers. A new country — Canada — and a new people — Canadians — were coming of age.

Who were the Loyalists?

Not everyone in the American colonies wanted to form a country separate from Great Britain. Even in the colonies that signed the Declaration of Independence, there were people who thought that the colonies should still be ruled by England. Many people believed that any revolution against a king was bad. Others thought that there were advantages to being ruled by England. They would be protected by the British Navy. There would be a market for their raw materials in Britain. Still others were farmers living far from the cities who really did not care who ruled.

The people who were opposed to the revolution were called Loyalists or tories. They called themselves Loyalists because they were loyal to the King. The rebels called them tories. A tory is someone who resists change.

Attacks on the Loyalists

One-third to one-half of the people in the American colonies remained loyal to the English king. The people who were fighting in the revolution were very unhappy about the Loyalists. The rebels attacked the Loyalists. Sometimes they tarred and feathered them — or even lynched them. They took property away from the Loyalists. They drove the Loyalists away from the homes they had lived in for years.

The revolution lasted from 1775 to 1783. During this time, many Loyalists left the American colonies. Some headed north to Quebec. Others went to England or the Caribbean. Many went to New York, the last big city to remain in English hands.

When the war ended, many of the new states passed laws that took away all the rights of the Loyalists. Anyone who had helped the British could be thrown in jail. Their homes and lands could be taken away. Many Loyalists decided to leave the United States.

Where the Loyalists Settled

100 000 Loyalists decided to leave. Nearly one-third went to Great Britain. Most of these people were among the richest and best educated of the Loyalists. Others went south to the Caribbean. About 40 000 came north to Nova Scotia and Quebec.

The Loyalists who came north settled in three main areas. Many settled in Nova Scotia and on vacant

American rebels punishing a Loyalist.

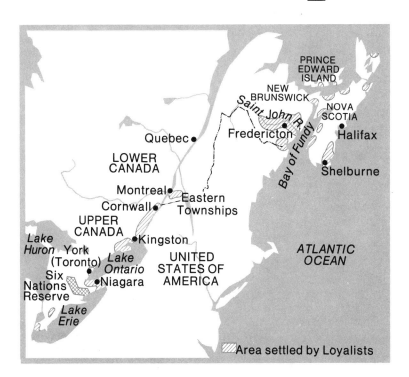

lands along the north shore of the Bay of Fundy. Others followed the St. Lawrence west to Lake Ontario and settled along the shores of that lake. And some settled south of the St. Lawrence River in Quebec. This area came to be known as the Eastern Townships.

During the Revolution, a number of Indian tribes fought with the British. Much of the Iroquois Confederacy was on the British side. After the war, many of these Indians decided to move to British territory. They settled along the Grand River, north of Lake Erie.

Joseph Brant (Thayendanegea)
BORN: Ohio, 1742
DIED: Burlington, Upper Canada, 1807
Son of a Mohawk chief, grew up under influence of William Johnson, a settler in the Mohawk Valley and Superintendent of Indian Affairs for the government of New York.
1755-1760 — fought on British side in war against French.
1761 — sent to school in Connecticut. Learned to read English, mathematics, some Latin and Greek, and farming.
1763 — persuaded Iroquois Confederacy not to join Pontiac's rebellion.
1776-1783 — Brant and the Confederacy remained loyal to Britain during the American Revolution. Fought well for the king.
1784 — Iroquois lands in the new United States claimed by Americans. Negotiated for new land in British territory. Granted land on Grand River for the Six Nations.
1785-1788 — Built Mohawk Chapel at "Brant's Ford," later to be designated a Royal Chapel by King Edward VII as a tribute to Brant.

A Mohawk village on the Grand River. This sketch on birchbark was made by Elizabeth Simcoe, whose husband was governor of Upper Canada in the 1790s.

The Loyalists in the Maritimes

In the 1770s George Ludlow had been a judge in New York. During the American Revolution the British government appointed him superintendent of police at Long Island, New York. Ludlow came to New Brunswick as a Loyalist in 1784. He was the first chief justice in the colony. He lived in this house on the Saint John River, 8 km from Fredericton.

Throughout the year of 1783, great fleets of ships sailed out of New York City harbour. They sailed north, carrying many Loyalists to their new homes. Thirty thousand men, women and children came to begin a new life in Nova Scotia.

Many went to the area along the Atlantic coast of Nova Scotia, south of Halifax. There, they built the new town of Shelburne. Others settled on the north shore of the Bay of Fundy. They found good farmland and abundant forests along the St. John River. A handful of Loyalists settled on Prince Edward Island.

The Loyalists Learn to Adapt

The Loyalists from many different backgrounds came to Nova Scotia. Some had been wealthy. They had been doctors, lawyers or merchants in their previous homes. They brought with them many of their possessions. At Shelburne, they built large houses and lived comfortable lives. But others brought little money with them and had to live on government grants.

Picture Gallery page 7

The formerly well-to-do Loyalists often were not prepared for the hardships of pioneer life. They had to clear land and build their own houses. Some found the new life very difficult.

Others adapted very well. They worked hard to establish a new life. For the Loyalists who had been farmers in the American colonies, life in Nova Scotia brought very few changes.

The Loyalists on the north shore of the Bay of Fundy wanted to be able to govern themselves. They did not want the people of Halifax to tell them what to do. The British government decided that a new colony should be created beside Nova Scotia. In 1784, the British government created the colony of New Brunswick.

Black Settlement in Nova Scotia

Among the Loyalists who came to the Maritimes were a number of blacks. Some of the black settlers were free men, soldiers who had fought on the British side in the war. Others were slaves, brought along by their masters as they left the United States. By 1788, there were more than 4000 blacks in the Shelburne area.

In the 1750s and 1760s, some slaves were sold in the British colonies of New England and Nova Scotia. Slavery was not legal in these colonies. But Loyalists who owned slaves continued to buy and sell them after they came to Nova Scotia. By the early 1800s, slavery began to die out in the Maritimes. In 1833, it was abolished throughout the British Empire.

Life was not easy for the blacks in Nova Scotia. Blacks were not allowed to vote. Land granted to the blacks was poor. Many blacks moved to the towns, where they could work as household servants or as labourers. Riots broke out in Halifax because blacks would work for lower wages than whites. Whites without jobs were angry about this.

By 1791, some of the blacks had decided to move to Africa. The African country of Sierra Leone was begun by blacks who left Nova Scotia. But other blacks continued to come to Nova Scotia. Some came from other British colonies. Others came from the United States as freemen or runaway slaves. Today there continues to be a large black community in Nova Scotia.

New Brunswick
When a new colony was established on the north shore of the Bay of Fundy, it was called after the family of George III, the English king. George was descended from the German House of Brunswick.

James Hayt Has For Sale
A Black boy, fourteen years of age in full vigour of health, very active, has a pleasing countenance and every ability to render himself useful and agreeable in a family. The title for him is indisputable.
Nova Scotia Advertisement circa 1784

Resurgam, the Loyalists' motto, means "I shall rise again."

The Loyalists in Upper Canada

Loyalists at a new town site.

By ship and by cart they came. On foot, on horseback, by large sailing ship and small boat, the Loyalists headed north. Those who came overland from the former Middle Colonies headed for the settled areas along the St. Lawrence River. Most of these Loyalists came from New York, Pennsylvania. Many were farmers. Some were English, but many were Dutch, German, Swiss and of other nationalities.

Some settled in the Sorel area near Montreal. They received small grants of land along the St. Lawrence. But most wanted to live in a community where English was the main language. And they wanted new areas of land that they could own and farm. Quebec provided neither of these things.

New Lands for the Loyalists

The answer was to travel west. The government of Quebec decided to open up the lands north of Lake Ontario for the new Loyalist settlers. It bought land from the Mississauga Indians from Cataraqui to the Trent River. Many of the Loyalists could settle here. The government also purchased an area west of Niagara. This was to make a new home for the Loyalist Indians.

General Frederick Haldimand, governor of Quebec, sent men out to survey these lands. They were divided into townships. Lots in the township would be governed by the same rules as under the seigneurial

Lady Simcoe's birchbark sketch of Kingston.

system. The head of a family was to get 100 acres (40 ha) with 50 acres (20 ha) for each member of the family. A single man was to receive 50 acres. Soldiers and officers from the army would get more land than ordinary settlers. Most of the settlers wanted to be close to Lake Ontario or the rivers flowing into it. It was easy to travel from one place to another by water.

The settlers needed places where they could buy goods they could not produce themselves. They needed foodstuffs in the first few years, until their

Ontario

Many Loyalists in Upper Canada settled near the lake the Iroquois called *Oniatario*, or "sparkling water." The name was shortened to Ontario and came to be applied to the province. Ontario's motto is *Ut incepit fidelis sic permanet*, Latin for "Loyal she began, loyal she remains."

farms were producing enough to feed them. And they needed such things as tea, knives and forks, dishes, clothing, guns, and pots and pans. They also needed places where they could sell their grain, flour and lumber. To fill these two needs, towns and villages grew up along the lakeshore. The two most important were Kingston and York.

Kingston and York

There had been a settlement at Cataraqui — the location of Kingston — ever since the first Europeans reached Lake Ontario. In 1673, Governor Frontenac built a fur-trading post there, which he named Fort Frontenac. In 1784, the first group of English-speaking people arrived. By 1790, there were 50 houses and stores. By the early 1800s, Kingston had become the largest and most rapidly growing town in the area.

The first town further west was on the site of an old Indian village called Toronto — the meeting place. Called York by the new English settlers, it quickly became the main trading centre for the area west of Lake Ontario.

The Loyalists who moved into the Lake Ontario region soon wanted to have their own government, separate from the French Canadians. In 1791, the British government passed the Constitutional Act. This act divided Quebec into Lower Canada and Upper Canada. It also provided for elected assemblies in the two colonies. The Loyalists had been used to this system in the American colonies. But this was the first time that the inhabitants of Quebec had had the chance to elect their own leaders.

Quebec After the Conquest

In 1760, Quebec City lay in ruins. Burnt-out buildings could be seen everywhere. Those left standing showed gaping holes in their roofs and walls. The British artillery fire during the siege of Quebec in 1759 had spared few buildings. Even the churches had been hit. The Basilica de Notre Dame, begun in 1647, was a charred shell. Red-coated British soldiers patrolled the streets.

Many of the fine houses of the city were destroyed. Others, still intact, had been abandoned by their owners. No longer could the sounds of laughter, music, and dancing be heard. Fine carriages no longer passed through the streets of the upper town.

In the lower town, where the working people lived, some houses were already being rebuilt. People were returning to their homes. But everything had changed. New France had ceased to exist.

The rich merchants had gone. Most of the government leaders had gone. Even before Quebec had fallen, they had begun to return to France, taking with them everything they could carry. The ordinary people, the peasants and workers, remained. The priests and nuns stayed too, to look after the spiritual needs of their people.

British Rule

Quebec was now under British rule. The Union Jack flew over the cities of Quebec and Montreal. French law was replaced by British law. The bishop and political leaders who stayed told the people to obey their new rulers.

The British at first expected to make Englishmen out of the French who remained in Canada. In 1763,

Everyday life did not change much for the working people in the lower town.

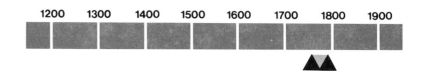

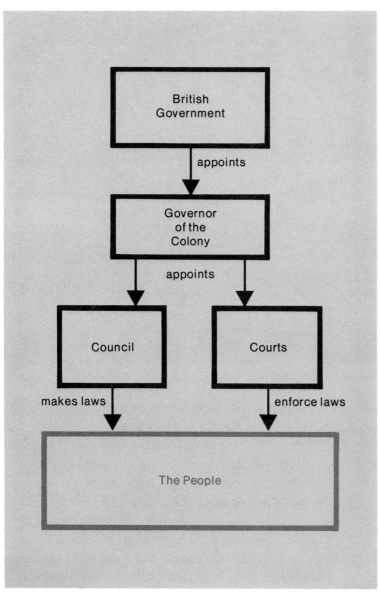

The system of government in Quebec from 1763 to 1791. In 1774, the Quebec Act restored the French system of law for everything but criminal matters. There was no elected assembly until 1791.

all French laws were thrown out. The rights of the seigneurs were reduced. English laws and customs would be used in the colony. Quebec was to be ruled in the English language.

British settlers came into the colony, in small numbers at first. English merchants, many from New England, replaced French merchants. A new, British, ruling class emerged. The fine homes were rebuilt. The fancy carriages passed through the streets again. The gap between the new British masters and the people of Quebec was great.

The Quebec Act and the Constitutional Act

Two acts of the British Parliament, however, helped protect the old way of life. The first was the Quebec Act of 1774. This restored French civil law. The daily life and business of the colony would continue according to the old laws. Only criminal law would be British. The rights of the seigneurs were restored. The Catholic church was also protected under the Quebec Act.

The second act was the Constitutional Act of 1791. The new Loyalist settlers wanted an elected assembly like the ones they had known in the American colonies. They felt that they could control the French Canadians through the assembly. The Constitutional Act gave the colonists the elected assembly. But it did something else. It divided the Quebec colony into two. The western part, the newly settled area where most of the Loyalists had moved, was called Upper Canada. The eastern part, where most people were French speaking, was to be called Lower Canada. Each part would have its own elected assembly.

Changing Life in Lower Canada

Under British rule, the habitants still worked their fields along the St. Lawrence. They still paid their rents to the seigneur. Fiddle music still rang out at lively country dances. Black-robed priests and nuns ran the churches and convents. Men went out to trade for furs and cut timber. Girls still married young and raised large families.

But the whole pattern of life had changed. The people of Lower Canada had become isolated. They were cut off from France. And there was a great gap of culture, language and religion between the Canadians and their new British rulers. Even the old economic patterns had changed.

The Decline of the Towns

Life in New France had been based on trade. Great shipments of furs were sent to France. Trade had made the towns of New France very important. Twenty-five percent of the population of New France lived in Quebec, Montreal or Trois Rivières. Among these people were traders, merchants, skilled craftsmen, civil servants, soldiers, priests, nuns and the servants of the wealthy families. Many left after the Conquest. Some went back to France; others moved onto the land.

The merchants and civil servants who now lived in the cities were British. But they did not bring their families, nor did the British soldiers stationed in Lower Canada. The population of the towns dropped sharply. By 1825, only 10 percent of the population of Lower Canada lived in the towns.

On the other hand, the population of the countryside continued to grow rapidly. The church and the

An habitant farm about 1850.

government had always encouraged the people of New France to have large families. In Lower Canada this trend continued. Couples married young. Families of 10 or 12 children were common. The population of Lower Canada doubled every 25 years or so.

This growth put great pressure on the farmlands along the St. Lawrence. Lands still covered in trees were cleared and farmed. New areas in the Eastern Townships, south of Montreal, were cleared. At first, most of the farmers in the Eastern Townships were Loyalists. Soon the seigneurial lands along the river were filled. French-speaking farmers began to move into the Eastern Townships too.

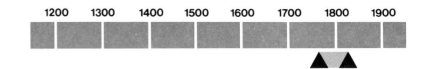

The Village

The fast growing rural population led to a new feature in the Quebec landscape: the village. Before the Conquest, farm homes were few in number, located near the seigneur's home. Now villages with many homes clustered around the local church sprang up. By the early 1800s, villages had been established about 10 to 12 km apart all along the St. Lawrence. As well as the church, the villages usually had a general store, a lawyer, a doctor, and sometimes a school. The village stood apart from the seigneury in Lower Canada. Most of the first people in the villages came from the towns. Later, villages were where young people moved as they broke away from their families.

Agricultural production was low. The habitants continued the old ways of farming. They used part of the land to grow grain — wheat, oats, and corn. The rest was left as untended meadow. The British tried to introduce new farming methods and new crops. They had little success, although the habitants did start to grow potatoes.

Some farms were more successful. Local merchants, notaries, even parish priests, acquired enough land to make a lot of money farming. This tended to make a wider split between the poor habitants who could barely make a living of the land and their richer countrymen.

The village of Charlesbourg north of Quebec in 1830.

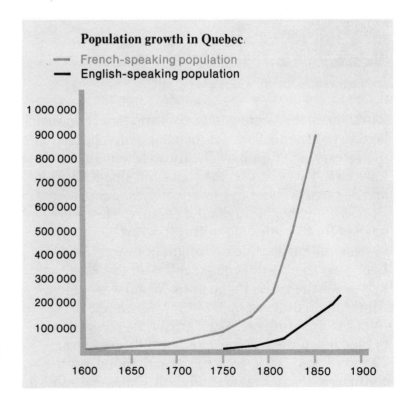

Population growth in Quebec

— French-speaking population
— English-speaking population

Timber, Furs and Urban Life

A timber raft on the river at Quebec, 1830.

Rural populations grew. There was no longer enough land to go around. Some of the young men headed into the forests to cut timber. The forests along the St. Lawrence River and on the Canadian shield held pine and oak trees. These trees were in great demand in Britain at the beginning of the century. They were needed for the ships of the Royal Navy.

Sawmilling became important in Lower Canada. Each year there would be great timber drives, bringing logs down the rivers to the mills. Wood was cut in winter, then dragged over the snow by horse to the river. After spring break-up, great rafts of logs were floated down the rivers to the sawmills. As Lower Canada's population grew in the early nineteenth century, a steady stream of French Canadians moved to the United States to work in the forests and sawmills of Maine.

The Fur Trade

The fur trade continued after the Conquest. British merchants took over the trade established by the French. They created a new fur-trading company, the Northwest Company, based in Montreal. The North-west Company sent explorers and traders out to the north and northwest to seek new supplies of furs. Soon, they were in fierce competition with the Hudson's Bay Company. Although the owners of the Northwest Company were British, most of the traders and voyageurs were still French.

Picture Gallery page 9

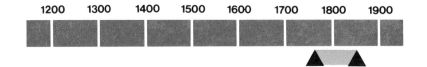

Notre Dame Street, Montreal.

Urban Life

The British controlled the town life of Lower Canada. They ran the businesses, owned the banks, factories, docks and shipyards. They created schools and universities such as McGill in Montreal. Most of the professions were dominated by the British. The one major exception was law. Because Lower Canada still used French civil law, French-speaking lawyers were important figures.

Montreal Overtakes Quebec

The most important city in the early nineteenth century was Quebec. Quebec was the capital of Lower Canada. The Governor General of the two Canadas lived there. Quebec was the centre for British wealth, culture and power. But, over time, Montreal overtook Quebec in importance and size. Montreal was better located for trade with the markets of the United States and Upper Canada. Many British merchants moved to Montreal. Factories were set up. Families like the Molsons established businesses and made fortunes that have lasted to this day.

During the first half of the 19th century, the gulf between English and French in Lower Canada widened. They were separated from each other by wealth, political power, religion, and language. English society had closed in around the French Canadians without absorbing them. They were cut off from France and had no ties to the British. In their isolation the people of Quebec created their own culture and society.

Pioneering

The Loyalists arrived in the 1780s. They wanted to have land of their own.

The British government wished to encourage settlers to come to British North America. They therefore offered settlers free land. Each Loyalist family would receive 100 acres (40 ha) of land. Each additional member of the family would receive an extra 50 acres (20 ha).

Loyalist soldiers were particularly encouraged to come. Officers received from 500 (200 ha) to 1000 acres (400 ha) each. Non-commissioned officers were given 200 acres (80 ha).

Finding Your Lot

Lots were chosen by a draw, so that they would be distributed fairly. The titles (deeds) to different lots were placed in a hat, and drawn by different settlers.

A guide would lead the family to their lot. If they were lucky they arrived with two oxen and a cart. All of their possessions were piled on the cart. When they arrived at their lot, the struggle to establish a new life began.

Clearing the Land and Building the First Home

Most of the land at this time was covered by forests of huge trees. Trees were often two metres in diameter, and up to 30 m high. There were no roads through the forest. Often the only route into the forest was by river or by Indian trail.

Newly arrived settlers first had to prepare a shelter. Usually this was made of branches. Sometimes it was covered by animal skins.

Pioneers get together to clear the site of a new town.

The next job was to make a clearing around the shelter. The huge trees had to be cut down. Logs were either set aside to make a log cabin, or were burned. The stumps were too difficult to take out of the

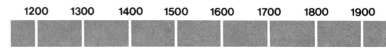

If there were neighbours in the area, they usually helped to build the first log cabin. If there were no neighbours, the whole family would work together to build it.

The first log cabin was usually very small, about 4 m by 6 m. Logs were notched to fit into each other. After the cabin was finished, the logs were chinked with clay, chinking kept out flies and mosquitoes and kept the heat in.

The cabin was built on the ground with an earth floor. It was only one storey high. Glass was expensive. Early log cabins had very few windows. At first, a hole was left on the roof to let out smoke from the fire. Sometimes a wooden chimney was built and covered with clay. As soon as possible, a stone fireplace was built for cooking and for heating the cabin in winter.

The farmer's land looked raw before the first seeding. Stumps stuck awkwardly out of the soil. The land was often charred and black from the log burning. A triangular harrow was dragged over the ground to mix the ashes and the soil.

Seeds were spread by hand. The first crops were usually potatoes and turnips. These crops could be stored easily over the winter. Other common crops were squash, pumpkin, corn and wheat.

Soil was pulled over the seeds with a hoe. With good soil, warm heat from the sun, and enough gentle rain, the crops would grow through the summer. With luck, the pioneers would have a small harvest in the fall. They hoped and prayed that there would be enough to last the family through the winter until the next spring. Then the same cycle was repeated.

But each year, the size of the clearing could be increased, and the harvest would be larger.

ground. They were usually left in the ground for four or five years until they had decayed, and could be pulled out. Sometimes stumps were then pulled to the side of the field to make a stump fence.

PIONEERING IN UPPER CANADA   141

Pioneer Life - A Partnership

Life for pioneer families was a partnership between all members. Each performed essential tasks. Without all working together, it was almost impossible to survive.

In her book *The Gentle Pioneers,* Audrey Norris described the life of the Stricklands, early pioneers in Upper Canada.

Samuel and Emma Strickland came to Upper Canada in 1825. They stayed at first in the town of Darlington, until they obtained a lot of land. In 1826 Samuel Strickland moved out to claim his lot, clear the trees and construct a log cabin. He left Emma, who was pregnant, in the town until their new home was ready.

One day, Emma's brother walked to his lot. He told him that Emma was dangerously ill. Samuel set out to walk back to the town, 56 km away. But Emma died giving birth to their baby son.

With his hopes for the future shattered, Samuel returned to finish clearing his land. His neighbours, the Reids, had looked after his crops in his absence. This kind of co-operation was common among pioneers, who had to survive in the wilderness.

He moved in with the Reids, who looked after the baby. He continued to look after the crops, cut trees, clear bush, and burn the dead wood. He had to look after livestock, plant crops, clear stumps and remove stones from the fields. He would make furniture and household materials. But there were many things that he did not have the time nor the knowledge to do. He couldn't spin or weave. He couldn't make bread, cheese and butter. He couldn't make clothing, quilts or rugs. He did not have the time to make candles, soap and other household utensils. And he alone could not look after his son, cook the meals and do the washing and mending as well as work the farm.

Besides, life in an isolated settlement was lonely. He could not continue without a wife. The Reids had a young daughter Mary. She agreed to be his new wife. Samuel and Mary were married, and raised a family of 13 children.

A family gathering at the Strickland farm some years later. Sam Strickland is the man on the right. His sister, Catherine Parr Traill, is seated and holding a child. She wrote several books about life in "The Backwoods of Canada." Another sister, Susanna Moodie, also wrote about "Roughing it in the Bush."

Catherine Parr Traill's description of the journey to her family's lot:

Our progress was slow on account of the roughness of the road. It was filled with many obstacles, including blocks of limestone, fallen trees, big roots and mudholes. Over the streams they have corduroy bridges, over which you go jolt, jolt, jolt, till every bone of your body feels like it is being dislocated. . . . I could hardly bear the thumping and bumping. Sometimes I laughed because I would not cry.

A corduroy road.

Roads and Transportation

Transportation was very difficult in pioneer communities in forested lands. At first there were no roads. Only occasional Indian trails could be found in some areas. The best lots were located on a lake or river. Then one could travel by boat. Usually these waterfront lots went to army officers or other privileged people.

The first roads were mere paths through the woods. They went over stumps and rocks, through mud and shallow streams. Wagons often stuck in the mud or were overturned by rocks.

The first improvement in the road was done by putting down logs, side by side, to prevent wagons from sinking into the mud. This was called a "corduroy road."

Without good roads, it was hard for pioneer farmers to get to market to buy supplies. Tea, salt, and sugar, and manufactured goods such as pots, guns and dishes all had to be bought. Without roads they could not get their grain or lumber to the mill. They had to sell their grain and lumber in order to get money to buy the necessities of life.

The government of Upper Canada was not interested in spending money to build roads in outlying areas. Many of the newly settled regions had few roads. This was one of the most serious complaints that pioneers had against their government.

Pioneer Bees and Social Life

Pioneer homes were often isolated from one another. Pioneer families had to do almost everything for themselves. The successful settler became almost self-sufficient. Some things, however, could not be done by one person or family. Clearing the land, building a log cabin or raising a barn required several people. To solve these problems, pioneers had a "bee" — gatherings of people to carry out a project — to help one another.

Logging, clearing, barn-raising, quilting or moving bees were all organized to do a necessary job. In addition, they provided a chance to meet neighbours and to exchange news. The eating, drinking and dancing following a barn-raising bee were enough to attract people from miles around. And what better way for young men and women to meet a future wife or husband?

Most pioneer families regarded Sunday as a day of rest. When they could, they went to church on Sunday.

A Methodist circuit rider.

The first church services were held in a home, or courthouse, hotel, or other building. The Methodists had ministers who travelled on horseback from home to home. They were called "circuit riders." Pioneer families greeted them eagerly as visitors who could bring news.

Religion

Later, as the community developed, churches were built. Each religious group had its own church. A village might have several churches. After Sunday morning services, which frequently lasted two or three hours, they would stay to chat and exchange news. Churches became centres for libraries and study groups. They were also used for socials and concerts, for Thanksgiving festivals in the fall, and for picnics in the summer.

Parties

In pioneer times, there were few organized forms of entertainment. A common activity on a Sunday was to have a "visit" with neighbours or relatives. Parties, for birthdays, weddings, anniversaries, or to welcome a new settler, were for the whole family. Children came and went with their parents. They stayed at the party until they were tired, and then went to sleep on a bed or in a quiet corner on a chair.

Dancing was the most popular activity at parties. Drinking was common, despite the concern of the churches. Whiskey was made from local grain, and was very cheap. Almost every road crossing came to have a tavern or inn. Pioneers frequently gathered in these local taverns to talk, to exchange stories, and to drink.

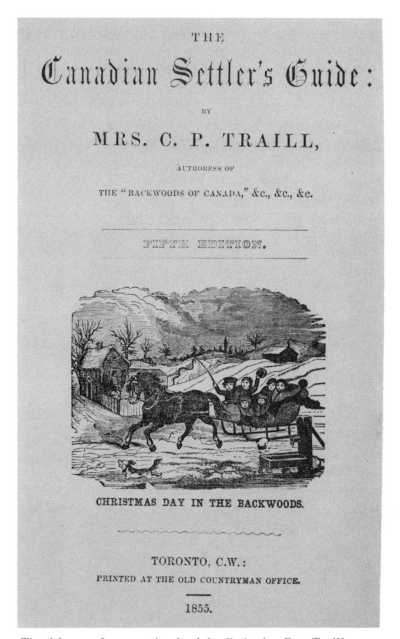

CHRISTMAS DAY IN THE BACKWOODS.

TORONTO, C.W.:

PRINTED AT THE OLD COUNTRYMAN OFFICE.

1855.

The title page from another book by Catherine Parr Traill.

A Raising Bee

We arrived in our lot in August, 1832. By the end of October we had cleared a few acres, and were ready to build our first log cabin. We invited our neighbours to come to help, and on the set day, 16 turned up. The work went merrily along, aided by large amounts of Canadian whiskey. It seems that this is necessary in order to get the job done. We also provide a feast of salt pork, potatoes, rice pudding and a huge cheshire cheese. Everybody worked together, whether they were rich or poor, regardless of their class.

By the end of the day, the four log walls were up. I was disappointed that they had not cut the doors or even a window, there also was no roof, and we had only a dirt floor. However, in the next few days, my husband was able to finish this first part of our new home. Some of the ladies came over a few days later for a moving bee. Before the snow arrived, we were quite happy to have a roof over our heads, in our new log home in Canada.

Adapted from "Backwoods of Canada" by Catherine Parr Traill.

Pioneer Clothing and Pioneer Schools

Pioneers made their own clothing from what they had at hand. Jackets and moccasins were made from deerskins. Warm blankets and rugs were made from bearskins.

Some pioneers planted flax which was made into linen. Linen was woven into fabric for shirts and dresses.

As soon as enough land was cleared, pioneers tried to get farm animals. Cows were raised mainly for milk or meat. Sheep were raised for wool.

Pioneer women knew how to turn raw wool into clothing. The raw wool was prepared and cleaned.

Women spent many hours at a spinning wheel turning the wool into spun yarn. Then the wool was dyed, using local herbs or weeds. Finally it was woven into fabric to make jackets, shirts, dresses, blankets and quilts.

Women gathered together to make beautiful quilts at quilting bees. At the same time, they had friendly conversation. In a time before radio, newspapers or television, it was the best way to find out the latest news. For pioneer women living in isolation in the woods, quilting bees and other social gatherings were essential.

Learning to spin.

Schools

Pioneers needed their children to help around the farm. However, most wanted their children to get an education. Education meant learning the "three Rs": reading, 'riting and 'rithmetic. Many of the activities in a modern school would be considered "frills" in a pioneer school.

The first schools were usually held in someone's home. Then, as the community grew, a schoolhouse was built. The local families contributed money to pay for a schoolhouse, and to pay the teacher's salary. Salaries for teachers were very low. As a result, good teachers were rare.

The first schools were log cabins. Children sat in rows, facing the teacher. In the middle of the room was a huge box stove. Children had to bring in wood and look after the fire themselves.

The "March of Intellect," a sketch of a country school made by a school inspector in 1845.

Discipline was very harsh. If students (usually boys) misbehaved, they were hit on the hand or the bottom with a birch stick. If they were very bad, they were taken "out to the woodshed" by the school master, for more punishment.

Very few children other than the children of the wealthy, went to school beyond the age of 12.

Egerton Ryerson

BORN: Charlotteville, Upper Canada, 1803
DIED: Toronto, Ontario, 1882
Fifth son of a Loyalist family, educated at local grammar school, where there was an excellent teacher. Became a Methodist even though he had been brought up an Anglican.
1825 — Entered Methodist ministry.
1829-1840 — Editor of Methodist *Christian Guardian.* In the paper, he attacked the clergy reserves — lands granted by the crown to the Anglican Church in Upper Canada.
1833 — Supported the Reformers but came out against William Lyon Mackenzie's rebellion.
1841 — first president of Victoria College in Cobourg (later to become part of the University of Toronto).
1844-1876 — Chief Superintendent of Education for Upper Canada.
1844-1845 — Toured Europe to see educational systems. Disliked the snobbery of English schools but liked some free schools he saw in Europe.

Worked to get better teachers, books, and libraries in every town. Wanted more than the "three Rs" for children. Promoted teaching of history, geography, nature study, music. Asked that copies of famous paintings and statues be placed in schools so students would understand art. Education was not to cram students with knowledge but to fit them for life. Children's minds were "the most precious wealth of the country."

Difficulties and Rewards of Pioneer Life

Not all pioneer settlers prospered. Life was always difficult. However, most settlers struggled to make a new life in Canada. After years of hard work, most found great satisfaction in their new home. After a few years, rough pioneer communities began to change. Soon pleasant homes and farms were dotted over the landscape. Where once there had been brown stump-studded fields, there were gardens and orchards with apple, plum and crabapple trees.

Eventually, a grist mill was built to provide a means of grinding grain into flour. As more land was cleared, crops were bigger. Farmers could then save some cash from their sale of wheat, oats or barley crops.

Often, a sawmill was built to provide sawn boards. This meant that pioneers could now build a new house with board siding to replace the log walls. These boards were called clapboards.

Some wealthier settlers built homes of stone. Many of these original stone homes still exist in farming areas of Ontario, Quebec, Nova Scotia and New Brunswick.

London, Ontario (Upper Canada), in 1840.

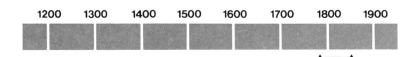

Brewer's Mills near Kingston, 1831.

This cartoon, "The Emigrant's Welcome to Canada," appeared in England about 1820.

A letter from a settler who gave up:

I bought a lot of wild land, but found I had been deceived. I lived for two months in a shed they call a shanty, eaten alive by mosquitoes. I could get nothing to eat but salt pork. All my English farming knowledge was quite useless. It broke my heart to work among stumps, and never see a well-ploughed field. I thought of my wife and children in England. I could not bring them here from the comforts they have known. Homes in Canada are worse than our English cow houses. So I shall just go home.
Adapted from Backwoods of Canada *by Catherine Parr Traill*

What is Canada good for?

It is a good country for the honest, hard-working craftsman.

It is a fine country for the poor labourer. After a few years of hard toil, he can have his own log house and land. He can look forward to his children having their own farms when they grow up.

It is a grand country for the rich man. He can buy and sell land and make a great profit in a few years.

But it is a hard country for the poor gentleman who does not know how to work with his hands.
Adapted from Backwoods of Canada *by Catherine Parr Traill*

Insects

The insects are troublesome, particularly the black flies. You do not feel their bite until you see a stream of blood flowing from the wound. Later it starts to swell and itch. These "beasties" delight in biting your throat, ears and cheeks. The swelling often lasts several days.

The mosquitoes are also annoying. To keep them out of the house we light little heaps of damp chips. The smoke drives them away. But it does not work completely and the smoke is quite a nuisance.
Adapted from Backwoods of Canada *by Catherine Parr Traill*

Questions

Can You Recall?

1. What proportion of the people in the American colonies remained loyal to the British King?
2. Some of the Loyalists went back to _____ . Others went south to the _____ or north to _____ and _____ .
3. In what part of the Maritimes did the Loyalists settle?
4. What was the name of Toronto in the early 1800s?
5. What did the Quebec Act do to protect the old French way of life? Why did it anger the Americans?
6. By 1825, only _____ percent of the people of Lower Canada lived in the cities.
7. What was the name of the fur-trading company started in Montreal to compete with the Hudson's Bay Company?
8. What is a corduroy road?
9. What is a circuit rider?
10. Many early pioneer homes in Upper Canada were made of _____ .

Ideas for Discussion

1. Role playing. Hold a discussion between an American rebel and a Loyalist. Each person should explain why he or she stayed or left the United States after the American Revolution.
2. The Quebec Act was intended to encourage the French Canadians to be loyal to the British king. Explain the ways in which it did this.
3. Make a list of jobs done by men and women in pioneer times. How do these compare to the jobs done by men and women today?
4. Explain how a "bee" worked. Discuss why such events were so important to the pioneers.
5. Discuss the connections between pioneer farms and early towns. How did the towns depend on the farms? What did the farmers need from the towns?
6. Hold a debate on the question: "Resolved that it would have been better to be a young person in pioneer times than it is to be a young person in Canada today."

King Street, Toronto, 1836.

Do Some Research

1. Write a short report on the history of settlement in your own community. Your report should include information on:
   a) when the first settlers came to your area;
   b) who the first settlers were;
   c) where they came from;
   d) what conditions they encountered;
   e) what native people they met;
   f) what signs of early settlement can still be seen in the area. If possible, include maps and illustrations with your report.
2. On a map of present-day Canada, locate the main areas of Loyalist settlement. Find out about the people who live in one of those areas today.
3. The picture on page 136 is by Cornelius Krieghoff. Go to the library and find as many examples as you can of Krieghoff's pictures of life in Lower Canada. Make a report to the class about life in Lower Canada. Use Krieghoff's paintings to help explain some of the points in your report.
4. Make a month-by-month chart of the things a pioneer family would have to do during their first year on their land. Assume that the family arrives in April.

"Winter Landscape," another painting by Cornelius Krieghoff.

5. The Constitutional Act of 1791 divided the colony of Quebec into two colonies called Upper Canada and Lower Canada. Locate the two new colonies on a map. Is Upper Canada "above" Lower Canada? Find out why the colonies were given these names.

Be Creative

1. Loyalists, like many people moving to a new land, had mixed feelings about leaving their homeland. Pretend you are a Loyalist migrating to Nova Scotia. Write a letter to a friend in England explaining why you decided to leave the United States. In your letter, give at least two reasons why you wanted to stay and at least two reasons why you finally decided to leave.
2. The British government tried to give the Loyalists the best start possible in their new homes. Below is a list of things that the governor gave to a group of Loyalists who started a settlement at Kingston. Make a visual display showing how each was used and its importance to the pioneers.

The governor issued to Loyalist settlers:	
boards, nails and shingles	1 hammer
80 squares of window glass	1 knife
guns, amunition and 1 axe for each male over 14	2 scythes
	1 sickle
1 plough	1 broad axe
leather to make horse collars	clothing for 1 year
2 spades	2 horses
3 hoes	2 cows
1 hand saw	6 sheep
seeds (wheat, corn, peas, oats, potatoes, flax)	
1 grindstone for each 3 families	
1 blacksmith for each township	

3. Hold a bee to accomplish something your class needs done or to do something for your community. You could clean up a park or playground, remove litter alongside a river or lake, or make something for the school. Remember to arrange for food and entertainment after the work is done.

War and Rebellion
ADVANCE ORGANIZER

1

In 1812, the Americans tried to complete their control of North America. They declared war on Canada. But Loyalists, British forces and French Canadians resisted. The American invasion failed.

2

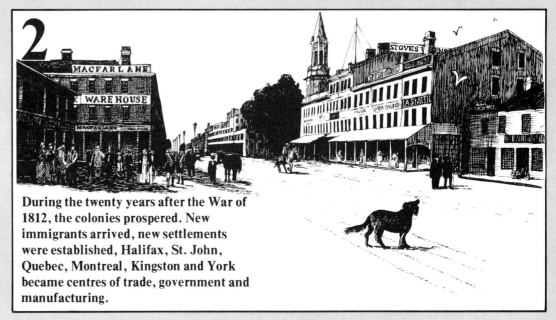

During the twenty years after the War of 1812, the colonies prospered. New immigrants arrived, new settlements were established, Halifax, St. John, Quebec, Montreal, Kingston and York became centres of trade, government and manufacturing.

3

Many French Canadians in Lower Canada were not happy being controlled by a small number of wealthy English. They wanted more control of Lower Canada by French Canadians. They called themselves the *Patriotes*. Louis Joseph Papineau became their leader.

After many years of being ignored, the French Canadians began to rebel. In November, 1837, Papineau led an armed rebellion. The rebellion was crushed by the British forces. For many French Canadians, this was a bitter reminder of the British Conquest of 1763.

Word List

Confederation	garrison	rebellion
discontent	immigrant	recommend
equality	investigate	Reformer
exile	*Patriote*	treason

4

In Upper Canada, many pioneers and farmers were also unhappy with British rule. They wanted cheaper land, more roads and public schools. William Lyon Mackenzie became the leader of these Reformers. When the government would not pass the laws they wanted, Mackenzie's supporters began to arm. In December, 1837, Mackenzie led a rebellion in Upper Canada. Though the rebellion was quickly crushed, it showed the British that there was much discontent in the colonies.

5

In 1838, Lord Durham was sent from England to Canada to investigate the problems that led to the rebellions. He recommended giving more control to the local elected representatives. Durham's Report did much to put Canadians on the road to self-government.

The War of 1812

In the early 1800s, Britain and France were at war again. Britain tried to weaken France by stopping trading ships from travelling to and from French ports. Britain also tried to stop some American ships from going to France.

Some British sailors had deserted from the British navy. They fled to the United States. Some joined the crews of American ships. British ships stopped American ships and removed these sailors. The Americans thought that these actions violated their rights as an independent country.

Conflict Between Settlers and Indians

Meanwhile, Americans began to move west across the Appalachian Mountains to the Ohio valley. They were looking for new land to settle and farm. The Indians who lived in this area, led by Tecumseh, wanted to stop them. They looked upon these newcomers as invaders and fought against them.

British fur traders, from their base in Montreal, continued to trade with the Indians in the Ohio valley. To keep the friendship of the Indians, the British provided them with guns and ammunition.

The Americans thought that the British were encouraging the Indians to fight against the settlers. A group of Americans who called themselves *War Hawks,* wanted to organize the American army to fight against the British in Canada. This would be a chance to get rid of the British forces still in North America. After the British were driven out, Canada could become part of the United States. Canada could provide a great deal of new land for American settlers.

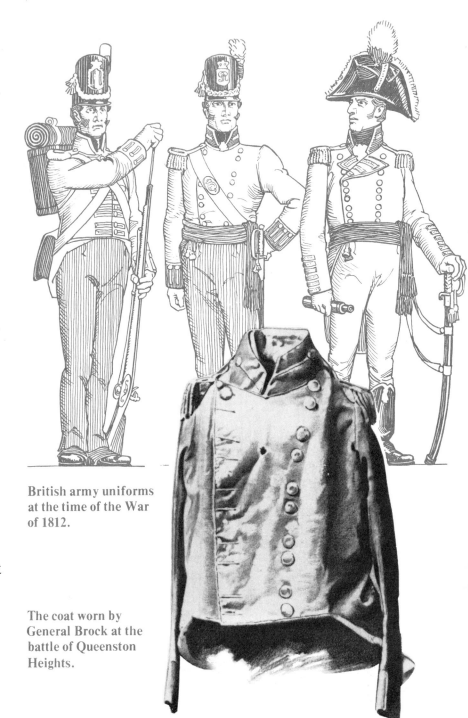

British army uniforms at the time of the War of 1812.

The coat worn by General Brock at the battle of Queenston Heights.

| 1200 | 1300 | 1400 | 1500 | 1600 | 1700 | 1800 | 1900 |

For all these reasons, the United States declared war on Britain in 1812. The Americans believed that the war would be short and victory easy. They thought that the more recent settlers in Canada would welcome the invading army. Two-thirds of the 80 000 people in Upper Canada in 1812 had come to the province after the arrival of the Loyalists. Many had come not because they were loyal to Britain, but because they wanted cheap land.

The War Begins

The Americans prepared to invade Upper Canada from Detroit. American soldiers under General Hull crossed into Upper Canada. However, they were ambushed and defeated by Indians under their leader Tecumseh.

General Isaac Brock was leader of the British forces. He was aware that most people expected the Americans to win easily. He knew that to stop them he would have to win a quick victory. Brock wanted to prevent any American invasion to give courage to British and Canadian soldiers. Brock had an army of about 700 British and Canadian soldiers and 600 Indians. The American forces under General Hull had moved back to Fort Detroit. On August 15, Brock crossed the Detroit River. The war whoops of the Indians, and the fear of fierce battle with Indians and British soldiers were enough for General Hull. On August 16, 1812, 2300 American soldiers surrendered at Fort Detroit without firing a shot. The victory was a great boost to British and Canadian morale. Brock was knighted for it. He became Sir Isaac Brock.

Tecumseh (Shooting Star)
BORN: On banks of Mad River, Ohio, 1768
DIED: Battle of Moraviantown, 1813
Son of a Shawnee chief. When American settlers moved into the Ohio valley, joined the British.
Told his people: "The Pale Faces who fought against our fathers, the British, are our enemies. They came to us hungry, and they cut off the hands of our brothers, who gave them corn. We gave them rivers full of fish, and they poisoned our fountains. We gave them mountains and valleys full of game, and they gave our warriors rum and trinkets — and a grave."
1812 — assisted at capture of Detroit. Was a great admirer of Brock. When asked about Proctor, who gained command after Brock's death, commented: "General Brock said, 'Tecumseh, come, *we* go.' General Proctor says, 'Tecumseh, *you* go.' Proctor's no Brock."
1813 — After battle of Moraviantown, buried by his tribe in secret grave near the Thames River.

General Hull's proclamation to the people when his troops entered Canada, July 12, 1812:
In the name of my country, I promise you protection for yourselves, your property and your rights. Raise not yours hands against your brothers. You should give a hearty welcome to the arrival of an army of Friends. You will be liberated from tyranny and oppression and become free men.

General Brock's reply, July 22, 1812:
Are you prepared, inhabitants of Upper Canada, to become willing subjects, or even slaves, to a foreign oppressor? If not, arise and join with the king's army to repel the invaders. Do not let your children be ruled by a foreign master. They would blame you for parting too easily with the greatest inheritance on earth — sharing in the name, character and freedom of Britons.

Queenston Heights and After

Brock felt that the decisive battles of the war would be fought on the Niagara frontier. He hurried to the Niagara area and organized his soldiers to resist an American invasion. On October 13, the Americans crossed the Niagara river at Queenston. The invasion began in darkness, at 4 a.m. By dawn, over 500 American soldiers were on the Canadian shore. General Brock led an attack upon the Americans, which stopped their advance. But he was killed during this battle.

Later that day, British, Canadian and Indian forces attacked the Americans and captured the heights at Queenston. After a bloody battle, the Americans withdrew across the river. Many surrendered. Almost 1000 soldiers were captured. This was more than the total number of forces under Brock's command.

These two battles, Detroit and Queenston, prevented an early American victory. American forces continued to attack Upper and Lower Canada for the next two years. But they had failed in their attempts at a quick victory. British and Canadian morale improved. They were now confident that they could resist the Americans, despite the much larger American army.

The battle of Queenston Heights.

The War in Upper Canada

The battles along the Niagara frontier continued for the next two years. British, Canadian and Indian forces won battles at Stoney Creek, Beaver Dam and Lundy's Lane. The Americans won several other victories. In 1813, they captured the capital of York (now Toronto). They burned the government buildings. A large warship being built in the dry dock in the harbour was destroyed. In 1814, the British got their revenge. They invaded Washington, the American capital, and burned down the White House.

The War in Lower Canada

In 1813, the Americans attempted to capture Montreal. The invading army was defeated by a force of British and French Canadian soldiers under Lieutenant Colonel Charles de Salaberry.

De Salaberry was the first French Canadian officer to serve in the British army. He recruited a French Canadian regiment which fought in the War of 1812. They won the battle of Chateauguay over a large number of American soldiers. The French Canadians showed that, like English Canadian settlers, they did not welcome American "liberation."

The End of the War

By 1814, the war was a stalemate. The Americans had not been successful in conquering the Canadas. Many Americans had lost their will to continue the war. The Treaty of Ghent ended the war in 1814. It left the boundaries of the two countries as they had been before the war. It marked the last time that Americans would try to take over Canada by force.

But the war had done much for Canadians. They had resisted an American invasion, in spite of overwhelming American advantages. It had made many Canadians suspicious and afraid of the United States. It had given birth to the beginning of a Canadian national feeling. Henceforth, many British settlers would think of themselves as Canadians.

From an address by General Brock to the Upper Canada legislature, July 27, 1812:

We will teach the enemy a lesson. A country defended by free men, devoted to their king and constitution, can never be conquered.

Laura Ingersoll Secord

BORN: Great Barrington, Massachusetts, 1775
DIED: Chippewa, Ontario, 1868
Father, Thomas Ingersoll, major in rebel army during American Revolution.
1793 — Ingersolls moved to Niagara peninsula, Upper Canada, to find good, cheap land. Town of Ingersoll is named after the family. Laura managed her father's tavern in Queenston.
1798 — Married James Secord, a Loyalist.
1812 — rescues James (wounded in knee) from battlefield after battle of Queenston Heights.
1813 — American officers occupying Queenston billeted in Secord house. Secords overheard them planning to attack British at Beaver Dam. Laura walked 30 km through enemy territory to warn Lieutenant FitzGibbon at Beaver Dam.
1832 — James appointed Inspector of Customs.
About 1838 — Laura, disguised as man, helped James arrest party of smugglers.
1841 — James died. Laura almost penniless.
1860 — after many petitions to the government, Laura's deed finally recognized with gift of 100 pounds from the Prince of Wales.
This is the legend of Laura Secord. Few facts are actually known about her life.

Halifax During the War of 1812

Much of the War of 1812 took place at sea. Each side attacked the other's merchant ships as well as warships. Posters urged young men to join ships with promises of a share of the booty captured. War prizes were brought into Halifax harbour. For Halifax was the chief British garrison and naval base on the east coast.

The star-shaped Citadel, a fortress begun in 1749, sat on a hill above the town. North of it was the naval dockyard, where naval vessels were built and repaired. Wood from the rich forests of the colony was used to build ships and to repair masts and spars. Smaller boatyards turned out fishing boats. The fishermen's wharves and market were busy, colourful places.

The Halifax Merchants

Halifax was also a town of merchants in the early 1800s. Ship chandlers' and provisioners' shops lined Water Street. Other merchants sold timber to markets in Britain. Most of the goods sold in Halifax shops were imported from Britain or New England. Several merchants grew wealthy selling these imported goods.

Shop clerks worked as many as twelve hours a day. They began early in the morning, often before daylight. The floors had to be swept, fires lit, candles and lamps trimmed, and stock arranged. Many young clerks lived in the shops where they worked. Their bedrooms were cubbyholes beneath the shop counters.

The Town Clock, set into the hill beneath the Citadel, was very useful. Many people had no watches. The time was also called out by the night watchman going about his rounds: "Ten o'clock and all's well." Often, he could not call "all's well." Drunken soldiers and sailors would get into fights. Fires were common. Halifax was largely wooden houses, built close together. Homes were heated with wood or coal fires. Candles or oil lamps lit the rooms.

Fires were fought by volunteer groups called Fire Clubs. There were several rival fire clubs; they competed to see which club could be the first to reach a fire. The volunteers would be alerted by the ringing of the fire bell. When the bell rang, they would rush from their jobs, often in their best clothes. Fires were fought with bucket brigades. Long lines of sweating leather-caped firemen passed leather buckets from hand to hand.

Halifax had no water mains and no running water in homes. The water supply came from big wooden pumps in the streets. Most streets were unpaved. Water Street was paved in 1816-17. But the pavement began to sink into the mud almost at once. Wooden sidewalks ran along the main street. There were no sewers or public garbage collection. Outhouses stood in every yard. Pigs and other animals were kept in backyards. Streets were filthy. Slops were emptied into the gutters, often to stand in smelly pools. There were no streetlights.

Schools

There were no public schools. It cost money to send a child to school, even though the Education Act of 1811 gave government money to meet some school costs.

An important school after 1818 was the National School, run by the Anglican Church. On the ground floor of the National School was a large room holding 200 boys. A room overhead held as many girls. Each room had one teacher. Older children helped by teaching the younger ones. Students who did well could go on to Dalhousie College (built 1819-20).

Most students left school at about 14. Boys were apprenticed to a merchant, professional man or engineer. Those without education learned a craft, worked in the mines and forests or became fishermen or unskilled labourers. Mothers tried to prepare their daughters for good marriages. Girls from poorer families went to work as servants or married young.

Leisure Activities

Young people in Halifax during the War of 1812 could amuse themselves in many ways. There were warships to look at as they came into the harbour, military parades to watch. In summer there was swimming or playing in the woods behind the town. In winter there was skating on the pond near the Citadel.

Holidays were times for celebration. Coronations and royal birthdays were marked by parades, dances and other gala events. Horse races on the Public Common were attended by everyone.

In 1812, Halifax had about 20 000 residents — half of them civilians. But when the war ended, the British moved their naval station to Bermuda. Fewer soldiers were posted to the Halifax garrison. Merchants suffered and there were fewer jobs for labourers in the shipyards. Crop failures in 1816 and 1817 added to the slump. In 1817, Halifax's population was only 11 000. The boom years of the war were over.

Discontent in Lower Canada

The system of government in Upper and Lower Canada was the same. The people in each colony had the right to elect an assembly. However, most of the power was in the hands of the governor. The governor appointed his own council. Usually, he chose people from among the wealthy British merchants. In Lower Canada this group was called the Chateau Clique, which meant the group close to the governor's palace or chateau. The Chateau Clique wanted to run the colony in a way that would help trade.

The majority of the people in Lower Canada were French, Catholic and farmers. The farmers wanted roads so they could get their wheat and lumber to the towns. The merchants wanted a canal system which would help trade with areas outside Lower Canada.

Then there were arguments about taxes. The Chateau Clique wanted a tax on land. Small farmers would have to pay this. The farmers suggested a tax on imports and a sales tax. The merchants would have to pay these taxes. The assembly and the governor's council could never agree on how to raise money.

English Attitudes

The English leaders did not want to listen to the French. They thought of the French Canadians as uneducated, ignorant peasants. They thought that it was only a matter of time until the French Canadians gave up their way of life and their religion and became more like the English.

This upset the French. The French leaders — priest, lawyers, doctors and other educated people — knew that they had to protect the rights of the French. They were proud to be French and did not plan to change. They set up a group in the assembly and called it the *Patriotes*. This group led the French Canadians in their fight against the English governor and his council.

> The die is cast; the British government have decided to make Lower Canada the Ireland of North America. One duty now remains — let them study the History of the American Revolution.
>
> *From* The Vindicator, *a Patriote newspaper, 14 April, 1837.*

One method the *Patriotes* used to get the British government to listen to them was to boycott British-made fabrics. They used only homespun cloth. Even in the Legislative Assembly they proudly wore habitant costume — homespun coat and pants, bright woven sash and knitted hat.

Selling homespun cloth at the market in Montreal.

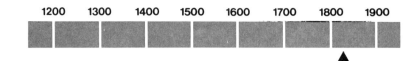

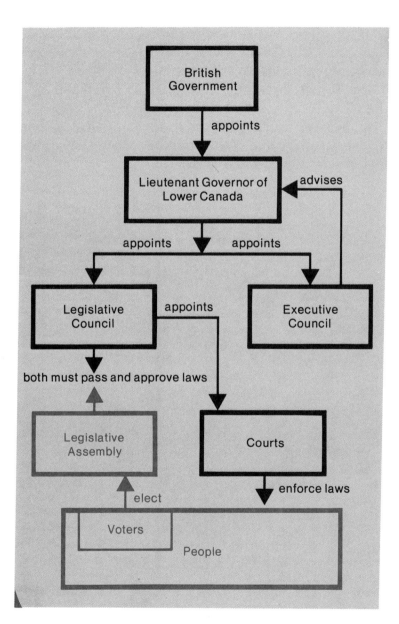

The system of government as set up by the Constitutional Act of 1791.

Louis Joseph Papineau

The leader of the *Patriotes* in the 1820s and 1830s was Louis Joseph Papineau. Papineau wanted the elected assembly to control all government tax monies. The governor and the British said no. Papineau began to look to the United States for ideas. He began to talk about getting rid of the British monarch and having an elected president. He thought the only way to accomplish this would be to have an armed rebellion.

It was not only the French who were against the government. Others, especially Irish Catholics, felt just as strongly. One *Patriote* leader was Dr. Wolfred Nelson. His opinion was, "The time has come to melt our pewter plates and spoons into bullets."

The *Patriotes* organized a group called *Fils de la Liberté*. This translates as "Sons of Liberty," the name of a rebel group in the American colonies before the American Revolution. The *Fils de la Liberté* carried banners showing an American eagle with a Canadian beaver in its beak. Other banners said, "Death to the Legislative Council."

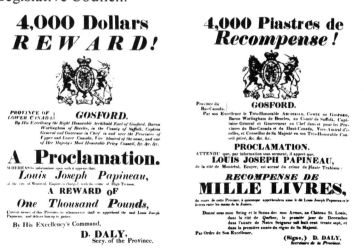

The Rebellion of 1837 in Lower Canada

In November of 1837, French *Patriotes* and anti-French British groups rioted in the streets of Montreal. The British thought a rebellion was about to start. They ordered the arrest of about 20 *Patriote* leaders, including Papineau. The British forces went to arrest these leaders.

The leaders would not surrender peacefully. In a battle at the village of St. Denis, the British forces were defeated. Twenty British soldiers were killed or wounded. This battle made the French forces think they could win the rebellion.

But their hopes were doomed. In December, 1837, a large British force attacked more than 500 rebels in the village of St. Eustache, north of Montreal. More than 70 rebels were killed and the rebels defeated. The British burned some of the buildings. Then they looted and burned a nearby village.

St. Denis was the only battle the rebels won. At St. Charles, two days later, British troops killed 40 *Patriotes* and captured 30. Only three British soldiers were killed.

The End of the Rebellion

This was the end of the rebellion. Papineau fled to the United States. From there he went to France. In 1845 he returned to enter government again. Twelve of the *Patriote* leaders were tried for treason, found guilty and hanged. More than 50 rebels were exiled to Australia.

The rebellion had been lost even though it had a good deal of support from ordinary people. The French Canadians were very bitter about their defeat. They thought the burnings, looting, the executions and the exiles, were very unfair treatment. For many, it was a reminder of the British Conquest in 1763. For some the anger over these events would last until the present day in Quebec.

Louis Joseph Papineau
BORN: Montreal, 1786
DIED: On his seigneury "La Petite Nation," 1854
1811 — called to bar as a lawyer.
1812 — present at capture of Detroit as a militia officer.
1814 — elected to Lower Canada Legislative Assembly.
1815 — chosen to be speaker of Assembly.
1820 — asked by governor to join Executive Council but found his advice ignored and soon resigned.
1822 — when British parliament wanted to unite the Canadas, went to London to oppose the bill. Union would mean the French would be a minority in their homeland. As leader of the *Patriotes* was impressed by American ideals of government. But never really believed in armed rebellion.
1837 — by now, was preaching patience and against violence, but the *Patriotes* and their supporters were too angry. Fled to United States. Tried to persuade Americans to help the rebels.
1839 — went to live in Paris, France.
1845 — returned to Canada under a general pardon. Re-entered assembly but never became leader again.
1854 — retired from politics to farm on his seigneury on the Ottawa River.

At St. Eustache, the rebels occupied the church. After the British forced an entry, they set fire to it. The rebels had to jump from the windows to escape. As they jumped, British soldiers picked them off with their guns.

Discontent in Upper Canada

Upper Canada grew quickly in the years between 1814 and 1830. Many settlers had made their homes there. Some were Loyalists or sons and daughters of Loyalists. Others were recent immigrants from the British Isles.

But many were later immigrants from the United States seeking cheap land. They did not feel any great loyalty to Britain. In the United States, they had voted in elections to elect the men who governed them. They believed that all people were equal. They did not think that wealthy people should have more say in government than poor people did. Although most did not want Canada to join the United States, they liked the American ideas of freedom and equality.

Mackenzie criticized members of the Family Compact in *The Colonial Advocate:*

They are the most amazing collection of sturdy beggars, parsons, priests, pensioners, army people, navy people, bank directors, land jobbers ever established to act as a screen for rotten government. They cost the country about 40 000 pounds a year. They tomahawk good laws which might help the people. And they don't like to be called a "nuisance."

Locks leading from the Ottawa River up to the Rideau Canal. Parliament Hill is on the right.

Many did not like the system of government in Upper Canada. As in Lower Canada, the governor was appointed by the British government. He appointed his own advisers to the executive council and the legislative council. These people were usually wealthy merchants, landowners or army officers. Most lived in large towns, such as Kingston or York.

The Family Compact

The government passed laws that favoured the wealthy people in the colony. Most of the governing group came from a few wealthy families. This group was called the Family Compact.

The only people who could vote in Upper Canada were adult, male, white landowners. They elected the assembly. The people they elected were usually small landowners or farmers. This group had different views from the people in the Family Compact. They wanted change or reform, and were called Reformers.

The pioneer farmers wanted roads through the forest, to get to the town markets. Roads were very poor. The Family Compact wanted to spend money on canals to help the merchants. Most of the money available went to the building of the Rideau, Welland and St. Lawrence Canals. There was little left for roads.

Land Issues

The farmers also wanted cheap land. They did not like the fact that some lots had been set aside for the use of the government (the Crown). They also were opposed to land being given to the Anglican church. They wanted this land to be sold to settlers or used for public schools. The farmers were also unhappy because land companies had bought large amounts of land cheaply. Now they were selling it at a high price. Most of these land companies were owned by members of the Family Compact.

The Reformers and the Family Compact also followed different religions. Most of the Family Compact members were Anglican. Most of the Reformers were Methodist. The Methodists wanted free public schools, paid for by taxes. The Compact wanted private schools run by Anglicans.

The Family Compact remained in control of the government. The governor and the councils refused to pass the laws the reformers wanted. By the 1830s the Reformers were beginning to think about other ways of gaining control. "If we cannot get what we want through government," they said, "we may have to resort to armed force." Some Reformers and some government representatives thought the situation was similar to that in the American colonies in the 1770s. Would the American Revolution be repeated in Upper Canada?

The farmer who wrote this joined a group of rebels and was killed in an uprising at Amherstburg near Windsor in 1837.

I have been in Canada since I was a little boy. Most of my time has been spent in looking after a growing and much-loved family. I have had to make my own roads and bridges, clear my own farm, educate myself and my children and be my own mechanic. I have had my bones broken by fallen trees, my feet cut by my axe, and suffered nearly everything except death. I have waited year after year in hope of better days. I hoped that the government would care less for themselves and more for the people. Every year I have been disappointed.

The Rebellion of 1837 in Upper Canada

Brave Canadians! Do you love freedom? I know you do. Do you hate oppression? Who dare deny it?

The words screamed out from a handbill that was distributed around the province. The writer was William Lyon Mackenzie. By the mid-1830s, he was leader of the Reformers. He had been editor of a newspaper, *The Colonial Advocate,* which attacked the Family Compact. The Family Compact wished to silence his criticisms. They sent a gang to smash his printing presses and throw them into Lake Ontario.

Mackenzie decided to run for the assembly to keep up his opposition to the government. He was elected as the member for York. He spoke so harshly about the policies of the Family Compact he was expelled from the assembly four times. Each time, he was re-elected.

Mackenzie supported better roads, cheap land and reduced power for the governor and councils. He thought more power must be given to the elected assembly. Then the province could have good government for and by the common people.

By 1837, Mackenzie had decided that the Family Compact would not give up their power willingly. He thought rebellion would be necessary. He travelled from town to town, trying to convince people to join his cause. At one meeting, his supporters held up banners reading "Liberty or Death." This had been one of the slogans of the American Revolution.

During 1837, the rebel farmers began to drill in the backwoods farm areas. In November, rebellion broke out in Lower Canada. The British Army left quickly to fight that battle. The rebel leaders in Upper Canada decided that this was the time to act. The farmers called on all rebel supporters to meet on the outskirts of York at Montgomery's Tavern.

From a report to the legislative assembly on grievances against the government:
Q — What price did the Canada Company pay the government for the Huron tract?
A — About one shilling per acre.
Q — What are they selling the land for?
A — For about 12 or 13 shillings per acre.

Strike, the conflict is begun.
Freemen, soldiers, follow me!
Shout — the victory is won —
Canada and Liberty!
Poem in The Colonial Advocate

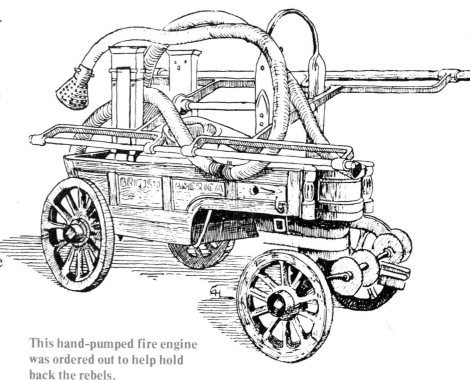

This hand-pumped fire engine was ordered out to help hold back the rebels.

The Outcome of the Rebellion

On December 5, the rebels marched down Yonge Street, the main street of York. At the other end of the street stood the government forces of Loyalist farmers and some soldiers. The two had a brief fight. The rebels were not expecting to meet organized opposition. The government forces fired a volley from their muskets. The surprised rebels quickly scattered. Mackenzie realized the armed rebellion was finished and fled to the United States. Although there were a few minor fights, the rebellion was over.

Why did the rebellion fail? It was not well organized. Not all of the rebel supporters showed up for the battle. The rebellion did not have the support of the majority of the people. Many people were suspicious of Mackenzie and his "American" ideas. Although they wanted change, they did not want to use violence to get it.

Even though the rebellion had failed, it worried the British. They did not want more violence in the colonies. They certainly did not want a repetition of the American Revolution. In 1838, they sent Lord Durham from England to see what was happening. Lord Durham reported that the colonists would be unhappy as long as the governor and his advisers ignored the Reformers' wishes.

He recommended that the elected assembly should have more control over the executive council. This form of government, called *responsible government,* was introduced in Canada in 1849.

After the rebellion, Mackenzie tried to get supporters to join him on an island in the Niagara River, 5 km above the Falls.

William Lyon Mackenzie
BORN: Dundee, Scotland, 1795
DIED: Toronto, Upper Canada, 1861
1820 — came to Canada as a shopkeeper.
1824 — founded his newspaper *The Colonial Advocate.*
1826 — attacks on Family Compact led to raid on his printing presses by a group of young Compact members.
1828 — elected to legislative assembly.
1835 — elected first mayor of Toronto.
1837 — led rebellion in Upper Canada. Set up provisional government on Navy Island.
1838 - 1849 — lived in United States, writing for newspapers. Did not like system of government. Said if he had seen American system before, he would never have rebelled.
1849 — allowed to return to Canada.
1851 - 1858 — member of assembly again, but had little influence.
1858 — given house in Toronto by friends. Mackenzie House is open to the public.
Grandson William Lyon Mackenzie King was prime minister of Canada from the 1920s to the 1940s.

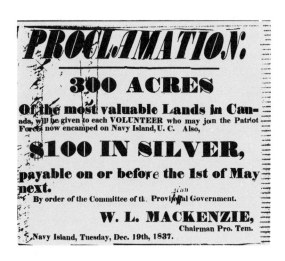

PROCLAMATION:

300 ACRES

Of the most valuable Lands in Canada, will be given to each VOLUNTEER who may join the Patriot Forces now encamped on Navy Island, U. C. Also,

$100 IN SILVER,

payable on or before the 1st of May next.

By order of the Committee of th. Provincial Government.

W. L. MACKENZIE,
Chairman Pro. Tem.

Navy Island, Tuesday, Dec. 19th, 1837.

Lord Durham's Report

The Rebellions of 1837 were quickly crushed in both Lower and Upper Canada. The *Patriotes* and Reformers had failed to change the government by force of arms. But even though the rebellions had failed they taught the British government an important lesson. The British could no longer ignore the fact that many people in the colony were unhappy.

Following the rebellions, the British government sent Lord Durham to Canada to find out why the people were so upset. Lord Durham was instructed to work out a better type of government for Upper and Lower Canada. He was also told to try to work out a plan for uniting the maritime colonies — Prince Edward Island, Nova Scotia, New Brunswick and Newfoundland.

Lord Durham spent much of 1838 in Canada. He talked to many people from both Upper and Lower Canada about the rebellions of the year before. At the end of the time, he wrote a report.

Lord Durham's Recommendations

Lord Durham said that the colonists in both Upper and Lower Canada would be unhappy as long as the governor and his council ignored the reformers' wishes. He recommended that the elected assembly should control the executive council. The executive council would be a cabinet, just like that of the British Parliament. The council could be thrown out by a vote of "no confidence" from the assembly. This gave the assembly control of the government. This form of government is called *responsible government.* Basically, Lord Durham was recommending that the British colonists in Canada have the same say in their own affairs that British citizens enjoyed at home.

Lord Durham felt that the causes of the rebellion in Lower Canada were more than just unhappiness over the government. He thought that the main problem was the clash between the British and the French-speaking Canadians. Lord Durham had little sympathy for the French Canadians. He thought that they would have to give up their language and way of life. Then the battles would end.

The Act of Union

Lord Durham suggested that Upper and Lower Canada be rejoined. This would give the English population more power. In 1840, the British Parliament passed the Act of Union. The legislative assemblies of the two colonies were joined together in 1841. Upper Canada was now called Canada West and Lower Canada became Canada East. The Act of Union restricted the use of French as an official language. In 1848, the British Parliament amended the Act of Union, and the restrictions on the use of French were removed.

Durham thought that the four Atlantic colonies should be joined together. In his report, he commented on the abuses of the rich landowners in Prince Edward Island. He believed that favouritism had to end if people were to come to the maritime colonies to stay. A new, stronger form of government was needed to overcome those abuses of power. But, when Lord Durham wrote his report, he dropped the idea of Maritime Union.

Lord Durham's report was the first step toward Confederation: a union of the British colonies in North America. It was also the first step to true self-government in Britain's North American colonies.

Responsible government was granted to Nova Scotia in 1846. The Canadas received responsible government soon after. But it would be 20 more years until Confederation.

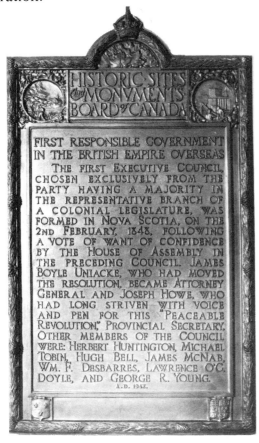

Lord Durham's attitude to French Canada:
I entertain no doubt of the natural character which must be given to Lower Canada, it must be that of The British Empire; that of the majority of British Americans; that of the great race which must be predominant over the whole North American continent.

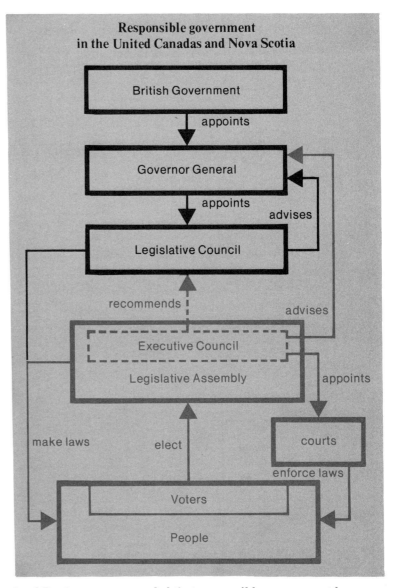

Lord Durham recommended that responsible government be granted to the British colonies in North America. A system of government like this was set up first in Nova Scotia and soon after in the united Canadas.

Kingston in the 1840s

Capital to be moved to Montreal read the headline in the Kingston *Chronicle and Gazette*. Readers of the weekly newspaper in 1843 were shocked. The news meant the end of their dreams for the city. They had hoped that Kingston would be the most important city in Canada.

In June 1841, the capital for the colony had been moved to Kingston from Toronto. Many fine buildings were built in the new capital. The most impressive was the City Hall, built of local stone. It had cost $90 000. Visitors from Montreal and Toronto agreed it was the finest building in all Canada.

Here was Kingston's public market. Farmers brought their produce to the market for the city's kitchens. In the City Hall were the post office, government offices, a library and handsome meeting rooms. The City Hall was topped by a beautiful dome. From a gallery round the dome, you could see the city, the surrounding countryside, Lake Ontario and the Thousand Islands.

Kingston City Hall in a photograph taken in 1855.

The view from the dome of City Hall in the 1860s.

Looking east, you could see Fort Henry set on a hill over the harbour. The British built the fort in 1836. Its position meant it could protect Lake Ontario and the St. Lawrence from possible American attack. Below the fort were barracks for sailors of the Royal Navy.

Kingston harbour was home port to some two hundred schooners and barges. The port was the centre for exporting grain, lumber and other products from Upper Canada. But the future did not look good. There was talk of improving the canals. Then large ships could travel directly from Montreal to Toronto or Hamilton. They would bypass Kingston entirely.

The steamboat, invented in 1807, had made its appearance on Kingston's waterfront. Steamboat companies made trips to Toronto and other places on Lake Ontario every day.

Ships and barges came to Kingston to be repaired. A marine railway, powered by four horses, pulled ships out of the water. Ships as large as 300 tonnes could be brought ashore for repairs.

The Kingston Penitentiary was at Portsmouth Harbour, 3 km west of the City Hall. A strong stone wall, with towers at each corner, surrounded the prison. In the mid 1840s, there were more than 400 prisoners. It was the only penitentiary in Canada at this time.

In the city itself were many fine houses, offices, stores, and churches. There was a university in Kingston, run by the Presbyterian Church. It still exists today as Queen's University. There was also the court house, a large stone building. Several of the churches ran schools. In 1845, there were five schools for girls and ladies, two for boys. There were two hospitals. One was run by the government, the other by Catholic nuns.

Industry

Kingston had other industries beside the shipyards. There was a large steam-powered grist mill, for grinding flour. Marble and limestone were quarried nearby. Marble monuments were made in the city. There were three tanneries, producing leather for shoes and boots. Three foundries turned out iron products — machinery, stoves, and other things needed in the growing colony. Other companies in Kingston produced carriages and wagons, candles, furniture, clothing and food products.

Kingston had been founded soon after the first Loyalists arrived in 1784. By 1842, its population had grown to nearly 8 000. When the capital was moved to Montreal, many people left. In 1845, there were only 6 123 people in Kingston.

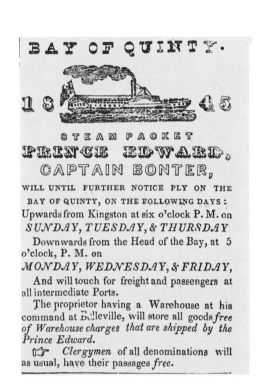

The University of Queen's College.

Questions

Can You Recall?

1. Why did the United States declare war on Britain in 1812?
2. Who was Tecumseh?
3. Who were the *War Hawks*? What did they want to do?
4. Who was the leader of the British forces in Upper Canada in 1812?
5. Name three battles of the War of 1812.
6. Where was the Citadel?
7. How many people lived in Halifax in 1812? in 1817?
8. Who were the Chateau Clique? the *Patriotes*?
9. In 1837, _____ led the *Patriotes* against the British.
10. The wealthy people who governed Upper Canada were called the _____ .
11. Who was William Lyon Mackenzie?
12. Why was Lord Durham sent to North America?
13. What was the Act of Union? What did it say?
14. Which colony was the first to have responsible government?

Ideas for Discussion

1. The Americans thought that it would be easy to conquer the Canadas, and that many people in these areas would welcome the American forces. Why was this not so?
2. Compare life in Halifax in 1812 and life in Kingston in 1841. Which city would you rather have lived in? Why?
3. French Canadians have often been unhappy with their government since 1763. Some reasons for this unhappiness came out during the 1830s. Explain these reasons. Show how they led to the rebellion of 1837 in Lower Canada.
4. One method the *Patriotes* used to express their anger was to boycott British goods. What is a boycott? Do you think a boycott is a good way of getting things changed? People still use boycotts today as a way of objecting. Can you think of some examples?
5. Antoine Gérin-Lajoie was 14 when the rebellion of 1837 took place in Lower Canada. He later wrote the song "Un Canadien errant." About whom is he writing? What does the song tell you about his feelings towards his country and his people?
6. Discuss how the following matters helped cause the rebellion in Upper Canada:
   a) the system of government;
   b) the lack of good roads;
   c) the position of the Anglican church;
   d) the Family Compact.
7. What is responsible government? How does it work in Canada today?

Un Canadien errant

Un canadien errant,
Banni des ses foyers,
Un canadien errant,
Banni de ses foyers,
Parcourait en pleurant
Des pays étrangers.
Parcourait en pleurant
Des pays étrangers.

Un jour, triste et pensif,
Assis au bord des flots,
Un jour, triste et pensif,
Assis au bord des flots,
Au courant fugitif
Il adressa ces mots,
Au courant fugitif
Il adressa ces mots:

"Si tu vois mon pays,
Mon pays malheureux,
Si tu vois mon pays,
Mon pays malheureux,
Va, dis à mes amis
Que je me souviens d'eux,
Va, dis à mes amis
Que je me souviens d'eux."

Once a Canadian lad,
Exiled from hearth and home,
Wandered, alone and sad,
Through alien lands unknown.
Down by a rushing stream,
Thoughtful and sad one day
He watched the water pass
And to it he did say:

"If you should reach my land,
My most unhappy land,
Please speak to all my friends
So they will understand.
Tell them how much I wish
That I could be once more
In my beloved land
That I will see no more.

"My own beloved land
I'll not forget till death,
And I will speak of her
With my last dying breath.
My own beloved land
I'll not forget till death,
And I will speak of her
With my last dying breath."

Do Some Research

1. Find out more about one of the following aspects of the War of 1812:
   a) the role of General Brock and the battles in defence of Upper Canada;
   b) Colonel de Salaberry and the battle of Chateauguay;
   c) the war at sea and the battle between the *Chesapeake* and *Shannon*;
   d) the British invasion of Washington;
   e) the treaty of Ghent.
2. Do some research on the following canals and waterways. Trace the route of each on a map. When were they built and why? What is each used for today?
   a) the Lachine canal;
   b) the Rideau canal;
   c) the Trent-Severn waterway;
   d) the St. Lawrence Seaway.

The Kingston-York stage pulls into Finkle's stage stop.

3. Write a short report on *either*
   a) the Citadel in Halifax;
   b) Fort Frontenac in Kingston;
      or
   c) Fort Henry in Kingston.
   Include in your report the reasons for building the fort, its history and what it is like today. Illustrate your report with pictures and plans of the fortifications.

Be Creative

1. On a map of eastern Canada, mark the locations of the battles in the war of 1812 and the rebellions of 1837.
2. Write the words for a fighting song that could have been sung by the Americans invading Canada or the British forces resisting the invasion during the War of 1812.
3. Write a dialogue that might have taken place between Louis Joseph Papineau and the leader of the Chateau Clique. Have each explain what he thinks is best for Lower Canada and why.
4. Write about the journey between Kingston and York from the point of view of one of the passengers in William Weller's Kingston-York stage coach. Why are you making the trip? Describe some of your experiences on the road.
5. Role-playing. Divide into two groups. One group will be merchants and government officials of the Family Compact and the governor Sir Francis Bond Head. The other will be farmers and Reformers led by William Lyon Mackenzie. Have each group discuss among themselves what they think is best for the colony of Upper Canada and why. Then have the two groups meet and have a debate.
6. Draw a picture of the battle of Yonge Street between the government forces and the rebels.
7. Try to find a copy of the music or a recording of "Un Canadien errant." Learn to sing the song either in French or in English.

Expansion
ADVANCE ORGANIZER

1

In the early 1700s Europeans had not yet come to the western part of Canada. The native people lived as they had done for hundreds of years. But their way of life was soon to be threatened.

In 1778, a British sailor, Captain James Cook, landed at Nootka Sound on the Pacific shores. He was followed by other British, Spanish and Russian explorers. European influence on the Canadian West had begun.

2

By 1793, an explorer from Montreal had reached the Pacific Coast. Alexander Mackenzie was the first European to cross North America to the Pacific. He was followed by Simon Fraser, David Thompson and others.

Fur traders for the Hudson's Bay Company and North West Company pushed into all parts of the Canadian West.

3

In 1811, Lord Selkirk planned a settlement for Highland Scots in the Red River area near the present city of Winnipeg. The pioneers came by sea, landing at Hudson Bay. There were no roads. The settlers made their way inland to the Red River. In spite of great hardships, the colony survived. It was the first European settlement in western Canada.

4

The Indians at first welcomed these new visitors. They did not know that the settlers would later put an end to their roaming way of life on the Prairies.

5

The Hudson's Bay Company set up fur posts on the west coast in the 1840s. Fort Vancouver and Fort Victoria established the British in this area.

6

The discovery of gold, first near the Fraser River, then in the Cariboo region, attracted prospectors from all over the world. To preserve control, Britain created a new colony named British Columbia in 1858.

7

Governor James Douglas maintained law and order over the unruly miners in British Columbia. The new British colony developed and grew, nearly 5000 km away from the Canadas across the continent.

The Great Migration

In the early 1800s, the French leader Napoleon led France in wars against much of Europe. In Britain, the war effort against France had tied up manpower and industry. Few people had left the country during the war to come to Canada. With the return of peace in 1815, a new wave of immigration began.

"The Emigrants' Farewell." This cartoon was published in London in 1832. Few people left their home country because they wanted to. Many were afraid of life in a strange land. They left because conditions at home forced them to emigrate.

Why? Many soldiers and sailors found themselves without jobs. The end of nearly a century of wars was marked by rapid growth in population. Changes in land use led to many poor peasant farm families being driven off the land. Those who owned land found they did not have enough to share among all the children.

This was the time of the "Industrial Revolution." People, driven off the farms, moved to the cities seeking work in factories. But, in the factories, machines often seemed more important than workers. Unemployment was high. Even those who found jobs remained poor. They lived in crowded rows of tiny houses. Soot from the factory smokestacks darkened everything around them.

Many people heard about free land in Canada. Others heard about work in shipyards and sawmills. They saw a chance to start a new life.

Over the next fifty years, large numbers of people from England, Scotland and Ireland made the long voyage to North America. Some settled in the maritime colonies of Nova Scotia and New Brunswick. Others moved west to the cities and towns of Lower Canada and the free farm lands of Upper Canada.

Each year saw nearly 25 000 immigrants arrive. By the 1850s, the combined population of Upper and Lower Canada was nearly two million.

English settlement

The Loyalists were followed by a steady stream of settlers from the mother country, England. Some were soldiers who chose to remain after their tours of duty in Canada had ended. Others were civil servants who had come over to help run the colonies. Merchants came, seeking new markets. There were teachers and clergymen, doctors and lawyers. Men and women worked side by side clearing the forests of Upper Canada to create new farms.

The Scots

The English were not the only ones to prosper in the Canadian colonies. Many successful pioneers came from Scotland.

Scottish settlers came from two different areas. Some came from the cities and farming villages of the Lowlands. Others came from the Highlands, where the fiercely independent clans had not been defeated by the English until 1746. The two groups had different experiences in Canada.

The Lowland Scots had several advantages. They spoke English and were often well-educated or skilled trades people. And they were Protestants. Their Presbyterian faith stressed hard work and temperate living. Being Protestant also meant they were accepted by the English majority, which still had strong anti-Catholic views.

Hard work paid off for many of these Scots. From their numbers came merchants, such as the fur traders Simon Fraser and Alexander Mackenzie. Others were bankers. George Brown, a leading Toronto politician and publisher, was a Scot. So was Sir John A. Macdonald, Canada's first prime minister.

In the Scottish Highlands, sheep had become more important than people. Landlords wanted to raise sheep for the English woollen mills. They drove farming families off the land. Some were marched straight to ships waiting to take them to Canada — not knowing where they were going!

Some of the Highland Scots settled in Nova Scotia. Others were taken to the unfamiliar landscape of the prairies by Lord Selkirk to start the Red River colony. Many spoke no English; their language was Gaelic. They were poor farmers with little education and few skills. Most were Catholic. These factors tended to keep them from mixing easily with the English majority. In Nova Scotia, they kept many aspects of Highland life alive, including speaking Gaelic, long after they were gone in Scotland itself.

Among other immigrants to Canada in the 1800s were many black slaves from the southern United States. Slavery had been abolished throughout the British Empire in 1833. The underground railroad was a network of people who helped the blacks escape. Some settled in Upper Canada. Others joined the existing black communities in Nova Scotia.

Mary Shadd
BORN: Wilmington, Delaware 1823
DIED: Washington, D.C. 1893
Abraham Shadd, Mary's father helped run underground railroad, Mary trained as teacher and taught slaves in Delaware.
1851 — moved to Canada. Settled in Windsor. Set up school for freed slaves. But unlike some other black leaders, wanted blacks educated with whites. One of first women to give public lectures in Canada. First woman to run a newspaper, *The Provincial Freeman,* which aimed to educate and establish black community in southern Ontario.
1861 — outbreak of Civil War in the U.S. Returned there to recruit black soldiers for army.
1883 — graduated as lawyer (aged 60).

Irish Immigration

Life was rough for the Highland Scots, but it was worse for the Irish. The English conquest of Ireland, completed in the 1600s, left the Irish very badly off. The best lands were given to English lords. Protestant English and Scots were brought in to work the land. The Catholic Irish were forced onto the poorest lands. They could not get the education or training needed to enter the professions or skilled trades.

Most were tenant farmers, working for English landlords. They had only small plots of poor soil for their own families. Their main crop was potatoes. Families were large and hunger common. Feelings of anger against the English conquerers were strong. Farmers rioted to protest these living conditions.

There seemed no hope of change. Some Irish, braver than most, set out to find a new home in North America. Many settled in the cities of Lower Canada. In the 1820s, a group led by Peter Robinson founded the community of Peterborough in Upper Canada. But it wasn't until the 1840s that vast numbers of Irish were forced to leave their homeland.

The Irish Potato Famine, 1846

In 1845 a disease spread through the Irish potato crop, destroying many acres of potatoes. The people eagerly looked forward to the next crop.

In May and June 1846, the fields were green, and it looked like a prosperous crop. However, by July the dreaded disease appeared again. In the fall, when the Irish dug up their potatoes, they found that the potatoes had turned to soft, smelly mush. There was little or no other food. Many Irish starved to death.

Leaving Ireland seemed the only answer. Some looked for work in British ports — Glasgow and Liverpool. Others came to North America.

In 1847 over 100 000 emigrants came from Ireland to Canada. Of these, it is estimated 17 000 died at sea on the voyage, 20 000 died in Canada, and 25 000 had to go to hospitals when they arrived in Canada. Of the survivors, approximately 30 000 went to the United States. Only about 30 000 who left Ireland actually stayed as immigrants in Canada.

Passengers could only be allowed on deck in fair weather, when they would not be in the way of the sailors operating the ship.

1200	1300	1400	1500	1600	1700	1800	1900

The Irish in the Cities

Irish immigrants were not prepared for pioneer farming. Most were penniless when they arrived. Many were weak or sick and unable to attack the hard job of clearing the land. Denied education and

Ships sailed from Canada to Britain carrying timber. Rather than return empty they would be filled with emigrants looking for a cheap passage. The crews were completely unprepared to look after hundreds of people on a transatlantic voyage.

Emigrants usually travelled in the "steerage." This was a section of the ship below decks. It was about 24 m long by 7 or 8 m wide and 1.6 m high. On each side of an aisle 1.5 m wide were double rows of berths made of rough planks. Six adults were assigned to each berth. Four rows of 13 berths could hold 308 people. Their baggage, utensils and food were crowded into the aisle. Some passengers brought hammocks to sleep in — if they could find a place to sling them. In the semi-darkness, children played. The confusion and noise are easy to imagine.

Here is a description of the voyage across the Atlantic in 1847.

"Before the emigrant has been a week at sea he is a changed man. How can it be otherwise? Hundreds of people — men, women and children of all ages — huddle together. They have no fresh air. They wallow in filth. They are often sick. People with the fever lie among the healthy. They get no food or medicine, except what other passengers can give them. They die without spiritual guidance. They are buried at sea without the rites of the church.

"The food is generally very poor. There is not enough water for cooking and drinking. No one can wash. The beds are filthy, and teeming with lice or other bugs."

opportunity in the past, they brought few skills with them. As a result, they drifted into the cities of Montreal, Quebec or Toronto, where they could get unskilled labouring jobs.

By the 1840s, 20 percent of Montreal's population was Irish; 14 percent of the residents of Quebec City came from Ireland. The Irish were among the poorest people in the cities. They did the heaviest and dirtiest of work. The women found work as lowly servants. The men worked as labourers. In Quebec City, the Irish were hired to load timber on the ships. The Irish section of Montreal was located near the docks. It had the lowest income and poorest housing in the city.

The Irish in the Country

Some of the Irish immigrants went to the country. They moved onto the forest lands of the Canadian Shield, north of Montreal. Some were farmers, scratching a living from the thin soil. Others worked building the railways and new roads, or in sawmills, tanneries and breweries. They frequently were not well received by local residents. Many feared that they would bring dreaded diseases with them. Others did not accept the poorer standard of living of the uneducated Irish immigrants. The Irish tended to live near one another, in close association with their own Catholic church. In the Ottawa Valley, the Irish slowly intermarried with the French-Canadian population.

They were often harshly treated by the English Protestant settlers of Upper Canada. Many of the first generation of Irish immigrants lived out their lives in poverty. But their children and grandchildren established themselves, and became successful citizens.

The Fur Trade and Exploration

On the shores of Hudson Bay, at the mouth of the Churchill River, stand the restored ruins of Fort Prince of Wales. The fort is the size of a city block. Its walls are up to twelve metres thick at their base and five metres high. Made of granite stones, it was built to last forever.

It didn't. It was built by the English of the Hudson's Bay Company in the 1730s. The first time the French attacked it, it was surrendered almost immediately. But the French couldn't burn it down or blow it up. Today, it stands as a monument to the Hudson's Bay Company and the trade the company thought it could capture at the bay.

The company wanted to handle all its fur trade at trading posts like Fort Prince of Wales along the bay. They expected the Indians to come to the posts to trade. There should be no need for the traders to go to the Indians.

Trade Moves Inland

Unfortunately for the Hudson's Bay Company traders, the French had other ideas. They travelled overland from Quebec to the West. They set up a line of trading posts close to where the Indians lived. The Indians were quite happy not to have to go all the way to the bay. Fewer and fewer brought the prized thick, glossy furs to Hudson Bay.

As a result the Hudson's Bay Company traders were forced to move inland. Henry Kelsey and Anthony Henday, among other explorers, headed overland. They set up posts along the great rivers that led south and west from Hudson Bay.

Sir George Simpson was Governor of Rupert's Land for nearly 40 years. Rupert's Land was the territory granted to the Hudson's Bay Company. Simpson made regular tours of inspection. He believed that a man should always look his best. Why was it important for him to dress well when visiting the fur forts?
Note the piper. How would music help the paddlers?

The fur trade became important to the native people's way of life.

1200 1300 1400 1500 1600 1700 1800 1900

When the British took over New France, a new company of traders called the North West Company was formed in Montreal. They joined with French traders and took over their trading posts. The North West Company was soon in fierce competition with the Hudson's Bay Company. The traders of the North West Company moved further and further west, setting up posts all across the northern and western plains. The traders and explorers even moved across the Rocky Mountains, tracing the westward flowing rivers to the Pacific.

Soon, there were two strings of fur-trading posts stretched across the west. Alexander Mackenzie, David Thompson, Simon Fraser and other explorers for the two companies began to map and explore the vast western regions. They also headed north toward the Arctic Ocean, still seeking both a passage across the country and the thick furs that were produced in the coldest regions.

Fort Prince of Wales, Hudson Bay

Alexander Mackenzie

BORN: Outer Hebrides, 1764

DIED: Mulnain, Scotland, 1820

1774 — came to New York, father a Loyalist officer. Mackenzie sent to live in Montreal.
1787 — became a member of the North West Company.
1789 — first overland expedition — found and followed Mackenzie river. It led him to the Arctic Ocean, not the Pacific.
1793 — second expedition reached Pacific Ocean at Bella Coola, B.C.
After his exploring years, became a successful merchant and consultant in the fur trade business. Advocated merger of Hudson's Bay and North West Companies.

The Red River Colony

Hudson's Bay Company ships carrying Swiss settlers to Red River meet ships of the Arctic explorer, William Parry, in Hudson Bay, 1821.

It was a spring day in 1811. A group of 100 nervous travellers from the Scottish highlands and the Irish countryside stood on the quay at Sligo, Ireland. They were bound for Hudson Bay. From the bay, they would head south to start a colony at Red River.

They had heard rumours that Red River was a terrible place. They had been told that the Indians were savages who would burn the settlers' houses and scalp their children. They had heard that there was no food at Red River, that it was terribly cold, that no one could live at Red River.

Yet staying at home seemed little better. Many of the travellers were small farmers from Scotland. They and their parents and grandparents before them had farmed small, rented plots of land. Now the land-owners had thrown them off the land, so that large flocks of sheep could be raised instead. The farmers could go only to the noisy crowded cities — or move to another country.

Lord Selkirk's Plan

One of the owners of the Hudson's Bay Company, Lord Selkirk, had obtained a grant of land from the company. He was going to start a colony on the land, the first colony west of Upper Canada and north of the 49th parallel of latitude. The Scots and Irish on the Sligo dock had decided to go to that colony.

Not everyone was pleased with Lord Selkirk's plans. The North West Company did not want settlers interfering with the fur trade. They tried to scare the settlers away by telling them how horrible the country was. But this group of settlers, and others after them, would not be frightened away.

There were problems along the way: poor weather, delayed sailings, the difficult journey overland from Hudson Bay to Red River. Once at Red River, food was scarce, the wrong farming tools were sent, sheep were killed by wolves. The North West Company and the Métis tried to chase the settlers away. The Métis

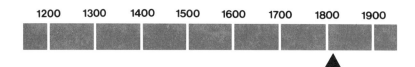

Different types of settlers.

A summer scene on the Red River near Fort Douglas.

were descended from the sons and daughters of European fur traders and their Indian wives. They felt that the land around Red River belonged to them and they wanted no settlers taking it away.

Métis Opposition

The Hudson's Bay Company tried to stop the Métis from hunting as they wished. The company tried to keep them from trading furs and pemmican as they wanted. In return, the Métis tried to frighten the settlers away and burned their houses. In one battle in 1816, 21 of the settlers were killed.

Yet the settlers were stubborn. Driven away again and again, they always returned. More settlers arrived and the Hudson's Bay Company brought in Swiss soldiers to protect them.

Finally, in 1821, the Hudson's Bay Company and the North West Company decided to join together as one company. The battle was over.

The problems of the colony were not over, however. Grasshoppers, floods, drought and disease all came over the next years. Yet the colony survived.

All the pictures on these two pages are by Peter Rindisbacher. He was a Swiss painter who came with his family to Lord Selkirk's colony in 1821 when he was 15. He sold his pictures of life at Red River to officers of the Hudson's Bay Company. In 1826, Rindisbacher moved to the United States. There, he painted for an American sporting magazine.

Exploring the Pacific Coast

Captain Cook's ships at Nootka Sound.

In a tavern in an Italian seaport sat an old Greek sailor named Juan de Fuca. Unsteadily he poured another glass of wine and continued his strange story. Many years ago he had sailed his ship north along the west coast of North America. Through storms and clear weather he had sailed, sometimes seeing nothing at all through the mist and the rain. But somewhere on his journey, at about the 46th parallel of latitude, he had come upon a wide opening in the coast, a tongue of water that led eastward. Perhaps this, he said, was the northwest passage that everyone else was looking for.

Did Juan de Fuca really make that journey? Or did he invent the tale? Nobody is sure. But there is a strait where the Greek sailor said there was one, and today it bears his name. Yet the man who is given credit for being the first European to visit these waters is not Juan de Fuca but Captain James Cook.

Captain Cook's Voyages

Captain James Cook is best known for his travels in the south seas, his trips around the world and his map making. On his third major voyage in 1778, Cook came north along the Pacific coast. He was looking for a northern passage over the top of North America.

He stopped briefly at Nootka Sound on the west coast of Vancouver Island to repair his ships and take on fresh supplies of water. He was the first European that the natives of the Northwest Coast saw. He was also the first European known to have landed on the west coast of what is now Canada.

Cook then proceeded up the coast until bad weather turned him south again. He left convinced that if any passage existed, it would be choked with ice. He and his crew then sailed for Hawaii, where Cook was killed by the natives.

His crew took with them some sea otter pelts that the Northwest Coast natives traded to them. This was the beginning of the fur trade along the Pacific coast.

Captain George Vancouver's Expeditions

Far to the south, the Spanish had heard that the British were taking an interest in this coast. Several years earlier, in 1775, they had sent out an exploring expedition headed by Bodega y Quadra. But Quadra had not stepped onto land. Now they sent out a new expedition and Quadra also went ashore at Nootka. He was soon followed in 1792 by expeditions under the English sea captain, George Vancouver, who had first travelled to the area with Cook. Vancouver sailed around Vancouver Island and mapped the area.

Russians and Americans

The British and Spanish were not the only ones interested in the Nootka area. As early as 1744, a Russian expedition under Vitus Bering sailed down the Alaskan coast. Now the Russians began to build fur-trading posts.

Even the newly independent Americans were getting into the act. Fur traders from Boston set up headquarters at Nootka.

Sometimes there was fighting as the four nations — England, Spain, Russia and the United States — vied for the fur trade and for possession of the area. Finally treaties were signed, giving Britain the rights to what is now British Columbia.

But by the time all the treaties were signed, they meant almost nothing. The sea otters, once so plentiful, were gone, hunted to extinction. There was

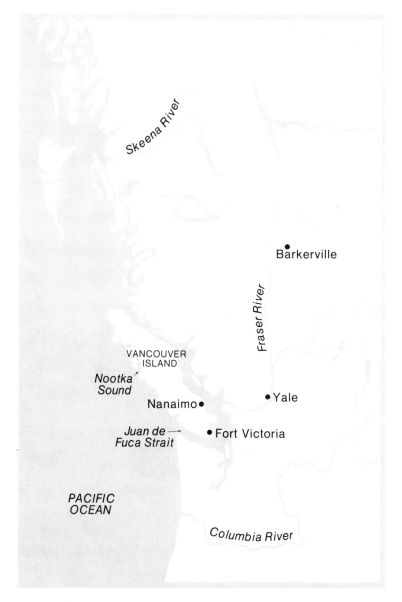

nothing left to fight over. The next people to be interested in this area would come, not by sea, but overland from Canada.

Captain Cook on the native people of the Northwest Coast:
The inhabitants are gentle, courteous and good-natured. I entered one of their homes. The homes are huge and are used by many families. They are made of cedar. The natives are very skilled. They split large boards up to five feet (150 cm) wide and two inches (5 cm) thick from the cedar logs.

Fort Victoria

The *Beaver* off Fort Victoria, about 1846. The S.S. *Beaver* was the first steamship on the Pacific coast.

By the 1840s, the Hudson's Bay Company had set up a network of fur-trading posts from Red River west through the plains and into the British colony west of the Rockies. The British called this area New Caledonia. It contained settlements at Fort Langley, Fort Vancouver and other forts in the north. But settlers from the middle and eastern United States were beginning to push westward into the area south of the 49th parallel. They claimed this area — called the Oregon Territory — for the United States. Fort Vancouver, the main Hudson's Bay Company post, was within this area.

The Hudson's Bay Company thought that the United States would probably soon take over the Oregon territory. James Douglas, one of the fur traders at Fort Vancouver, was sent north to find a new location for the Hudson's Bay Company headquarters. He decided to build a fort, to be called Fort Victoria, at the southern tip of Vancouver Island.

The fort was established in 1842 and quickly became the headquarters for the company. Settlers came to farm the land around the fort. Miners were brought from Britain to work in the mines at Nanaimo, north of Fort Victoria, where coal had been discovered.

New settlements were established on the mainland. In spite of these ports and posts, very few people lived in this vast area. Canada was 5000 km away. Sailing ships took many weeks to go around Cape Horn at the southern tip of South America and across the Atlantic to Great Britain. The colony was completely isolated. Would it become part of the expanding United States?

1200	1300	1400	1500	1600	1700	1800	1900

Panning for gold.

Yates Street, Victoria, 1862.

Gold on the Fraser River

In May of 1858, the Hudson's Bay Company steamer *Otter* was on her way to San Francisco from Fort Victoria. On board was the usual cargo of goods and people — and one very special addition. On this trip, the ship carried 800 ounces of gold, collected in New Caledonia and bound for San Francisco.

Almost the moment that the ship docked, the news was out. Gold in New Caledonia! Gold had been found to the north. Within a month of the *Otter*'s arrival in San Francisco, the first prospectors were beginning to stream into Fort Victoria. They had been idle since the 1849 California gold rush petered out. They were on their way to the Fraser River where, it had been reported, the gold had been found.

All through 1858, the rush went on. Fort Victoria changed from a sleepy fur fort into a bustling town. It was soon bursting with gold-seekers eager to find their fortunes. A tent town sprang up around the walls of the fort. Would-be miners took over every boat they could find. Some even built rafts to make their way to the Fraser River.

Catherine Schubert

BORN: Rathfriland, County Down, Ireland, 1835
DIED: Armstrong, British Columbia, 1918
1851 — after potato famine, emigrated to work as servant in Springfield, Massachusetts in order to send money home to family.
1855 — married Augustus Schubert, a carpenter. They moved west to St. Paul, Minnesota Territory. Opened grocery store.
1858 — moved to Red River to escape discontent of Indians in Minnesota. Set up farm and liquor store in St. Boniface.
1861 — lost everything in spring flood of Red River.
1862 — Augustus decided to join overland trip to Cariboo gold fields. With 3 children under age 6 and pregnant, Catherine insisted on going too. A terrible trip, especially across Rockies with winter approaching. Baby born outside Kamloops.
1863-1877 — While Augustus looked for gold, Catherine ran farm and inn at Lillooet, roadhouse serving meals at Quesnel, taught children at home and agitated for proper schools.
1877 — appointed matron at government boarding school at Cache Creek. Much loved by her students.
1881 — Augustus gave up mining because had never struck it rich. They settled on farm in Okanagan Valley near Armstrong.

The Gold Rush and After

Fewer than 1000 Europeans lived in New Caledonia at the start of 1858. By the end of the year, 10 000 people were living in the area.

That same year, Britain set up a new colony on the mainland. It was called British Columbia.

By now, the prospectors could no longer find gold along the sandbars of the Fraser River. They were looking for the source of the gold that had washed down along the Fraser. They headed north to the interior area called "the Cariboo."

The Cariboo Road

In 1860, they found the source of the gold. Towns like Quesnelle Forks, Barkerville and Keithley Creek grew up quickly along the creeks where the gold was found. Miners, merchants, wagon drivers and all manner of people set up house in these towns. A company of Royal Engineers was sent from England to British Columbia. Their first task was to build a road north along the fearsome Fraser Canyon from Yale, where the ships had to stop, to the goldfields. It was the first road built in the colony.

The coming of the wagon road opened up the interior of British Columbia. Now people and goods no longer had to make the difficult trip along the narrow trails. Now stagecoach teams pulled the coaches north. Roadhouses were built. Here, the coaches stopped for the night and new teams of horses were hitched up. Ranches and farms spread around the roadhouses.

Already life in the goldfields was changing. At first, prospectors had been able to reach the gold fairly easily. They could pan it in the streams or wash it out in their rocker boxes. But the loose gold was soon all

Ships could not travel beyond Yale, so the Cariboo Road to the gold fields was started here.

The Cariboo Road 140 km above Yale.

taken up. Then miners had to blast their ways into the hillsides and find ways of separating the gold from the rock. This was expensive and took many men. In the end, it cost more to recover the gold than the men could sell the gold for.

By the early 1870s, the fever for gold was over. Yet British Columbia had changed a great deal. The Cariboo road was built. There was a new townsite at New Westminster. Steamers ran the rivers. Victoria had become a bustling town, farms had been started. Hotels, stores and houses had been built. These changes outlasted the gold rush, and the westernmost section of British North America continued to grow.

Barkerville in the 1860s: "the gold capital of the world."

Questions

Can You Recall?

1. From what two parts of Scotland did immigrants to Canada come? Why did the two groups have different experiences in Canada?
2. In 1846, the _____ brought disaster to the people of Ireland.
3. Why did Irish immigrants to Canada often end up in poorly paid jobs?
4. How many people lived in Upper and Lower Canada in the 1850s?
5. The _____ Company and the _____ Company were rivals for the western fur trade.
6. Name three explorers who travelled west of the Great Lakes in the eighteenth and early nineteenth centuries.
7. In 1793, Alexander Mackenzie became the first European to cross the _____ to the _____ Ocean.
8. Who were the Métis?
9. Who was the first European to record setting foot on the Pacific coast of what was to be British Columbia?
10. What countries traded in the Nootka Sound area late in the eighteenth century?
11. What were the names of the two British colonies on the Northwest Coast.
12. Where did the gold rush of 1858 take place?

Ideas for Discussion

1. "The best settlers are the ones who start with nothing and have everything to gain by working hard." Discuss.
2. Explain why many Scots and Irish left their homes to come to Canada in the early 1800s.
3. Explain how the fur trade led to the development of western Canada.
4. In 1778, Captain Cook sailed into Nootka Sound. Native people on the Northwest Coast met Europeans for the first time. More than a hundred years later, Edward Sheriff Curtis took these pictures of native life. He also took many of the photographs you see in the chapter "The First Canadians." Curtis spent 30 years travelling through

western North America taking over 40 000 pictures of native people. He wrote 20 books in a series called *The North American Indian.* Many tribes invited Curtis to visit them and record their way of life. Why were these photographs so important to the native people?
5. How important was the gold rush to the the development of British Columbia?

Do Some Research

1. Find out more about the following events in Europe at the time of the Great Migration:
   a) the wars with Napoleon;
   b) the Industrial Revolution;
   c) the Irish Potato Famine.
   If you had lived in the British Isles at the time, which of these events might have made you decide to leave for a life in a new land? What other reasons might have led you to come to Canada?

2. Write brief biographies of the following:
   a) Simon McTavish, founder of the North West Company;
   b) George Simpson, governor of the Hudson's Bay Company;
   c) James Douglas, governor of British Columbia.

3. With a group of three or four other students prepare a report on the expeditions of the following explorers:
   a) Samuel Hearne;
   b) Simon Fraser;
   c) David Thompson;
   d) Alexander Mackenzie;
   e) Sir John Franklin.
   Mark the routes followed by each explorer on a map. Use a different colour for each explorer. Make a *legend* (explanation) for your map showing how you have marked the routes of each explorer.

4. With a small group of students, prepare a class presentation on the way of life of the Métis. Your presentation should include maps showing where the Métis lived, drawings of their homes, an account of their main activities and a statement by a Métis telling how he or she felt when the Selkirk settlers first arrived.

Be Creative

1. On a map of the world, trace the routes that took settlers from Europe to:
   a) eastern Canada;
   b) Red River;
   c) British Columbia.
   Write the story of a settler's journey to one of these places.

2. Imagine that you are one of the Selkirk settlers who arrived at Hudson Bay in 1811. Write a letter home describing what you saw when you arrived.

3. Each year, workers for the Hudson's Bay Company took trade goods to the trading posts in the Northwest and brought back furs. Imagine that you are one of the people shown at this portage and that you are on your way to Fort Edmonton. Describe your companions and tell of your experiences on this expedition.

4. Write a song that could be sung on the trail with a fur trader or in a gold rush camp.

5. Draw a series of pictures that show a prospector on his way to the Cariboo. The drawings should show him arriving in Victoria, making his way to Yale by steamer, following the trail north and arriving at the goldfields.

Confederation
ADVANCE ORGANIZER

1

Confederation. What does it mean? A confederation is a group of people or organizations brought together for a common purpose. The Confederation of Canada brought together a number of colonies. They became provinces in a stronger unit, the nation. Each province has its own government. But there is another level of government — the federal government — that governs for the people of all the provinces.

2

In the early 1860s, Canada was still seven separate British colonies and a large area owned by the Hudson's Bay Company. Each of the colonies had its own government, but all were subject to the laws of Britain.

Britain had become tired of ruling the colonies in North America. Running the colonies was expensive. Britain also feared the strength of the neighbouring United States. If they attacked, Britain would have to defend its colonies.

3

Many people in Canada wanted to see the colonies united. Some wanted to see an independent Canada, free of British rule. There was talk of joining the four Atlantic colonies into a Maritime Union separate from the other colonies.

Not everyone in the colonies was in favour of Confederation. There were those who wanted to remain British subjects. Some French Canadians felt that Confederation might mean the end of their separate identity and rights.

absentee	confederation	federal	proposal
civil war	conference	identity	republic
coalition	constitution	independent	resolution
common	delegate	parliament	union

4

A conference was called in Charlottetown, Prince Edward Island, to discuss the proposed Maritime Union. Political leaders from the Canadas joined the conference. The idea of a Maritime Union was quickly scrapped in favour of a larger Confederation.

A second conference was held at Quebec City to draw up the rules for Confederation. These rules became part of the British North America Act, the basis for Canada's constitution.

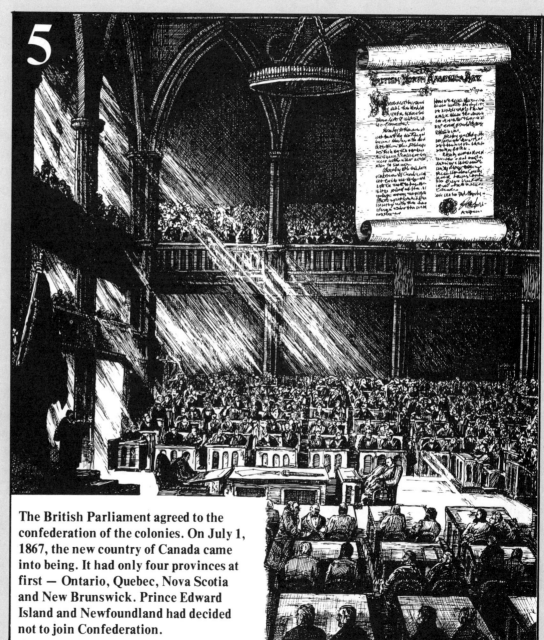

5

The British Parliament agreed to the confederation of the colonies. On July 1, 1867, the new country of Canada came into being. It had only four provinces at first — Ontario, Quebec, Nova Scotia and New Brunswick. Prince Edward Island and Newfoundland had decided not to join Confederation.

Introduction

What is now Canada was still seven separate British colonies in the middle of the nineteenth century. Each of the colonies had its own legislative assembly. Men elected to the assemblies made laws to govern the colonies. But the colonies were still subject to the laws of the British Parliament. In each colony there was a governor who represented the Queen of England. Defence of the colonies was handled by the Royal Navy and the British Army.

By this time, Britain was growing tired of ruling Canada. Running a colony was costly. So was keeping the navy and British soldiers in Canada. But Britain was afraid that the United States might invade Canada again as it had during the War of 1812.

Ever since the rebellions of 1837 many Canadians had wanted to be independent of Britain. Some wanted to form a republic, like France or the United States. Others wanted an independent country, but one still linked to Britain and the Queen.

Not everyone wanted an independent Canada. Some of the colonists wanted to remain British. They felt that Canada was not strong enough to be independent. Some worried that the French Canadians might take over the new country. Some French Canadians feared they would lose their religion and language rights. There were colonists who wanted to see Canada become part of the United States.

The American Civil War

Between 1861 and 1865, the Americans fought a civil war between the North and the South. During the war, the British supported the South. The cotton plantations of the South were important to Britain. Following the North's victory, some Americans wanted to use the northern army to invade Canada. Many Americans believed that it was their destiny to rule North America from the Atlantic to the Pacific, and from the Gulf of Mexico to the Arctic. They felt that it was only a matter of time until the United States took over the last British colonies in North America.

The British realized that the isolated separate colonies in North America were not strong enough to protect themselves against American attack. They would have to join together somehow to protect themselves.

Maritime Union

There was little agreement among the colonies about uniting to form one country. Some of the people of the four Maritime colonies wanted a separate Maritime union, similar to the union of the two Canadas in 1840. Others wanted the Maritime colonies to join the Province of Canada as four separate provinces. Many people in Newfoundland wanted nothing to do with the proposed union. They were happy to remain a British colony.

The people of the Maritimes had little contact with Canada. Most of their trade was with Britain, the United States or the West Indies. The only transportation route to Canadian markets was the St. Lawrence River. Ice blocked the river in winter, cutting off contact with the Maritimes.

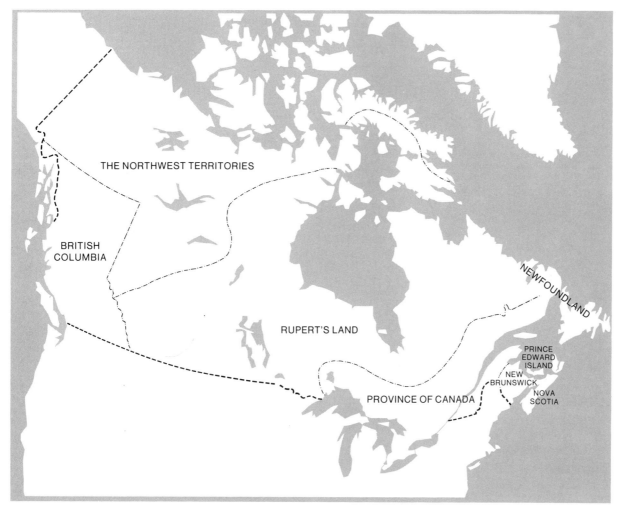

THE NORTHWEST TERRITORIES

BRITISH
COLUMBIA

NEWFOUNDLAND

RUPERT'S LAND

PRINCE
EDWARD
ISLAND

NEW
BRUNSWICK

NOVA
SCOTIA

PROVINCE OF CANADA

By the 1860s, British Columbia had an elected assembly. But she did not have responsible government like the British colonies in the eastern part of North America. Rupert's Land was run by the Hudson's Bay Company. The British Crown claimed the Northwest Territories, but there were no government officials in the area.

Stalemate in Canada

In the early 1860s, the government of the combined Canadas was in trouble. The Act of Union had created a stalemate. The balance between political parties and between French and English Canadians was so close that no party could stay in office for very long. In two years five governments had tried to run the colony.

In 1864, a coalition government was formed. This brought together members of all parties from both Canada East and Canada West. The government was led by John A. Macdonald from Canada West and George Etienne Cartier from Canada East. Both were Conservatives. They were joined by Reformers like George Brown and Independents like Alexander Galt.

The coalition government believed that the way out of Canada's problem was a federal union. Each region would govern its own affairs. A federal government would run the army, post offices, and other services. Their view of the federal union was not limited to Canada East and Canada West. They thought that the federal union, or Confederation, could include the Maritimes too.

The Confederation Debates

In the mid-1860s, in all of the colonies, there were discussions about forming a new, independent country in British North America. Everybody was talking about the proposed union. People took sides. Some argued for union, some against. Some wanted independence, others didn't. A few said that they were for joining the United States. Here are some of the important voices of the period and their arguments for or against Confederation.

Even though the official names were now Canada West and Canada East, people still talked about Upper and Lower Canada. We have followed their custom and referred to those taking part in the debate as being from Upper or Lower Canada.

John A. Macdonald (Upper Canada):

So satisfactory were the reasons we gave; so clearly did we show the advantages of the greater union over the lesser. The Maritimes at once set aside their own project. They joined heart in hand with us in entering into the larger scheme — trying to form, as far as they and we could, a great nation and a strong government.

Andrew R. Wetmore (New Brunswick):

An imaginary conversation commenting on the grant New Brunswick would get if it joined Confederation:
"Father, what country do we live in?"
"My dear son, you have no country, for Mr. Tilley has sold us all to the Canadians for 80 cents a head."

A Pro-Confederation Song

Come boys, let's sing a song,
For the day it won't be long
When united to our country we will be.
Then the Maple Leaf entwined
And the Beaver too, combined
With Old England's flag shall float upon the sea.

Tramp, tramp, tramp! The new Dominion
Now is knocking at the door.
So goodbye, dear Uncle Sam,
As we do not care a clam
For your greenbacks or your bunkum anymore!

From The Cariboo Sentinel, *19 June, 1869*

John A. Macdonald (Upper Canada):

We have hit upon the happy medium. We have formed a scheme of government that has the strength of a true union and yet preserves local freedom. We have taken advantage of the experience of the United States. We have avoided the defects of the American system — which brought on the present unhappy war in the United States.

The best interests and prosperity of British North America will be promoted by a Federal Union under the Crown of Great Britain, provided such a union can be worked out on principles fair to each province.

1200	1300	1400	1500	1600	1700	1800	1900

Antoine Aimé Dorion (Lower Canada):

The Confederation scheme is put before us on two grounds. The first is the need to deal with the problems that have arisen between Upper and Lower Canada. The second is the need to defend the country.

I have suggested a Confederation of the two Canadas to deal with the first problem. The local legislatures would deal with local problems. The central government would have control over commerce and other areas of common interest. I have never been in favour of bringing in other provinces. This could only bring trouble and embarrassment. There is no social, no commercial connection between the provinces — nothing to justify their union.

It is said that Confederation is necessary in order to better defend this country. Some people think that by adding two and two together you get five. But I cannot see how, by adding the populations of the maritime provinces to that of Canada, you can multiply them to make a larger force to defend the country.

In a period of four years, the Northern States have raised an army of 2 300 000 men. That is as many soldiers as we have men, women and children in the two Canadas. We are bound to do everything we can to protect the country. But we must not ruin ourselves to prepare for an invasion which — even with the help of Britain — we cannot stop. The best thing that Canada can do is keep quiet and give no cause for war.

Charles Tupper (Nova Scotia):

The fact is, that if the Maritime Provinces are known at all across the Atlantic, it is because we are next door to Canada. This is true despite our own immense resources.

D'Arcy McGee (Lower Canada):

The United States have frightful numbers of soldiers and guns. They wanted Florida and seized it. They wanted Louisiana and purchased it. They wanted Texas and stole it. Then they picked a quarrel with Mexico and got California. If we had not had the strong arm of England over us, we too would be part of the States.

The viewpoint of the United States Secretary of State:

I look upon Canada and see how a clever people are occupied with bridging rivers and making railroads and telegraphs. I say, "It is very well: you are building excellent states to be hereafter admitted to the American Union."

I know that Nature designs that this whole continent shall be, sooner or later, within the magic circle of the American Union.

The Debates Continue

Etienne Taché (Lower Canada):

In a federal union, general questions would be looked after by the federal government. Local questions would be looked after by local governments. This would be almost the same as if we had a separation of the provinces. Lower Canada would be able to preserve all the institutions it holds so dear.

John A. Macdonald (Upper Canada):

I would be quite willing, personally, to leave that whole country (the Canadian West and North) a wilderness for the next half-century. But I fear if the Englishmen don't go there, the Yankees will.

Alexander Galt (Lower Canada):

The railway will be a bond of union in time of peace and in time of need. We can only trust that we will stay friendly with the United States, but it is our duty to be prepared. If ill-feeling should arise, the intercolonial railway would be very important.

An Anti-Confederation Song

Hurrah for our own native isle, Newfoundland!
Not a stranger shall hold one inch of its strand!
Her face turns to Britain, her back to the Gulf.
Come near at your peril, Canadian Wolf!

Ye brave Newfoundlanders who plough the salt sea
With hearts like the eagle so bold and so free,
The time is at hand when you'll all have to say
If Confederation will carry the day.

Cheap tea and molasses they say they will give,
All taxes take off that the poor man may live:
Cheap nails and cheap lumber our coffins to make,
And homespun to mend our old clothes when they break.

If they take off the taxes how then will they meet
The heavy expenses of the country's up-keep?
Just give them the chance to get us in the scrape
And they'll chain you as slaves with pen, ink and red tape.

Would you barter the right that your fathers have won,
Your freedom transmitted from father to son?
For a few thousand dollars of Canadian gold
Don't let it be said that your birthright was sold!

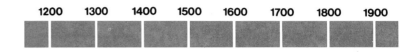

George Etienne Cartier (Lower Canada):

The question is as simple as this — we must either have Confederation or be taken over by the United States. Some feel that it is not necessary to form a Confederation to prevent being absorbed into our neighbouring republic, but they are mistaken. The English provinces, separated as they are at this time, cannot defend themselves. When we are united, the enemy will know that if he attacks any province — whether it be Prince Edward Island or Canada — he will face the combined forces of the Empire.

George Brown (Upper Canada):

I am sure that this union will inspire confidence in our stability. It will help us in all our affairs. It will mean investors will want to go into business here.

Union will break down the trade barriers between us. We will have control of a market of 4 000 000 people. The United States are rich because they have free trade with each other.

The intercolonial railway will give us ice-free ports all year round. Then goods will not have to pass through the United States in winter.

Joseph Howe (Nova Scotia):

Let us see what these Canadians want to do. They are not a very happy or united community. Two-fifths of the population are French and three-fifths English. This must ever be a source of weakness — unless the two groups are fused into one.

They are shut in by frost from the outer world for five months of the year. They are at the mercy of a powerful neighbour whose population outnumbers them eight to one.

A more unpromising basis for a new nation can hardly be found on the face of the earth. It would be politically insane to join Canada in Confederation.

Canada is a fine nation, with great natural resources. But it is hemmed in by icy barriers to the north and by a powerful nation to the south. It is cut off from deep-sea navigation for nearly half the year. It has two nationalities to bring together. It has no coal. Who will predict a bright future for her?

John A. Macdonald (Upper Canada):

Whatever do you, stick to the union. We are a great country. And we shall become one of the greatest in the universe if we stay together. We shall sink into insignificance and conflict if we allow it to be broken.

The Conferences

In 1864, a conference was called to discuss the possibility of a Maritime union. The conference was held at Charlottetown, the capital of Prince Edward Island. Lord Durham had favoured a union of the four Maritime colonies — Prince Edward Island, New Brunswick, Nova Scotia and Newfoundland — during his visit in 1838. Over the past 25 years there had been much talk about the possibility of a union. But nothing had been done about it.

Only three of the Maritime colonies were going to meet at Charlottetown. The fourth, Newfoundland, showed little interest in the proposed union. However, a fourth colony invited itself to the conference.

The Charlottetown Conference

The Canadian Governor General, Viscount Monck, wrote asking permission of the Maritime colonies for a Canadian group to attend the conference. The Maritime colonies said yes. Eight Canadian leaders were sent to Charlottetown. Among them were: John A. Macdonald, George Etienne Cartier, Alexander Galt, George Brown and Thomas D'Arcy McGee. Prince Edward Island gave the Canadian party a warm welcome, wining and dining them in style.

The discussion of Maritime union took less than an hour. The proposal was rejected quickly. The talk moved to a new proposal, brought by the Canadians.

The official photograph of the delegates to the Charlottetown Conference.

They suggested a larger union that would include all the British colonies in North America. The delegates began to create the design for what would be the new country of Canada.

The Quebec Conference

The colonial leaders met again in Quebec City, just over a month later. The Quebec Conference began on October 10, 1864. Newfoundland sent delegates too. After two weeks of secret meeting, the conference came up with a plan for Confederation.

There had been much heated discussion. Each of the colonies wanted something different from the proposed Confederation. Nova Scotia and New Brunswick wanted a railway built to link them with the markets of Montreal. Prince Edward Island wanted lands held by absentee landowners bought back. Newfoundland was not certain that it would benefit from Confederation at all.

Provincial Powers

One of the key issues discussed was: "How much power should each province have?" There was a wide range of views on the issue. Some thought that the provinces should have no powers. All power should rest with one legislature, as in England. Others felt that most of the powers should remain with the provincial assemblies. The Canadian delegates were worried about the provinces having too much power. The American Civil War was still going on. Many believed that the war came about because the states had too much power.

Each issue was slowly worked out. The construction of an intercolonial railway linking Canada and the Maritimes was promised. Unoccupied lands in Prince Edward Island would be bought back. The powers that the provinces and the federal government would have were agreed upon. These powers were outlined in a series of resolutions.

One step still remained before Confederation could take place. Each colony had to approve the resolutions passed at Quebec.

Joseph Howe
BORN: Halifax, Nova Scotia, 1804
DIED: Halifax, Nova Scotia, 1873
1817 — entered father's printing shop as "printer's devil" (apprentice errand boy).
1828 — editor of Halifax paper *The Nova Scotian.*
1835 — prosecuted for libel because of attacks on government in paper. No lawyer would take the case, so defended himself. Jury found him not guilty.
1836-1863 — member of legislative assembly. Worked for responsible government. Later, pressed for intercolonial railway.
1860-1863 — prime minister of Nova Scotia.
1863 — defeated in election by Charles Tupper.
1864 — invited by Tupper to Charlottetown Conference, but could not attend.
1865-1867 — came out against Confederation. Believed in some form of union, but thought Confederation proposals too rushed. Dislike for Tupper may have coloured his views.
1868 — persuaded to accept Confederation.
1869 — became member of parliament but uncomfortable in Ottawa. Felt his position was false.
1873 — appointed lieutenant governor of Nova Scotia a few weeks before his death.

The Fenians

The battle of Ridgeway.

Governor General Monck's appeal for volunteers:

The soil of Canada has been invaded by a lawless band of pirates. This state of things imposes upon the people of Canada the duty of defending their altars, their homes, and their property.

Tramp, tramp, tramp, our boys are marching!
Cheer up, let the Fenians come!
For beneath the Union Jack, we'll drive the Fenians back
And will fight for our beloved Canadian home.

The soldiers in the railroad coach shouted out their song over and over. Even their disappointing breakfast of herring and bread couldn't dampen their spirits. The soldiers were volunteers. They had answered the call to turn back the Fenian invasion of Canada. The day before, an army of 1000 Fenians had crossed into Canada at Niagara.

The Fenians were Irish Catholics. They were fighting to free Ireland from English rule. Many poor people had left Ireland after the potato famines of the 1840s. Most had gone to the United States. The American Civil War saw many Irish Americans wearing the uniforms of northern soldiers.

Now the Civil War was over. The Fenians wanted to use their military experience to fight the British. Canada was the nearest point of attack. The Fenians thought they would be supported by Americans and Irish immigrants living in Canada.

The Battle of Ridgeway

The Fenians crossed the Niagara River shortly after midnight, June 1, 1866. The Fenian soldiers wore green shirts, black belts, and workmen's trousers. Their officers were dressed in proper military uniforms — left over from the Civil War. Over each Fenian regiment flew a battle flag — green with a gold sunburst or a harp embroidered on it.

News of the invasion quickly reached Toronto by telegraph. Within 48 hours 20 000 volunteers were rushing from Toronto to Niagara by train and steamship. They were full of enthusiasm for the coming fight. Crowds of men, women and children filled Union Station. Others lined the docks of Toronto harbour. Some waved Union Jacks as they saw fathers, brothers or husbands go off to fight.

The Fenians, led by Colonel O'Neill, were moving toward Fort Erie. There they hoped to attack the railyards of the Erie and Ontario Railway. The citizens of Fort Erie hooked all the railcars together into one long train. The train was moved safely out of town.

The Fenians marched further into Canada. They ran into Canadian defenders at the village of Ridgeway. O'Neil's army was met by a militia unit led by Colonel Booker. Booker's ill-prepared soldiers were outnumbered. Sounds of gunfire, smoke and flying bullets broke the peaceful summer day.

At first the Fenians had the upper hand. But reinforcements soon arrived, sending the Fenians into retreat. The invaders were driven back to the Niagara River and were forced to surrender.

Thomas D'Arcy McGee
BORN: Carlingford, Ireland, 1825
DIED: Ottawa, Ontario, 1868
1842 — emigrated to Boston where wrote for *The Pilot,* a weekly paper for Irish Americans.
1845-48 — returned to Ireland. Edited anti-English newspapers. After Irish rebellion in 1848, escaped to New York.
1857 — invited to Montreal by Irish-Canadians. Founded newspaper *The New Era.*
1858 — elected to legislative assembly.
1864 — delegate to Charlottetown and Quebec conferences. Was very enthusiastic about "the new nationality." Helped persuade Maritime provinces to join. By now, shed anti-British ideas of the 1840s in Ireland.
1866 — condemned Fenian invasions.
1868 — on way home from late-night session at House of Commons, shot as a traitor to Ireland by a Fenian.
1869 — his murderer was executed in the last public hanging in Canada.

Fenians in French Canada

Later that month, a second group of Fenians invaded Canada East. Once again, they found they were not welcome. Irish Catholics and French Canadians did not join the Fenian cause against the hated English. The Fenians were soon driven off.

The Fenian raids posed no real threat to the British colonies in North America. However, they made the leaders of those colonies very conscious of how hard it was to defend themselves. Many in Canada felt that the Fenians could not have made their raids without help from the Americans. They wondered if the Americans might not be the next to invade Canada. The Fenian raids, and the fear of American invasion, strengthened the arguments for Confederation.

Confederation: A New Nation

Each colony had to approve the Confederation resolutions passed at Quebec. There was still little agreement. The Canadian assembly approved Confederation by a three-to-one margin. Prince Edward Island rejected it by the same margin.

The voters of New Brunswick threw out the pro-Confederation party in the 1864 election. A year later they voted it back in. Both Nova Scotia and New Brunswick finally decided to support Confederation. But they wanted the union to be different from the one proposed at Quebec. The two small colonies feared that they would be dominated by the Canadas. The Newfoundland elections of 1865 saw only 10 supporters of Confederation elected to the assembly of 30 members.

The Great Seal of Canada.

The London Conference

The final decisions on Confederation had to be made by the British parliament. The colonies were the property of the British Crown. A conference was held in London in 1866 to work out the final design of Confederation. At the London Conference, the Canadian colonies could only offer advice. They had no votes.

The resolutions of the London Conference differed little from those passed at Quebec. These resolutions became the British North America Act. This Act quickly passed in both the houses of the British Parliament on March 29, 1867.

A Royal Proclamation set July 1, 1867 as the day the new Dominion of Canada would come into being. The new country had four provinces: Ontario, Quebec, Nova Scotia, and New Brunswick. The B.N.A. Act (renamed the Constitution Act, 1867, when the Canadian constitution was "patriated" in 1982)

Two views on Confederation in Nova Scotia

This first day of July 1867 is the Birth Day of the Dominion of Canada. Nova Scotia today entered a partnership, forever, with New Brunswick and the Canadas. The booming of the cannon early this morning and the ringing of the Church Bells proclaimed the gladness. At midday the High Sheriff, Mr. Kaulbach, read the Queen's Proclamation. Then a salute of 50 guns was fired, after which three hearty cheers were given for Queen Victoria and three more for the New Dominion. The band finished off with God Save the Queen.

Died! Last night at twelve o'clock, the free Province of Nova Scotia. The dead was the offspring of English stock. She should have been an honour and support to her parents in their old age. Her death was brought about by unnatural treatment at the hands of some of her ungrateful sons.

made provision for other colonies to join. The designers of Confederation saw a day when Canada would stretch from Vancouver Island to Newfoundland. They chose a motto from Psalm 72 in the Bible. *A mari usque ad mare* is the Latin for "From sea to sea."

Queen Victoria in 1867. She is wearing black in mourning for her husband, Prince Albert, who died in 1861. She wore black for him until her own death in 1901.

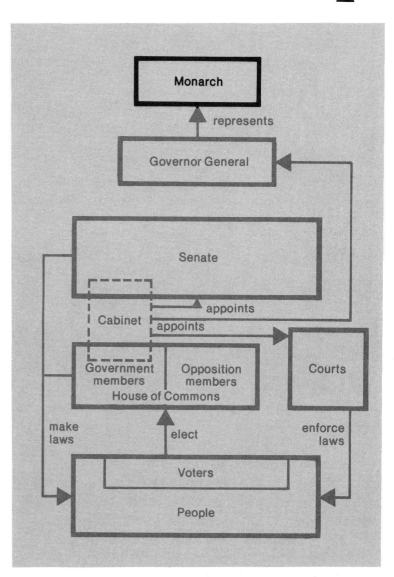

The federal system of government in Canada as set up by the British North America in 1867. The system of government in each province is similar. The monarch is represented by a lieutenant governor instead of a governor general. Provincial assemblies have no senate.

The Creation of the National Capital

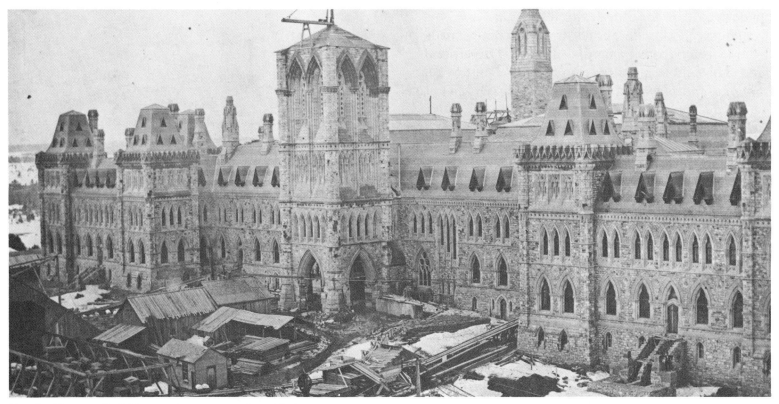

The Parliament Buildings under construction, 1864.

Ottawa had only been a city for twelve years when it became the capital city of the new nation of Canada. There were those who would argue that it really wasn't yet a city even then. More of an overgrown logging camp with a partly finished Parliament Building overlooking the Ottawa River, they said. Even Governor General Monck felt it was a silly place for a capital. Ottawa's roads were not paved. The dust in summer was so bad that he travelled by boat from his Rideau Hall residence to Parliament instead of riding in an open carriage through the dusty streets.

The Choice of Ottawa

Queen Victoria had chosen Ottawa as the capital city of the United Canadas in 1857. Before, the capital had shifted among Toronto, Kingston, Montreal and Quebec — an unpopular and inefficient way to operate a government. A report to the Queen recommended that Ottawa be chosen instead of any of the former capitals. Ottawa was a compromise choice. Both Toronto and Montreal were so jealous of each other's position that neither of them would do. Ottawa sat between Canada West (Ontario) and Canada East

(Quebec) at a point where the two provinces were joined by a bridge. The location far inland and away from the American border made it easier to defend than Toronto, Kingston, Montreal or Quebec. And the population of the city included both French and English-speakers. When the Queen's choice was made known, George Etienne Cartier led the support for Ottawa in the assembly.

When Confederation took place ten years later, Ottawa was chosen as the capital of the new country. It wasn't the only possibility considered. Some still felt that Toronto should be the capital, but Montrealers would have been upset. The people of Prince Edward Island thought that Charlottetown should be the capital. But then they decided not to join Confederation after all.

The Parliament Buildings

Besides, there were already those fine stone Parliament Buildings in Ottawa. Soon after Queen Victoria had named Ottawa the capital of the Canada colony, construction had begun on the Houses of Parliament. In 1860, the Prince of Wales had laid the cornerstone. The buildings were of limestone from New York and Pennsylvania, brought north by railroad. During the 1860s, the people of Ottawa watched the Parliament Buildings going up on the Hill overlooking the point where the Rideau Canal meets the Ottawa River. The sounds of hammers and chisels on stone rang out as skilled masons shaped building blocks and fancy decorations.

The Parliament Buildings were not yet complete when Canada became a nation in 1867. In fact it would be twelve more years before they would be completed. But sessions of Parliament were already meeting there in 1867. The original Parliament Buildings were burned down in 1916. The present buildings are an almost exact reproduction of the first Houses of Parliament — except for the Peace Tower.

July 1, 1867

Ottawa put on its best face for the first "Dominion Day" on July 1, 1867. It was a warm sunny Monday and everyone dressed up for the occasion. There were platforms and bleachers covered in red, white and blue bunting. Parties were held everywhere: there were picnics, garden parties, tea parties, dinner parties and dances. And there were speeches. Everyone was told what a great day it was. Lord Monck read the Royal Proclamation creating the new country of Canada. A transatlantic telegraph message from Queen Victoria was read to the people of Canada. It was sent along the new submarine cables laid a short while before. John A. Macdonald was knighted by the Queen — he was now Sir John A.

Artillerymen fired their cannons 101 times to salute the new nation. The Civil Service Rifle Company fired a "feu de joie" on Wellington Street. They forgot to remove the ramrods from their guns, however. The ramrods sailed gracefully through the air to land on Sparks Street. That evening there was a huge bonfire on Nepean Point. The celebrations were closed with a great fireworks display. The sky was filled with showers of light, silhouetting the Parliament Buildings. Everyone agreed it was a great beginning.

Questions

Can You Recall?

1. The Maritime colonies traded mainly with _____, _____ and _____.
2. The two conferences held in 1864 to discuss Confederation took place in _____ and _____.
3. Who were the Fenians?
4. In the end, which colonies voted for the Confederation resolutions passed at Quebec? Which ones voted against?
5. Who made the final decisions about the form Confederation would take?
6. What day did Confederation come into being?
7. Which city became the national capital?
8. Which colonies made up Confederation in 1867? Which provinces did they become?

Ideas for Discussion

1. Discuss the reasons that persuaded the British government that the Canadian colonies should unite.
2. List the reasons advanced against Confederation.
3. Explain why the Fenians attacked the Canadas.
4. The British North America Act gave certain powers to the federal government and certain powers to the provincial governments. On the right is a list of some of these powers.
   a) *In general*, why do you think the Fathers of Confederation gave certain powers to the federal government and others to the provinces?
   b) Why was it important that weights and measures be a federal matter?
   c) Why was education assigned to the provinces?
   d) When the Thirteen Colonies joined together to become the United States of America, they gave certain powers to the federal government and said that the states had all other powers. In Canada, it is the other way around. Discuss the advantages and disadvantages of each system.

Do Some Research

1. Find out more about the American system of government. Make a chart comparing and contrasting it with the Canadian system.
2. The people who worked on Confederation are known as the Fathers of Confederation. Find out who they were and where they came from. Write a short biography of one of them on a piece of cardboard. If each student chooses a different person to write about, you will have a class set of "biocards" on the Fathers of Confederation.
3. A class project. The symbols used on pages 196 to 199 are taken from the coats of arms or the flags of the provinces of Canada. What is a "coat of arms"? Find out about the coats of arms of Canada, the ten provinces and the two territories. Paint pictures of them and display them where other students in your school can see them. Under each coat of arms, write a paragraph explaining the symbols used on it.

Federal Powers	Provincial Powers
Federal taxes	Provincial taxes
Trade and commerce	Managing provincial lands
Weights and measures	and timber rights
Money and banks	Most hospitals and charities
The federal civil service	The provincial civil service
The military and the navy	City and town affairs
Shipping	Licences for shops, taverns,
Fisheries	etc. (in order to raise money)
Indian affairs	Property and civil rights
Citizenship and immigration	Immigration to the province
Criminal law and	Most courts and prisons
penitentiaries	Education
Transportation between	Transportation within the
provinces or to other countries	province
All matters not assigned to	All matters of a local nature
the provinces	

Be Creative

1. Hold a debate on the topic: Resolved: that the British colonies in North America should join together as one country.
2. Write a poem that could have been read on Canada's first birthday.
3. Make a picture gallery of drawings related to Confederation. You could include portraits of some of the Fathers of Confederation, a drawing of the July 1 celebrations plus a drawing of the Parliament Buildings.
4. Look at the pictures of people living in Canada at the time of Confederation. Imagine you are one of these people. Are you for or against Confederation? Write a letter to a friend explaining your attitude. Describe what you did on July 1, 1867.

Businessmen.

A habitant.

At the station.

Teamsters.

Factory workers.

Joining the Pieces
ADVANCE ORGANIZER

1

In 1867, Canada had four provinces. Much of northern and western Canada was still mainly inhabited by native people, living much as they had for centuries. The Hudson's Bay Company owned most of these lands.
The new Canadian nation purchased Rupert's Land and the Northwest Territories from the Hudson's Bay Company in 1869. Canada wanted to bring settlers to farm the Prairies.

2

The Métis and Indian people of the West were fur traders and buffalo hunters. They were afraid that farming settlers would bring an end to their way of life.

3

The Métis rebelled against the Canadians. They formed their own government to protect their rights. Among the leaders of the Métis was Louis Riel. A force of British soldiers ended the rebellion. In 1870, Manitoba became the fifth province of Canada.

4

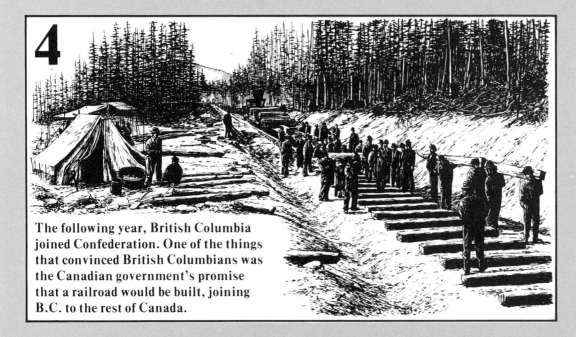

The following year, British Columbia joined Confederation. One of the things that convinced British Columbians was the Canadian government's promise that a railroad would be built, joining B.C. to the rest of Canada.

5

Once the railroad was completed, more immigrants came west by train. Some settled in cities that grew up along the rail line. Others came to farm the rich lands of the Prairies.

Word List

dependent   rebel
depression   reserve
persecute   surveyor
provisional   transcontinental

6

Settlement of the Prairies destroyed the way of life of the western native peoples. Traders brought alcohol that ruined many lives. Canadian and American hunters killed most of the buffalo, the main source of food for native people of the area.

7

The North West Mounted Police was established in 1873 to deal with the problems created by non-native settlement of the Prairies. Treaties were imposed upon the Indians, putting them on reserves, and making them dependent upon the government for support.

8

The Métis and Indians, led by Louis Riel, rebelled once again in 1885. The army and NWMP were brought in to put down the second Northwest Rebellion. The Métis and their Indian allies were defeated. Louis Riel was hanged for treason.

9

In 1873, while the Prairies were being settled, Prince Edward Island joined Confederation. The Canadian government promised to buy back the island's farm lands from landowners living in England, and would pay for a railway across P.E.I.

The H. B. C. Sells Rupert's Land

The king of England had granted a charter to the Hudson's Bay Company. This charter gave the company the rights to all the land drained by the rivers flowing into Hudson Bay. This was an immense region. It included most of the Prairie provinces, northern Ontario and northern Quebec. The Hudson's Bay Company called this land Rupert's Land. For the next 200 years, only a few settlers and fur traders joined the Indians and Métis in this land.

Prince Rupert (1619-1682) was a cousin of Charles II, the king of England. During the English Civil War, Rupert had fought bravely for his uncle, Charles I. He was granted the charter for the Hudson's Bay Company in 1670. Rupert's Land was named after him. 200 years later, Rupert's Land became part of Canada.

The Pas, in what is now Manitoba, in 1857, twelve years before Rupert's Land was sold to Canada.

1200 1300 1400 1500 1600 1700 1800 1900

The sale of Rupert's Land did not end the fur trade. This trader is sorting fox, beaver, mink and other furs at a Hudson's Bay Company warehouse in the 1890s.

After Confederation, Canada began to look longingly toward this great western land. John A. Macdonald dreamed that Canada would stretch from the Atlantic to the Pacific Ocean. Canadians did not see anything on the land that they really needed. But they were afraid that if Canada did not take over this land, the United States would. And there would end the Canadian dream.

The American Threat

American settlers were already moving into the area south of the 49th parallel and west of the Great Lakes. Unless the Canadian government acted, the area north of the parallel would become American as well.

In 1869, the Canadian government began to talk to the Hudson's Bay Company about the sale of Rupert's Land. The company wanted one million pounds and the right to keep selected land. The Canadian government did not want to spend that much. The two parties could not agree. The British Colonial Office offered to help the two come to an agreement. Finally they agreed to a price of 300 000 pounds for the land.

Indians and Métis

In 1869, Rupert's Land became a part of Canada. The Canadian government and the Hudson's Bay Company thought the problems were over. But neither had thought very much about the feelings of the people who lived in this land they were buying and selling. Their neglect of the rights and feelings of the Indians and Métis was to cause two rebellions, in 1870 and 1885. Some of these resentments have lasted to the present.

The First Riel Rebellion

The armed Métis reined in their horses and blocked the path of the men headed north. The two groups talked quietly. Then the shouting began. The men tried to push past. The Métis would not let them. Finally, they wheeled around and galloped back south.

The leader of the group turned back by the Métis in 1869 was William McDougall. McDougall was the governor Canada had sent to take over Rupert's Land. Why did the Métis refuse to let him pass?

For years, the Métis had thought of the land around Red River as their own. They lived a life that revolved around the buffalo hunt. Each year — and sometimes twice a year — the Métis men left their homes and farms along the Red River. They headed out in huge cart trains, looking for the herds of buffalo. Once the buffalo were seen, the Métis would make

camp and the hunt would begin. The buffalo provided food for the Métis for the rest of the year. Most of the Métis lived on farms along the river, but farming took second place to the buffalo hunt in their lives.

The Surveyors Arrive

Now Canada was eager to take over the Northwest. Even before the sale was complete, the government sent surveyors to mark out homesteads along the Red River. The homestead survey lines cut across the long narrow Métis farms which were laid out like those along the St. Lawrence River.

The Métis protested. Sometimes they stopped the surveyors from doing their work. Now Ottawa was sending a governor to the territory without even consulting the people who lived there.

The Métis head for the buffalo plains.

Some of the rights the people of Red River demanded:

The right to elect their own legislature.
Protection for their homes and farms.
A railway within five years.
A military of local inhabitants only.
Use of English and French in the legislature, courts and all public documents.
Representation in the Canadian Parliament.
All existing customs to be respected.

The execution of Thomas Scott.

After the Métis turned the governor back, they held a meeting at Red River. There were long arguments over what they should do next. Finally, a young Métis, Louis Riel, suggested they write a bill of rights. The bill of rights demanded that the people of Red River should choose their own government. The bill asked that Red River be represented in the Canadian parliament. Both French and English should be official languages in the area.

The Métis Provisional Government

Some Métis were afraid the bill of rights would not be enough. They feared that the Canadians who had already settled in Red River would take over and let the governor in. The Métis decided to set up a "provisional government." This temporary government would look after the colony until an agreement could be made with Canada.

The Canadians in the area refused to obey this government. The Métis grew even more angry with the Canadians. They arrested the noisiest and threw them into prison. The Canadians escaped and were recaptured. A young Métis and a Canadian were killed.

Now Louis Riel offered a bargain. The Métis would let the Canadians go free if they would promise to stop making trouble. Some of the Canadians made this promise, but others refused.

Riel decided to put one of the Canadians, Thomas Scott, on trial for insubordination. Insubordination — refusing to obey the leaders — was a crime punishable be death according to Métis law. In the buffalo hunt, refusing to obey could endanger everyone.

Scott was tried and found guilty. He was executed by a firing squad on March 4, 1870.

Manitoba Joins Canada, 1870

The news of the death of Thomas Scott quickly reached Eastern Canada. People in Ontario and Quebec took sides. English Protestants in Ontario were furious. They thought Scott had been killed because he was a Canadian and a Protestant. They thought the Métis involved should be arrested or simply shot.

French Catholics in Quebec were just as angry. They thought the Métis were being persecuted because they were French and Catholic. They demanded that Riel and his followers be left alone.

In the middle of the argument, delegates from Red River arrived in Ottawa. They came because they had been told by Bishop Taché, who had been sent to Ottawa by the Métis, that the Canadian government would talk to the provisional government. However, when the Métis delegates arrived, they were arrested. In the end they were released, and the two sides sat down to talk.

The Manitoba Act

The Canadian government agreed to give the provisional government most of the things it had asked for. These things were set forth in the Manitoba Act. The Red River area would become a province of Canada called Manitoba. It would have all the rights the other provinces had. Some 570 000 ha of land were to be set aside for the Métis. The French language and Catholic religion were to be protected by the act. A cash grant and annual subsidy would be given to Manitoba when it became a province. Manitoba joined Canada in 1870.

Had the act ended there, all would have been well. But the Manitoba Act also sent a company of soldiers west to restore order at Red River. The force, under Colonel Wolseley, arrived at Red River in the summer of 1870 after a difficult trip north of Lake Superior.

By this time, the Métis had disbanded their forces. They thought that the Canadian government would

The Riel family homestead at St. Vital near Winnipeg. Riel's family had lived in Red River since 1807. His grandmother, Marie Anne Gaboury, had been born in Quebec. She married a fur trader, Jean Baptiste Lagimodière, and came west with him. She was the first white woman in the Canadian West. She died here in 1878 at the age of 96.

not arrest or try the leaders of the rebellion. But when the soldiers arrived, Riel and his fellow leaders were worried. They had heard that some of the soldiers were going to try to capture or kill Riel. The Métis leaders went into hiding.

More Disputes

Some of the soldiers treated the Métis badly, as did other Canadians at Red River. The Métis fought back. There were fights and arguments every day. Some Canadians tried to take over land that the government had promised to the Métis. Some Métis decided that the only thing to do was to move further west, away from Manitoba.

In the 1874 elections Louis Riel ran and won a seat in the House of Commons. But he did not go to Ottawa for fear he would be arrested. In the next election, he ran again and won again. This time he was expelled because he did not show up.

In 1875, the fate of the Métis leaders was resolved. Everyone except Riel and another leader, Ambrose Lepine, was pardoned for any part in the rebellion. Riel and Lepine were pardoned only on condition that they stay outside Canada for the next five years. Manitoba had been born, but had lost one of her most magnetic leaders.

Manitoba
There are at least two theories on the origin of the name Manitoba. One is that it is based on the Cree word Manitou "The Great Spirit." Another is that it comes from an Assiniboine word meaning "lake of the Prairies."

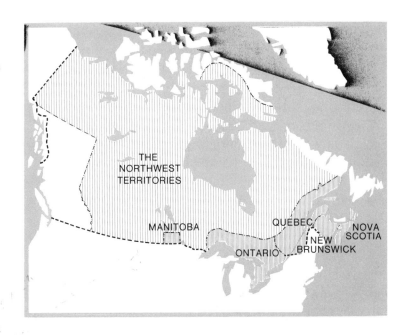

Before the railway, the Red River cart was the basic form of transport in the Canadian West.

British Columbia Joins Canada, 1871

By the mid-1860s, the Cariboo gold rush was over in British Columbia. There was still gold to be mined in the Cariboo. But it was no longer easy to wrench it from the ground. Special new equipment and a great deal of money were needed to mine for gold.

The miners drifted away, seeking another gold strike. The wagon trains no longer rushed up the Cariboo road loaded with passengers and tons of freight. The gold patrols no longer returned laden with the precious gold dust. Life was quiet in Victoria and in the Cariboo. It was not easy to make a living.

Costs of the Gold Rush

The two colonies of British Columbia and Vancouver Island were still paying the costs of the gold rush. They had to pay for the Cariboo road. There were the costs of the laying out of the new townsites. The police who patrolled the road and the gold fields had to be paid. There was little money available in the colonies. To make things worse, the two colonies could not seem to agree on anything. Each was jealous of the other and blamed the other for its problems.

But both knew that they must join together if they were to last. In 1866, they did join. They took the name of British Columbia, and continued to quarrel with each other.

Joining together did not solve their problems. The leaders of the colony tried to think of possible solutions. British Columbia could join the United States — and there were many who thought she should. The United States looked like a rich country. But the colony was British by birth and tradition. Most people on the mainland thought it would be better to join Canada.

Victoria in 1862, the height of the gold rush.

John Helmcken

Most people on the island opposed joining Canada. Then John Helmcken was chosen as the new governor of the colony. He thought it would be a very good idea to join Confederation. The colony decided to see what kind of a deal it could make if it joined Canada.

The Canadian government made a good offer. Canada agreed to take over British Columbia's debts. A cash bonus would be paid for every person living in the province. The naval base at Esquimalt would remain where it was. The province could decide for itself when it was ready for full representative government.

The most important promise was that a railway would be built. British Columbia felt alone out on the west coast. It wanted some way of communicating with the rest of Canada. The Canadian government promised that it would begin work on a transcontinental railway within two years. The railway would be completed within 10 years.

British Columbia accepted the promises. On July 20, 1871, Canada's sixth province entered Confederation. Canada now stretched from sea to sea, from Atlantic to Pacific.

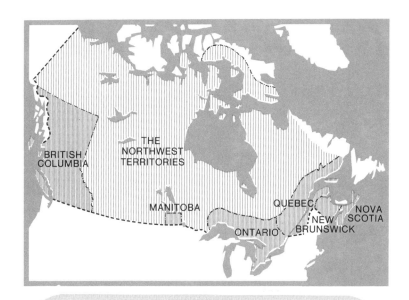

British Columbia
The first British settlements on the Northwest Coast were called New Caledonia. However, in the 1860s, Queen Victoria gave the area a new name: British Columbia after the discoverer of America.

Matthew Baillie Begbie (The Hanging Judge)
"The biggest man, the smartest man, the best-looking man and the plaguey-est man that ever came over the Cariboo Road."

BORN: off the Cape of Good Hope, Africa, 1819
DIED: Victoria, British Columbia, 1894
Attended Cambridge University. Stories say he preferred sports, acting, cards and women to studying.
1858 — sent to British Columbia as first judge at height of gold rush. Held court in barns, tents and fields as well as courthouses. Many legends grew round him: based decisions on what he saw as justice, not on written law. Always made his opinion known: a man accused of sandbagging another in a barroom brawl was found innocent by the jury. Begbie disagreed and said, "Prisoner at the bar, you can go, and I truly hope the next man you sandbag will be one of the jury." One story is that he heard men in the street below his hotel window plotting to shoot him. Emptied his chamber pot on their heads. Probably not fair to call him "the hanging judge." If a murderer was found guilty, hanging was the only sentence the law allowed. He often worked to have death sentences commuted by the governor.
1861 — reported that "Nearly all inhabitants respect and obey the laws. They prefer peace and order to the violence and bloodshed of other gold-mining regions."
1870 — made chief justice of British Columbia.

Prince Edward Island Joins Canada, 1873

Summerside,
Prince Edward Island.

Few changes came to Prince Edward Island until well into the nineteenth century. Most of the island was still owned by people who lived in Britain. The tenant farmers could not own their own land. The owners of the land were not willing to make many improvements.

The islanders were granted their own assembly in 1851. The new government was run along the same lines as those of the Canadas and Nova Scotia. The population of the island increased slowly. By 1861, there were 81 000 people living on Prince Edward Island.

Fishing, farming and shipbuilding remained the major occupations on the island. In 1861, 89 fishing establishments were based on the island. Between 1861 and 1870, 914 ships were built in the docks of Charlottetown.

It was in Charlottetown that the Maritime governments first met to talk about union. There they were joined by the Canadians. Out of the Charlottetown Conference came the proposal for Confederation. But when it came time for Confederation, Prince Edward Island chose not to join the new country of Canada.

A shipyard at Murray River.

Tourists could stay at the Point Pleasant Hotel, Stanhope.

Mackerel fishing.

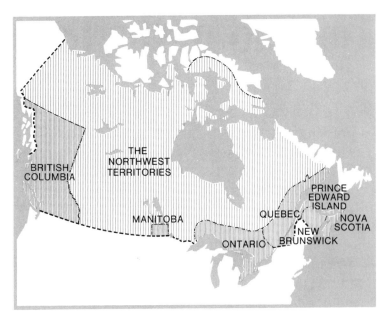

P.E.I. Has Second Thoughts

By the early 1870s, the people of the island were having second thoughts about Confederation. The island government had decided to build a railway which would cost a great deal of money. The colony was poor. The islanders realized that they must either pay heavy taxes to pay for the railway, or join Canada and have Canada pay the cost of the rail line.

They decided to join Confederation. Canada promised to give Prince Edward Island $800 000 to buy back land from absentee owners. A grant of $50 for every person living on the island would be given to the Prince Edward Island government. Canada would pay the railway debt. Canada promised to start and maintain a steamer service between the island and the mainland. And Canada took over the operation of some of the island's public services.

On July 1, 1873, Prince Edward Island became the seventh province of Canada. Two years later, under the Compulsory Purchase Act, the province was able to buy back much of the land held by absentee owners.

Toronto in the 1870s

Toronto in the 1870s was a prosperous and fast-growing city of 100 000 people. It was a centre of government, of commerce, and of banking. There were as yet few heavy industries to block the view of the lake or fill the sky with smoke. Hamilton and Montreal were the industrial cities then; Toronto was more important as a trading centre.

The railways had made Toronto the important commercial centre it was. In the 1850s, railways had been built linking Toronto with Montreal, Kingston, Hamilton, London, Collingwood, Windsor, and Sarnia. By the 1870s, branch lines reached to towns as far away as Sudbury and Owen Sound. The tracks of the Great Western, the Northern, the Grand Trunk, and the Toronto and Grey Bruce Railways fanned out from Toronto Harbour like the fingers of a giant hand. There they met steamships and sailing schooners carrying goods from Europe and the United States.

Passenger trains travelled these lines too. Everyone one was on the move. Farms kids from Haliburton, Belleville, and Woodstock took the train to the big city, looking for adventure — and jobs. Families took the train to Niagara-on-the-Lake for picnics and excursions. Businessmen rode the trains to sell their goods.

Yonge Street.

Union Station

The pride of Toronto's waterfront in the 1870s was the new Union Station. The cornerstone had been laid in 1872 and only a year later, its three graceful towers were reflected in the waters of the lake. Passengers entering the city at Union Station saw the busy movement of boats just outside their carriage windows. People sailing and rowing for pleasure crossed wakes with the steamers bringing cargoes to the docks.

The view from Toronto Island in Lake Ontario.

Commerce

Leaving Union Station, the newly arrived traveller would step out to the busy prosperity of Front Street. The shops and offices of successful merchants and traders lined the street. Horse-drawn carriages and streetcars competed for space along the asphalt-paved roadway.

Walking east along Front brought you to Yonge Street. This had been Toronto's main street since the early 1800s when it was the main trail from the lakeshore to the newly cleared settlers' lands to the north. Yonge and Front was the site of several banks, the first signs of Toronto's importance as a banking centre. If you went north on Yonge, you would come to Timothy Eaton's new store at the corner of Queen. But for the more impressive banks and stores you turned west on King Street. Wooden sidewalks, gaslamps, and cast-iron hitching posts reminded you that Toronto was still a young city, but fast growing up in the modern world.

News from Europe and America could be printed in Toronto papers the same day events happened, thanks to the telegraph system that crossed the Atlantic and stretched through North America. The University of Toronto, located in Queen's Park, was home to many of the newest ideas in science and medicine. Toronto was definitely a city with a future. Still, it would be another fifty years before it would be as important as Montreal as an industrial centre. And it would be another hundred years before it reached the population of Montreal.

King Street.

Maggie, Eaton's first delivery horse.

The North West Mounted Police

A greeting card from C Division, Battleford, 1895.

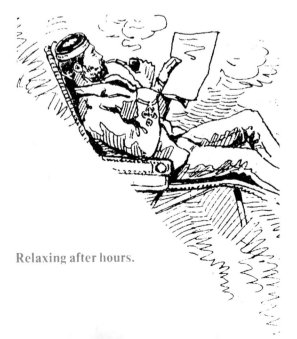

Relaxing after hours.

Canada, the Hudson's Bay Company and Britain had signed a treaty that made the Northwest a part of Canada. But the treaty was really just a piece of paper. Once you travelled beyond Manitoba, there was no sign that anything had changed in the Northwest.

Yet a great deal was changing south of the border in the United States. These changes were affecting the Canadian Northwest. As settlers moved into the American Midwest, some straggled north into Canada.

The Whiskey Traders

The Indians who lived on the Canadian prairies had furs to sell to fur traders. Some of the American settlers were fur traders. Many offered whiskey and other alcohol to the Indians in return for the furs. Often, the Indians accepted the exchange. But the whiskey was helping to destroy the life of the Indians. The Indians knew this and hated the traders.

The Indians also stole the traders' horses. For them, horse-stealing was a sort of ritual. It proved that the thief was a man. But the traders thought that horse-stealing was a crime. They wanted to punish the Indians for their acts.

Early in 1872, a group of whiskey traders had their horses stolen. They came upon a camp of Indians. The traders had been drinking. They didn't bother to find out if these Indians had stolen the horses. They swept down upon the Indians, firing their rifles. The Indians' guns were slow and old-fashioned. The Indians too had been drinking whiskey. They could not fight back effectively. Many Indians were killed. One trader died.

News of the battle, known as the Cypress Hills Massacre, reached Ottawa. Canada did not want to see war break out between the Indians and settlers as had happened in the United States. Prime Minister John A. Macdonald and his government had been thinking about how to keep peace in the west. They now decided to form a police force to patrol the Northwest.

The NWMP Heads West

In 1874, the North West Mounted Police signed up their first recruits. By mid-year, 300 men were on their way west. The idea of 300 men trying to control such a huge amount of territory at first seemed ridiculous. Thousands of troops had only made things worse in the United States. But the North West Mounted Police would not try to control things by force. They would be there as peacemakers. They were to prevent battles, not to take part in them. They would impress the Indians and the settlers with their fairness.

The force marched west to Fort Whoop-up, one of the posts of the whiskey traders. No one was there. The traders had fled south. The police built a post nearby. They built and manned other posts in the prairies. As they rode in their red tunics across the plains, they soon became a familiar sight.

The aim of the Canadian government succeeded. The mounted police were able to act as peacemakers in many conflicts between Indians, settlers and traders. Over the next ten years, the Indians began to see the police as their friends.

Official motto of the NWMP:
Maintiens le droit (Uphold the right).

Unofficial motto:
They always get their man.

The Indian Treaties

A person finds a piece of land. He decides it is his land. He begins to live there. But how can he convince the people who already live there that it is his?

He can kill the people who already live there. He can try to persuade them to go away. Or he can try to buy the land from them.

This problem faced the Europeans who came to North America. Several nations claimed part of the continent. Yet the Indians who already lived in North America could be said to own the land.

At first, the Indians did not see the problem. They did not believe the land belonged to anyone. It was there to be used by everyone. But the Europeans insisted that they owned the land.

Sometimes, they "bought" the land from the Indians. The most famous example of this is the buying of Manhattan Island for trinkets and glass beads. Sometimes, they made friends with the Indians and shared the land. This happened in such places as Acadia. Sometimes they made war on the Indians and drove them out of the land. This often happened in the Thirteen Colonies and later in the United States.

Everyday life: preparing fish.

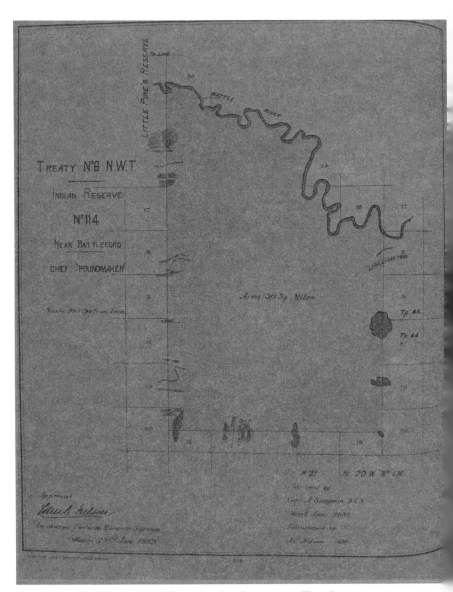

A survey of the Cree chief Poundmaker's reserve. The Cree and Blackfoot had long been enemies. But Poundmaker greatly admired Crowfoot. To help keep peace, Crowfoot adopted Poundmaker as his son.

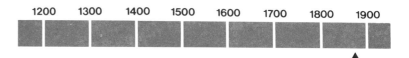

Settlers Move West

As Canadian settlers moved onto the plains, it was clear that none of these solutions would work. There was nowhere else for the native people to go. It would be difficult for settlers and nomads to share the same land. The Canadians did not want to go to war with the Indians. But they were determined to have control of the land.

The Canadian government wanted to sign treaties with the Plains Indians. This was not a new idea.

Chief Crowfoot. The chain holds the lifetime CPR pass granted to him as one of the terms of the treaty.

Treaties had been signed with the Six Nations Indians in the eastern provinces. The government had set aside land, called *reserves,* for the Indians to live on. The same idea would be used in the west.

The North West Mounted Police went out to talk to the Indians about the treaties. Treaties were signed between the Canadian government and a number of nations and tribes. Finally, only the great Blackfoot nation had still not signed.

Treaty with the Blackfoot Nation

In 1876, 4000 Blackfoot and their chiefs met in one place to sign the treaty. The treaty gave to the Blackfoot reserves of one square mile for each family of five and $12 for each member of the Blackfoot Confederacy. It gave the Blackfoot permission to hunt and fish anywhere in the Northwest. Each year, the government would pay $25 to each chief, $15 to each minor chief and $5 to every other native.

The government promised to give the Indians cattle and farming equipment and to teach them to farm. It promised to feed the Blackfoot in times of need.

Crowfoot, the most important Blackfoot chief, signed the treaty on behalf of the confederacy. He did so mainly because he trusted the North West Mounted Police. He saw the settlers were moving into the Northwest. He saw that the Indians could no longer hunt the buffalo. He saw that the old way of life was dying and he thought the treaty offered a chance at a new way of life. But Crowfoot did not realize how completely the treaties marked the end of the Plains Indian way of life.

The Railway

A railway to the west! Tracks of steel spanning the country, across the mountains to the Pacific! It seemed a magnificent idea, an idea to unite a country. But there was a snag. Building a railway across 5000 km of rocks, mountains, muskeg, swamp, rivers, canyons, lakes and prairie was not an easy job.

It would not be cheap, either. The first question for Prime Minister John A. Macdonald was where the money to build the railway was to come from.

There were two choices. The government could pay out the money itself. Or, it could pay a private company to build the railway. The government did not want to build the railway. It did not even want to run a railway once one was built. It decided to find a private company to build the railway.

Two companies were interested in the job: one Canadian, one American. Macdonald wanted a Canadian company to do the job. Yet the American company seemed better equipped. The American company promised Macdonald they would get rid of their American owners. They also paid Macdonald's Conservative party large amounts of money to be used in the next election.

The Pacific Scandal

The Liberal opposition found out about the money paid by the railway company to Macdonald. It appeared to be a bribe paid by the company to get the railway contract. This event was called the Pacific Scandal. As a result the Prime Minister and his government had to resign. The Liberals led by Alexander Mackenzie, won the next election, in 1874.

The new Prime Minister, Alexander Mackenzie, wasn't at all sure that the country could afford a trans-Canada railway at this time. He did very little to advance the railway. Over the next ten years, a few surveys were made. But only a few short lines of track were laid.

The British Columbia government became impatient with the delay. It demanded that the railway begin at once or British Columbia would leave Confederation. Mackenzie promised to start the railway.

The railway work began again. When Macdonald was re-elected in 1878, he stepped up the pace of the work. Surveyors fanned out, looking for the best route for the track. The contract was let to the Canadian Pacific Railway Company. The government gave the company 25 million dollars to start work. The CPR was

Donald Smith, drives the last spike.

also given 10 million hectares of valuable land in the Prairies and Northern Ontario.

The CPR hired William Van Horne to be its general manager. Van Horne believed that anything was possible. In one summer, his men laid close to 900 km of track.

Muskeg and Mountains

This was while they were still working on the easy part, across the flat prairie. At either end of this track lay trouble. At one end were the Rocky Mountains; at the other, the hard rock and muskeg of Northern Ontario. Progress was slow through these areas. Van Horne's men blasted their way through the Kicking Horse Pass in the Rockies. But they still didn't know if they could get through the Selkirk Mountains to the west. Van Horne was lucky; Major Rogers discovered a pass. To the south, Andrew Onderdonk and his crews of Chinese labourers inched their way along the Fraser Canyon.

In the east, railway workers (or navvies) blasted their way through the rock of northern Ontario. So great was the need for dynamite that Van Horne had factories built to produce the blasting powder along the route. In other areas, mile after mile of track twisted and sank under the swampy muskeg.

Yet, somehow, the line was finally completed in 1885. A train loaded with people sped west. It halted at Craigellachie, in the Selkirk Mountains. There, railway president Donald Smith drove in a spike to mark the completion of the railway. Two days later, the train steamed into Port Moody. The first Canadian trans-continental crossing by rail was complete.

Telegram from John A. Macdonald to Sir John Abbott, advisor to the group with the contract to build the railway:

I must have another ten thousand; will be the last time of calling; do not fail me; answer today.

This telegram was revealed by the Liberals in 1873. It led to the Pacific Scandal and the defeat of the Conservatives in the next election.

"WE IN CANADA SEEM TO HAVE LOST ALL IDEA OF JUSTICE, HONOR AND INTEGRITY."—The Mail, 26th September.

William Cornelius Van Horne
BORN: Chelsea, Illinois, 1843
DIED: Montreal, Quebec, 1915

1857 — telegraph operator for Illinois Central Railway. Worked way up in American railway system.
1874 — general manager of bankrupt Southern Minnesota Railway. Attracted wheat shippers with subsidy to farmers who settled along the tracks. Gave free lunches to work crews so they worked harder. Helped farmers struck by grasshopper plague, saving wheat — which the railway then shipped.
1882 — general manager of CPR. The job: to lay 4700 km of track as soon as possible.
1885 — present at driving of last spike.
1886 — started annual inspection tours from Montreal to the Pacific. Later would ride these tours in his own railway car, The Saskatchewan.
1888 — elected president of CPR. Encouraged settlers in the Northwest with "cent a mile" fares for homesteaders. Built hotels and set up round-the-world tours on CP steamships to provide full services for tourists.
1900 — "retired" from CPR, built railway in Cuba.

Building the Railway

Making a road bed.

A Chinese work gang.

A Red Letter Day For Canada — June 28, '86 WHEN THE CANADIAN PACIFIC RAILWAY OPENS PACIFIC OCEAN

A trestle bridge is completed.

The Great Western Railway's Engine No. 8.

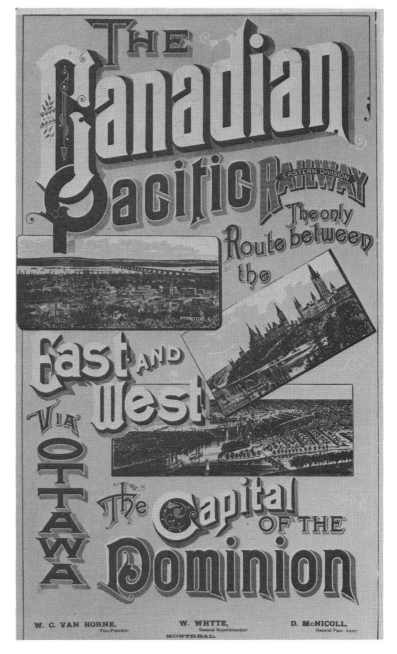

Communications

The railway helped bring together the vast nation of Canada. Now it only took days to travel from one end of the country to the other, not weeks or months. More rapid forms of communication were also being developed in the second half of the nineteenth century.

Raising a telegraph pole in the Rockies.

The Telegraph

Scientists began to understand the use of electricity in the late 1700s. By 1831, an American, Joseph Henry, had the idea of sending signals along a wire by means of an electrical current. A short time later, Samuel Morse invented a code using short and long pulses (dots and dashes) to represent letters of the alphabet. In 1843 he sent messages on his telegraph from Washington to Baltimore. Telegraph is from two Greek words meaning "distance" and "writing."

The first telegraph in Canada was built in 1846 between Toronto and Hamilton. The new invention was so useful it spread rapidly. By 1850, Bytown (now Ottawa) was linked to Montreal by telegraph. Three years later, an underwater cable was laid between New Brunswick and Prince Edward Island.

In 1858, the New York, Newfoundland and London Telegraph Company laid a cable across the Atlantic from Ireland to Newfoundland. Just four weeks later, the line went dead. No further attempts were made until after the American Civil War. Then, a special ship, the *Great Eastern,* was used for the job. In 1866, the first successful cable was brought ashore at Heart's Content, Newfoundland.

The telegraph and railways grew together. The CPR found it was easy to run telegraph wires alongside the railway track, joining Vancouver to Montreal. Railway stations doubled as telegraph offices. By 1890, it took only a few minutes to get a message from one side of the country to the other. The railway companies still run the telegraph system in Canada.

The Telephone

Meanwhile a young Canadian named Alexander Graham Bell was experimenting with hearing aids. His research led him to a new use for telegraph wires — transmitting the human voice. There are great arguments as to whether Bell invented the telephone in Canada or in the United States. He himself said he had the idea at his home in Brantford in 1874. But the details were perfected in Boston in 1875. The first long-distance call in history was made the following year from Brantford to Paris, Ontario.

Bell took little part in bringing the telephone to everyday use. He moved on to experiment in other fields. Later at his home at Baddeck, Cape Breton Island, Nova Scotia, he became interested in flight. Experimenting first with kites and gliders, he improved on the Wright brothers' airplane design. His plane, the *Silver Dart* was built in Canada. It made its first flight in 1909 from Baddeck Bay.

A telephone operator in Lauder, Manitoba.

Radio

In 1901, an Italian inventor named Guglielmo Marconi came to Signal Hill in St. John's, Newfoundland. Here, he received the first radio signal sent across the Atlantic. Radio has been important to the development of Canada in this century. Radio transmitters and receivers can go where telegraph and telephone wires do not exist.

These inventions have kept Canadians in contact with each other. The telephone, radio, and now television are important tools in many Canadian homes.

Sandford Fleming
BORN: Kirkcaldy, Scotland 1827
DIED: Halifax, Nova Scotia, 1915
1845 — came to Canada as surveyor and engineer for the Northern Railway.
1849 — rescued famous painting of Queen Victoria from a fire which destroyed the parliament buildings in Montreal.
1851 — designed Canada's first postage stamp "the threepenny beaver." Chief engineer of intercolonial railway.
1871 — appointed to supervise surveys for the CPR. Surveyed Yellowhead, Kicking Horse, Eagle and Rogers passes through the Rockies.
1879 — invented "Standard Time": proposed dividing world into 24 zones. Within each zone the time would be the same. 25 countries agreed to try the idea in 1884. This is the system the world uses today.
Father of an idea for a cable (telegraph) system throughout the British Empire.
1887 and 1894 — represented Canada at Imperial Conferences.

Métis and Indian Grievances

After the Riel Rebellion in 1870, many of the Métis from Red River headed west. Settlers were crowding into the new province of Manitoba. The Métis decided they could no longer live there. They wanted to continue their traditional way of life, hunting the buffalo and doing some farming. They felt this would not be possible where there were many settlers.

The Canadian government had promised them land around Red River. But few Métis actually received any. Some sold their land very cheaply to new settlers. Canadian settlers simply took over some Métis lands. Other Métis simply decided to leave for the area around the Saskatchewan River to the west.

Métis Land Claims

For 15 years, the Métis, Indians and white settlers in the area lived peaceably together. But gradually all of these groups grew unhappy with the government in Ottawa. The Métis were annoyed with the way that land was being divided up under the township system. They wanted long river lots according to the traditional Quebec pattern of settlement. But the western survey was dividing land up into township squares. The Métis also resented being treated the same as any newly arrived homesteader. They had been in the area for many years. They did not think they should have to wait three years to claim land they believed was theirs.

The white settlers were just as unhappy. They thought that the Canadian government was ignoring the wishes of the residents of the Northwest. They and the Métis sent letters of protest to Ottawa. Some wrote columns in local newspapers. They all wanted the Canadian government to pay more attention to what the local people wanted.

The government in Ottawa did not seem to hear anything that was being said out west. The people of the Saskatchewan Valley decided that something would have to be done about this.

Riel Returns

In 1884, the Métis decided to send for Louis Riel. Riel had spent the past 15 years in eastern Canada and in the United States. For a little while, he had been in hospital in Montreal. After he left hospital, he married an American Métis woman and went to teach school in Montana.

A Métis family.

1200	1300	1400	1500	1600	1700	1800	1900

He decided to come back to help his people in the Saskatchewan Valley. Riel rallied the Métis, some whites and many of the Indians behind him. The Indians had even greater problems than the whites or Métis. Many of them were facing starvation. For years, they had lived from the buffalo. Buffalo provided their food, some of their clothing and many other things for them. But, as more and more hunters, white and Indian, hunted the buffalo with repeating rifles, more and more buffalo were killed. The coming of the railway signaled the end for the buffalo. Now, the Indians had no food to eat.

The government tried to provide a little food. The members of the North West Mounted Police tried to help. But too little help and too little food was provided. The Indians wanted to show the Canadian government that they could not be left to starve.

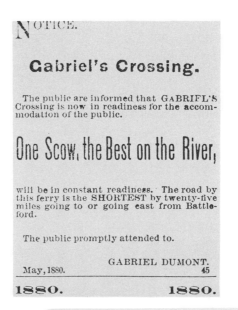

NOTICE.

Gabriel's Crossing.

The public are informed that GABRIEL'S Crossing is now in readiness for the accommodation of the public.

One Scow, the Best on the River,

will be in constant readiness. The road by this ferry is the SHORTEST by twenty-five miles going to or going east from Battleford.

The public promptly attended to.

GABRIEL DUMONT.

May, 1880.   45

1880.   **1880.**

According to the treaties, the government had to provide the Indians with food in times of need.

Gabriel Dumont
BORN: St. Boniface, Manitoba, 1837
DIED: Batoche, Saskatchewan, 1906
1850 — at 13, fought first battle when 100 Métis held off 2000 Sioux for two days. A crack shot, learned battle tactics on the buffalo hunt.
1872 — with the buffalo nearly gone, turned to farming near South Saskatchewan River. Ran a store and ferry at Gabriel's Crossing (churchgoers crossed free on Sundays). Elected president of local Métis government.
1884 — went to Montana to ask Riel to lead Métis.
1885 — as Riel's military commander-in-chief, wanted to use guerrilla tactics and techniques of buffalo hunt, but Riel wanted pitched battles. After battle of Batoche escaped to U.S. Toured with Buffalo Bill's Wild West Show as the sharpshooting "Prince of the Plains."
1893 — returned to Batoche under terms of amnesty (pardon) granted in 1886.

THE NORTHWEST REBELLION   235

The Battles of the Northwest Rebellion

The Indians were the first to break the shaky calm that prevailed along the Saskatchewan. Early in 1884, they demanded food from a farm instructor at Crooked Lake. The man refused. Faced with starvation, the Indians took over his storehouse. The Mounted Police were sent to the scene. They found the Indians barricaded inside the storehouse. After a while, the police talked the Indians into coming out. Only the instructor was injured in the incident.

The same thing happened again later in the year on another reserve. Once more, the police, aided by the Cree chief Big Bear, were able to calm the Indians.

The volunteer army heads west.

At Duck Lake, Dumont turned the idea of the buffalo pound into a military tactic. He lured Crozier's men into a shallow valley surrounded by sharpshooters. He later used the same technique at Fish Creek to delay the troops.

1200	1300	1400	1500	1600	1700	1800	1900

Riel's Demand

But the peace could not continue. The government in Ottawa refused to hear the pleas of the settlers, Indians and Métis. By March of 1885, the people of the West were tired of waiting. More and more, they talked of open, armed rebellion. On March 18, Riel and his Métis followers took several government officials prisoner. They took over a church and cut the telegraph lines to Prince Albert. A provisional government was formed at Batoche. Riel sent a message to Mounted Police Superintendent Leif Crozier. It demanded that Crozier surrender the police fort at Fort Carlton. Riel vowed that if Crozier refused, full-scale war would begin. Crozier would not obey.

A short time later, police and volunteers from Prince Albert rode out to join battle with the Métis. In the battle at Duck Lake, the Métis were the victors, forcing the enemy to retreat.

The Indians under Big Bear and Poundmaker decided to join the Métis forces. They would rather die in battle than die of starvation or live as poor farmers. But the combined forces were doomed to lose the war.

News of the rebellion reached eastern Canada. A military force was quickly formed to go to the West. Three thousand soldiers steamed west over the newly completed Canadian Pacific Railway line. North of Lake Superior the line had not yet been built. The soldiers slogged across muskeg and frozen ground. Their arrival in early April to join the police and volunteer western force of 5000 men meant the end of the rebellion.

The End of the Rebellion

In battles at Fish Creek and Batoche the Métis were defeated by the soldiers. The Cree chiefs Big Bear and Poundmaker won early battles — but then were defeated by the superior numbers of the military force. Big Bear surrendered. Poundmaker was taken prisoner by the North West Mounted Police.

Riel's brilliant military lieutenant, Gabriel Dumont, escaped to the United States. But Riel was tired of the battle and of exile in another country. He wanted to justify his ideas and his defence of his Métis people. He surrendered to the Mounted Police.

Riel was then arrested and charged with treason.

The steamship *Northcote* was carrying military supplies. Dumont's men lowered a wire ferry cable that ran across the river. The cable sheared off the *Northcote's* masts and smokestacks. The ship drifted out of control past the Métis and their rifles. But three days later, the rebels lost the battle of Batoche.

The Death of Louis Riel

Louis Riel on trial.

In June of 1885, Louis Riel faced a courtroom in Regina, fighting a charge of treason. The eyes of all of Canada were focused on the trial. English-speaking Protestants in Ontario insisted that the traitor Riel must die for his acts of treason. French-speaking Catholics in Quebec insisted that the hero Riel must leave the courtroom a free man.

In Quebec, a Riel Defence Committee was set up. Three lawyers were chosen to defend Riel. They decided that Riel had only one defence against the charge of treason. He must plead not guilty by reason of insanity. They felt that there was evidence to hold up this plea. Riel had spent some months in an insane asylum in Montreal. He had visions. He thought he was talking directly to God. Some of his ideas seemed crazy to other people.

The day of my birth I was helpless and my mother took care of me. Today I am a man, but I am as helpless before this court in the Dominion of Canada as I was the day of my birth. The Northwest is also my mother; it is my mother country. Although my mother country is sick, some people have come from Lower Canada to help her take care of me. I am sure my mother country will not kill me any more than my mother did.

From Louis Riel's speech at his trial

We, on the jury, recommended mercy. The prisoner was guilty and we could not excuse his acts. But at the same time, we felt that the government had not done its duty. It did nothing about the grievances of the Métis. If it had, there would never have been a second Riel rebellion. We strongly condemned the dawdling of Macdonald and his government. If they had been on trial as accessories, the jury would have shown them little mercy.

We tried Louis Riel for treason, but he was executed for the murder of Thomas Scott.

Comments of members of the jury

Canadian Pacific liners steam into Owen Sound on Georgian Bay bringing the volunteers back from the second Riel Rebellion. Owen Sound was Canadian Pacific headquarters at this time.

Riel's Defence

But Riel would not accept this defence. He wanted to defend his ideas and his actions. He did not want everything he had worked for dismissed as the ideas of a crazy man.

Riel told the judge and jury that he had only led his people into battle because the government of Canada would do nothing for them. And he told them that he would rather die than have his actions accepted as the actions of an insane man. Riel got his wish. He was convicted of treason and sentenced to hang.

The debate over Riel raged on. The execution was delayed twice as both sides continued their arguments.

Finally, in November of 1885, Riel was hanged in punishment for his leadership of the Rebellion of 1885.

His death did not end the argument. It continues to this day. Riel is now regarded as the founder of Manitoba and the great defender of the Métis people.

The rebellion marked the end for the nomads of the prairies. Both Métis and Indian now had to conform to a life imposed by the railway and the settlers. The buffalo hunt was finished as a way of life. Métis and Indian alike must become part of a new kind of society.

Montreal in the 1880s

Montreal in the 1880s was a city of two cultures, just as it is today. Its population of 200 000 was divided between English and Scots living on the west side and French Canadians on the east. To be sure, there were poor Irish-Catholic labourers living on the east side of the city and some wealthy French-speaking Montrealers on the west. But in general, the city was divided by religion, language and geography.

Leisure Activities

Some things brought rich and poor, English and French, Catholic and Protestant together. Montreal was a city that knew how to have a good time. There were winter carnivals, torchlight snowshoeing in Mount Royal Park, and tobogganing on Fletcher's Hill. Summer saw horseracing, picnics and regattas. There were theatres, operas, fancy dress balls, and other entertainments. Sportsmen played cricket, baseball and lacrosse, and raced boats in the Grand Trunk Regatta, held off Nun's Island. Workers' groups would hire steamers for summer outings on the St. Lawrence.

But if a sense of pleasure was shared by all Montrealers, it could not hide the deep divisions that lay so close to the surface in the 1880s. Then, in 1885, the execution of Louis Riel widened the gap between English and French Montrealers.

The Northwest Rebellion

When the Northwest Rebellion broke out, Montrealers of both groups rushed to back the new Dominion. Three militia units — the Prince of Wales Rifles, the Garrison Artillery, and the 65th Regiment

The incline railway, Mount Royal Park.

Afternoon in Sohmer Park.

| 1200 | 1300 | 1400 | 1500 | 1600 | 1700 | 1800 | 1900 |

— were sent west to stop the Métis rebels. The 65th, the pride of the city, were a French-speaking unit. Bishop Fabre called on Montrealers to join in prayer and fasting in support of the troops.

The rebellion was quickly put down. In July, the troops came home. Thousands turned out to meet the returning soldiers. The warmest welcome was for the 65th, who had seen the heaviest fighting. They were proud but tired soldiers, wearing torn uniforms faded by the prairie sun. On their heads were all sorts of gear — from cowboy hats to Indian headdresses. A brass band played "Vive la Canadienne" and the bells of Notre Dame rang their welcome. Flags hung from every window as soldiers and welcomers marched through the streets. At the church, the *Te Deum* was sung, thanking God for their safe return.

But joy soon turned to tension, as it became certain that Louis Riel would be hanged. Each day the newspapers carried stories of Riel's trial, sent east from Regina by telegraph.

"Parking" in Jacques Cartier Square.

The Execution of Louis Riel

Riel was executed on November 16, 1885. That night, 400 students marched through downtown Montreal. They carried red, white and blue flags — draped in black. As they marched, they sang "La Marseillaise," the hymn of the French Revolution. The marchers stopped only once, to burn a dummy dressed as Sir John A. Macdonald.

The next morning, all of Montreal's French-language papers carried editorials attacking the execution. They accused the Conservative government of betraying the rights of all French-speaking Canadians.

Many Montrealers agreed. The next Sunday, 40 000 turned up at a mass meeting to protest the death of Riel. They met in the Champ de Mars. There, the crowd heard 30 speakers express the same sentiment. Wilfrid Laurier, soon to be Prime Minister of Canada, said, "If I had been on the banks of the Saskatchewan, I would have shouldered my musket too." Honoré Mercier, a strong French Canadian nationalist, sparked the crowd's wildest cheers. His opening words "Riel, our brother is dead, victim of his devotion to the cause of the Métis of whom he was leader, victim of fanaticism and treason," stirred their hearts. Jeers filled the air as Mercier and others attacked Macdonald for the death of Riel and for the anti-French feelings of English Canada.

That night, the split between the two sides of Montreal was deeper and more visible. Over the years, fueled by events such as the Manitoba Schools Question, the Boer War, and Conscription, it would continue to grow wider.

The Klondike

Ho for the Klondike! The cry rang out around the world. Once more, prospectors were on their way north and west, lured by stories of gold in the Klondike, in Canada's Yukon.

In 1896, prospector George Carmack found an area rich in gold. A single shovelful of gravel produced $10 worth of gold. Other local prospectors soon joined him on Bonanza Creek, near the Klondike River. When these gold miners went down to Victoria and San Francisco later in the year, the news was out. Prospectors began to pour north to the Klondike.

The Chilkoot Pass.

Deadhorse Pass

But how could they reach the Klondike? Boats took the prospectors north to Skagway. From there, they must make their way over the Chilkoot Pass between the Pacific coast and the interior of the Yukon. The pass soon became known as Deadhorse Pass, because of the number of horses and mules that died on the trip. They were not alone. Prospectors died too of starvation or exhaustion.

Miners tried to reach the Klondike by a variety of other routes. Some tried to work their way north

Faith Fenton and H.J. Woodside travelled with the NWMP detachment to report on the gold rush for their newspapers.

Yukon

The Yukon Territory takes its name from the Yukon River. The river flows through the territory and Alaska to the Bering Sea. *Yukon* is a Kutchin word meaning "Great River."

"Guess you know the name 'Yukon' means 'Great River.' Well, you don't know nothin' about the Great River till you see that ice go."

From *No Man Stands Alone* by Amy Wilson

through the interior of British Columbia. Others worked their way to Edmonton and then went overland through the Peace River country. The gold rush helped to open up both these areas to settlement.

The gold rush also meant a boom for Victoria and Vancouver. Both had suffered from the results of a depression in the early 1890s. Now, Vancouver's population doubled and Victoria began to prosper again.

Law and Order

The sudden arrival of thousands of people in the Klondike caused problems. A detachment of North West Mounted Police was sent to the Yukon to maintain law and order. Again, as on the prairies, the Mounties managed to prevent violence. They stopped prospectors from fighting over claims. They prevented robbers from stealing gold from prospectors.

The gold rush brought about the creation of the Yukon as a separate territory of Canada in 1898.

Questions

Can You Recall?

1. How much money did the Hudson's Bay Company want for Rupert's Land? How much did they actually receive from Canada?
2. What was the most important event each year for the Métis?
3. List three of the rights demanded by the Métis in their bill of rights?
4. Who was the leader of the Métis in 1870?
5. What was British Columbia promised in return for joining Confederation?
6. Give two reasons why Prince Edward Island joined Confederation.
7. What contributed most to the growth of Toronto as a business centre in the 1870s?
8. Define the word "treaty." Explain why Canada signed treaties with the Plains Indians.
9. Where and when was the "last spike" of the CPR driven?
10. What were two causes of the Northwest Rebellion in 1885?
11. On a map of western Canada, draw the routes used by miners to get to the Klondike.
12. Give two results of the Klondike gold rush.

Ideas for Discussion

1. Why were the Protestants in Ontario so opposed to rights for French-speaking Métis in Manitoba? Discuss this question in the light of the rights the Métis asked for.
2. Who was Thomas Scott? Why was he executed? Discuss why the execution of Scott was important to:
   a) English Canadians;
   b) the Métis;
   c) Louis Riel in 1885.
3. Discuss whether or not the terms of the treaties between the Plains Indians and Canada, in your opinion, were fair. In giving your answer, think about the events and conditions that led up to the Northwest Rebellion of 1885.
4. Suggest some reasons why the construction of the railway was an important condition for British Columbia joining Confederation.

5. "Modern technology helped the Canadian government defeat the rebels in the Northwest Rebellion." Explain the part played in the rebellion by:
   a) the railway;   b) the telegraph.
6. In his speech at his trial, Louis Riel said, "I know that through the grace of God I am the founder of Manitoba." What did he mean? In your opinion, is this statement true?
7. Describe the impact of the building of the railway on Canada's West.
8. Discuss reasons why women played little or no role in most of the events described in this chapter. How have things changed since that time?

Do Some Research

1. Prepare a research report on the NWMP and their importance in the years 1873 to 1900.
2. Why was it necessary to send surveyors out before the railway could be built? What is a survey? How is it conducted?

A party of surveyors for the railway starts a portage round rapids on the North Thompson River.

3. Go to the library and prepare an oral report for the class on one of the following:
   a) Louis Riel
   b) Gabriel Dumont
   c) Poundmaker
   d) Big Bear
4. Find out more about one of the inventions described on pages 232 and 233. Describe its development and its importance to Canadians.
5. Human activities have wiped out some animals and greatly affected the lives of others. Write a "biocard" about an animal that lives or lived in Canada or in Canadian waters. Use the biocard on the buffalo as an example. Here are some suggestions:
   a) sea otter
   b) passenger pigeon
   c) caribou
   d) black rat snake
   e) Atlantic salmon
   f) burrowing owl
   If students choose different animals, you can put together a class album of animal biocards.
6. Prepare a report comparing the British Columbia Cariboo gold rush of the 1860s with the Klondike gold rush.

Be Creative

1. Write a short story about a boy or girl visiting downtown Toronto in the 1870s.
2. Imagine that you are Superintendent Jarvis of the NWMP. You have just completed a long day on patrol and your cook is preparing supper. Write a letter to your family in Ontario describing the Saskatchewan landscape and the interesting people you have met today.
3. Make a large mural showing the construction of the railway in the 1880s.
4. Write and perform a short play on the trial of Louis Riel.
5. Write a newspaper article reporting the response in Montreal to the hanging of Louis Riel.
6. Make a visual display showing gold mining techniques used in the British Columbia and Yukon gold rushes.

Maple Creek, Saskatchewan. 1896, NWMP Superintendent Jarvis on patrol.

Buffalo (American bison)
The runner of the Plains.
BORN: on the Prairies of North America.
DESCRIPTION: male (bull) up to 2 m tall, weighing more than 1 t. Female, up to 1.5 m tall, weighing 315 kg. Brown, hump at shoulders, shaggy hair on head, neck, shoulders.
HABITS: grazing the Plains in large herds. Prefers grass, but will eat twigs and leaves. Prefers to eat in morning and late afternoon; midday is siesta time. Often on the move; prefers to plod slowly along, but can stampede at up to 65 km/h.
HISTORY: once, more than 60 million bison lived on the North American Plains. Europeans, and Indians once they had guns, killed almost all the buffalo, often just for their tongues or for "sport." Almost extinct at one time, several thousand buffalo now live, mostly in national and provincial parks.

Turn of the Century
ADVANCE ORGANIZER

1

By the 1880s, Canada stretched from sea to sea. But Canada needed people, and it needed new industries where those people could work. To achieve these things, Sir John A. Macdonald set out his National Policy.

2

In Ontario and Quebec, factories and other manufacturing plants were built. Iron and steel mills were started in Ontario towns. The iron was used to make locomotives and farm machinery. Along the St. Lawrence River, textile mills and clothing factories were built. The owners of these businesses became rich and powerful.

3

Life was hard for the workers in these factories. They worked long hours for little pay, often in dangerous conditions. Children as young as 10 worked full time. Workers started organizing themselves into unions to fight for better pay and conditions.

4

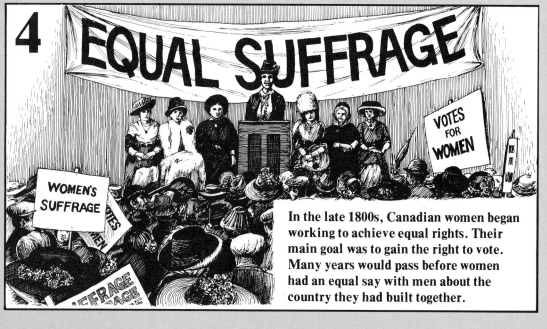

In the late 1800s, Canadian women began working to achieve equal rights. Their main goal was to gain the right to vote. Many years would pass before women had an equal say with men about the country they had built together.

Word List

conditions	industry	tariff
factory	policy	textile
illegal	reform	trade union
immigration	suffragette	workplace

5

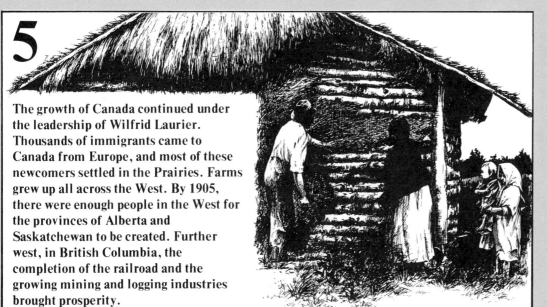

The growth of Canada continued under the leadership of Wilfrid Laurier. Thousands of immigrants came to Canada from Europe, and most of these newcomers settled in the Prairies. Farms grew up all across the West. By 1905, there were enough people in the West for the provinces of Alberta and Saskatchewan to be created. Further west, in British Columbia, the completion of the railroad and the growing mining and logging industries brought prosperity.

6

SHIPYARD CLOSED

In the Maritimes, things were not going as well. The great age of wooden ships was passing. Shipyards were closing. Industries in the Atlantic provinces were unable to compete with those of Central Canada.

7

Central Canada continued to prosper with the expansion of manufacturing. In the northern parts of Ontario and Quebec, mining and logging were important. Ontario began to overtake Quebec as an industrial centre.

8

Under Laurier, Canada became more active in world affairs. Laurier participated in Imperial conferences. Canadian troops fought in the Boer War in Africa.

The world was modernizing rapidly at the start of the twentieth century. Canada was enjoying prosperity as its population and industries grew. Sir Wilfrid Laurier predicted that the twentieth century would belong to Canada.

Macdonald and the National Policy

Cartoonists find some people more fun to draw than others. John A. Macdonald's features made him a favourite subject.

John A. Macdonald became the first prime minister of Canada in 1867. In his first six years in office, his government more than doubled the area of Canada by buying Rupert's Land from the Hudson's Bay Company. Manitoba, Prince Edward Island and British Columbia all became provinces of Canada.

During the 1870s things were not going well in Canada. There were few new industries in the country. There were few new jobs. Many people were out of work. This was Canada's first depression. The Liberals led by Alexander Mackenzie came to power in 1873. But they were not able to improve these conditions.

In 1878, another election was held. Macdonald and the Conservatives wanted to get back into power. They wanted to get Canada out of the depression. They decided on a new policy, which they called the National Policy. The National Policy had three main points: first, a tariff to protect Canadian industries; second, a transcontinental railway to link Canada from Atlantic to Pacific; third, increased immigration to provide workers and settlers.

Protection for Industry

First, the Conservatives wanted to protect Canadian industry. Manufacturing industries in the United States had several advantages over industries in Canada. Many of them had been started earlier and were prospering by the 1870s. Since the United States had more people, industries there had a larger market. Therefore, they could make more goods and sell them more cheaply than in Canada. This made things very difficult for Canadian manufacturers. Macdonald promised that, if his government were elected, he would make the Americans pay an extra tax to sell their goods in Canada. This extra tax on imported goods is called a tariff.

The Transcontinental Railway

Macdonald promised that the transcontinental railway would be completed. Then farm products from the prairies could go to Eastern Canada and Europe. Manufactured goods from Ontario, Quebec and the Maritimes could be sold in the West. British Columbia would have its promised railway to tie it to the rest of Canada.

Immigration

Finally, Macdonald promised to bring in more immigrants from other countries. These new settlers would fill the new farming areas in the West. They would also buy the things Canada's new industries were producing.

Macdonald and the Conservatives won the election in 1878. The National Policy, with its protective tariff, transcontinental railway, and increased immigration, came into effect.

Macdonald's first wife, Isabella, was a bedridden invalid. Because he could not entertain at home, he used to go to taverns. He began to drink too much. George Brown, the leader of the opposition, once scolded him in the assembly for his drinking. Macdonald replied, "The people would rather have John A. drunk than George Brown sober!" He used to enjoy drinking with D'Arcy McGee. One night he told him, "Look here, this government can't afford two drunkards, so you've got to stop."

George Etienne Cartier

BORN: St. Antoine, Verchères, Lower Canada, 1814
DIED: London, England, 1873
Probably descended from family of Jacques Cartier.
1835 — became a lawyer in Montreal.
1837 — fought on rebel side in 1837 rebellion. Fled to the United States. Returned the next year.
1848-61 — represented county of Verchères (where two centuries earlier Madeleine de Verchères had defended her family's seigneury against the Iroquois) in legislative assembly.
1857 — joined John A. Macdonald in the leadership of a government with representatives from both Canada East and Canada West.
1861-73 — represented Montreal first in legislative assembly, then in House of Commons.
1864 — leading French Canadian at Charlottetown and Quebec conferences. Persuaded French Canada to accept idea of Confederation.
1867 — minister of militia in first government of Dominion of Canada.
1868 — knighted by Queen Victoria for helping to bring about Confederation.
1872-73 — thought to be involved in the "Pacific Scandal" with Macdonald, but died before anything could be proved.
Author of a song which nearly became Canada's national anthem, *O Canada; mon pays, mes amours!* (Oh Canada, my beloved country).
In 1965, Ontario named the highway running from Windsor to the Quebec border the Macdonald-Cartier Freeway after these two Fathers of Confederation.

Macdonald had two sons by his first wife. One died young, but the other, Hugh John, became the premier of Manitoba. His second wife, Agnes, was the sister of his secretary, Hewitt Bernard. They were very happy together. But even so, there was tragedy in their lives. Their daughter, Mary, was crippled with water on the brain.

The Growth of Industry

Canada's population was growing. By 1900, seven million people lived in Canada. All of these people needed manufactured goods. They needed sawn lumber and ground flour, wagons to travel in, and binders and mowers to harvest their crops. They needed beer to drink, knives to cut their food, and shoes and clothing to wear. The new newspapers in the towns needed newsprint.

Some of these things had been made in Canada since the early days. But many of them had been imported from other countries. In the 1880s and 1890s, many more Canadian factories began to operate, to turn out the manufactured goods that Canadians needed.

Delivery Day at Stettler, Alberta in the early 1900s. After the farmers collected their new machines, they were entertained with a parade often led by the Massey band and a free dinner at a local hotel.

The Market for Goods

Several things made this possible. There were enough people that manufacturing in Canada became profitable. The railway could now carry goods to the western half of the country. And Macdonald's protective tariff made it easier for Canadian industry to compete with industry in other countries.

The need for new machinery led to the growth of steel mills. The building of the railways also caused a great demand for steel. New wagons, buggies and farm implements required steel. The first steel mill in Canada was located in Cape Breton. Later, mills were established in Hamilton, Ontario.

Most of the industry in Canada was located in Ontario and Quebec. One such industry was Massey

Farm Implements. In early pioneering days, farmers depended on the local blacksmith shop for their simple farm tools. But as more farmers moved to an area and as more complex tools were developed, factories were needed to make the tools.

The Masseys

Daniel Massey, a farmer near Newcastle, took over a bankrupt foundry there in 1847. He made ploughs, harnesses, kettles and other articles of iron and steel. Two years later, he moved to a newer, larger foundry and brought in his son, Hart, to help with the business. He hired more employees and made more tools.

The Massey firm developed automatic binders, mechanical rakes, reapers and mowers to replace the hand and horse-drawn tools that had been used on pioneer farms. By 1867, it was selling farm machinery all over Canada and in the United States and Europe.

Business was so good that Massey wanted to move to a more central location, with a larger factory. In 1882, the company moved to Toronto. This fast-growing city was a railway centre and had a good port and easy access to water transportation. In Toronto, Massey built a large factory, employing 1000 workers. As the demand for farm implements grew, other companies were set up. In 1891, Massey merged with its chief competitor, Harris, to become Massey-Harris.

In 50 years, the firm had changed from a small family operation to an industrial giant. Massey-Harris continued to grow. It became the world's largest producer of farm machinery and equipment. Today the company is known as Massey-Ferguson. It has factories in Canada and the United States, and sells farm machinery all over the world.

HALIL YOUSEF,
SHEPPARD'S HOTEL, CAIRO, EGYPT,
EGYPTIAN SALESMAN OF
THE MASSEY M'F'G CO., TORONTO.

Massey-Harris sold machinery all over the world.

The Labour Movement

A Toast For Labour

From The Ontario Workman, *1872*

Here's to the man with horny hand,
  Who tugs the breathing bellows;
Where anvils ring in every land,
  He's loved by all good fellows.

And here's to him who goes a-field
  And through the world is ploughing;
Or with stout arm the axe doth wield,
  While ancient oaks are bowing.

Here's to delver in the mine,
  The sailor on the ocean,
With those of every craft and line
  Who work with true devotion.

Our love to her who toils in gloom,
  Where cranks and wheels are clanking;
Bereft is she of nature's bloom;
  Yet God in patience thanking.

A curse for him who sneers at toil,
  And shuns his share of labour, —

The knave but robs his native soil,
  While leaning on his neighbour.

Here may this truth be brought on earth,
  Grow more and more in favour;
There is no wealth but owes its worth,
  To handicraft and labour.

Then pledge the founders of our wealth;
  The builders of our nation,—
We know their worth and now their health
  Drink we with acclamation.

The nineteenth century saw many new businesses and factories open in Canada. These shops and factories made everything from clothing and shoes to ships' boilers and locomotives. Men and women had to work long, hard hours to turn these things out. Workers were also needed to mine coal, iron and other minerals. Trees had to be cut down, canals dug, railroads laid. Sawmills and smelters took raw materials and turned them into timber and steel to build a new nation.

The owners of these businesses and industries did well. Many became rich and powerful. They lived in large houses surrounded by lawns and trees. They had servants to cook their food and raise their children.

Long Hours and Little Pay

In the factories men and women worked long hours for little pay. People worked 10 to 12 hours, six days a week. Many of the workers were immigrants. Their homes were small, if they owned a home at all. Most of them rented rooms in boarding houses.

Protection Island Coal Mine, Nanaimo, British Columbia.

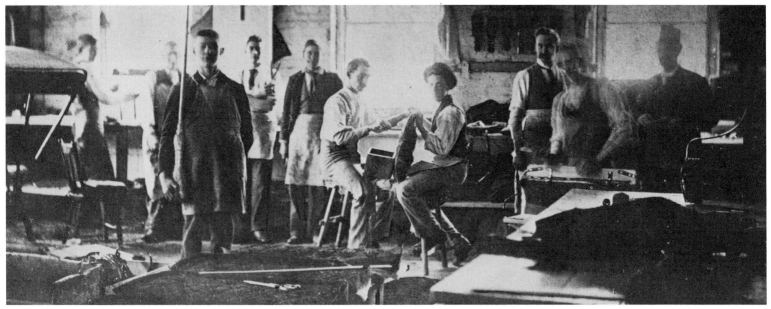

The McLaughlin Carriage Factory at Oshawa, Ontario, 1892. The company is now part of General Motors.

Canadian workers first began to organize to improve their working conditions in the 1830s. The first known Canadian trade union was set up by printers in Quebec City. They were soon followed by the shoemakers and tailors. In 1833, the carpenters of Montreal formed the Mechanics Mutual Protection Society. Their aim was to reduce the workday to 10 hours. The next year, the masons and stonecutters joined the fight. A strike that year led to a 10-hour workday.

The Growth of Trade Unions

1872 was an important year for Canadian workers. A combined effort by many unions led to the 9-hour workday. Trade unions began to feel that they could work together to improve conditions. That year also saw the passage of the Trade Unions Act in parliament. Trade unions were legally recognized at last.

The first Canadian trade unions were craft unions. Their members shared a common craft or trade — shoemaking, weaving, carpentry, boatbuilding. In the 1880s a new type of union came to Canada: the Knights of Labour. The Knights of Labour organized unskilled labourers in factories, mines and other large workplaces. They were active in all parts of Canada: in Quebec shipyards, in Hamilton foundries, in CPR shops in Winnipeg, and in the Nanaimo coal mines.

There was great resistance to trade unions from the men who owned the shops and factories. The less their workers were paid, the more money the owners made. Even many Reformers were opposed to trade unions. George Brown, one of the Fathers of Confederation, was the founder of the *Globe* newspaper in Toronto. He was sympathetic to many reforms for small farmers. Yet he was so opposed to trade unions that he fired any worker who tried to organize a union in his shops. He made speeches urging employers to "Stamp out the movement. Drive the union men from Canada." John A. Macdonald took advantage of this attitude to encourage workers to vote Conservative in the election of 1872. He stressed the anti-labour attitude of the Liberals. The workers supported him. The Conservatives won the election of 1872.

Child Labour and the Growth of Unions

A child miner, Manitoba, about 1910.

Child Labour

Ten little children working in a mine;
One was blown up in the air, then there were nine.
Nine little children through the factory gate;
One was caught in the machine, then there were eight.
Eight little children in the sweatshop heaven;
One of them pined away, then there were seven.
Seven little children, orphans in a fix;
One of them starved to death, then there were six.
Six little children in the glass works strive;
After the explosion, there were only five.
Five little children in department store;
One got consumption, then there were four.
Four little children go to work in glee;
Trolley killed one of them, then there were three.
Three little children in the mill did stew;
One caught pneumonia, then there were two.
Two little children all the spindles run;
One inhaled cotton dust, then there was one.
One little child forlorn skipped a day for fun;
But he was soon put in jail, then there were none.
"Suffer little children to come unto me,"
For they pay a bigger profit than the men, you see.

By Daniel Kissam Young, *The Industrial Banner*, 1905.

Children worked alongside adults in the workshops, factories and mines of nineteenth-century Canada. Some employers hired children as young as eight. A child could be paid much less than an adult worker. The less money an employer paid for workers, the greater his profit.

Children in cigar factories earned about $1.00 a week. (Adults earned the same amount in a day.) The factories were long sheds — ill-lit, hot, sweaty places. Beatings and other forms of punishment were common — sometimes for as little as talking to another child while working.

Young boys worked the coal mines of Nova Scotia. The shafts and tunnels of the mines were sometimes so tight that only a small boy on his hands and knees could reach the coal. For this hard and dangerous work, the boys were paid 60¢ to 80¢ a day.

In 1889, children of eight working in a Montreal cotton mill earned $92 a year. To earn this money, they worked from six in the morning until six at night, six days a week. Clothing factories were called "sweat-shops" because they were usually hot and airless. Many workers and machines were crammed into a small room. The Hochelaga Cotton Mill near Montreal employed 1100 workers in the 1880s. Of these, half were girls and young women. They were paid less than 75¢ a day. Men doing the same job earned a dollar.

The early trade unions fought for an end to child labour. They wanted it to be illegal to hire a child younger than 16. Change came slowly. Even in the early 1900s, one in every 30 factory workers in Canada was a child. In 1908, Ontario passed the first child-labour act in Canada. The new law made 14 the minimum age for working in factories.

The Struggle Continues

By the end of the nineteenth century, trade unions were firmly established in Canada. Thousands of men and women in all parts of the country were members. But the struggle was far from over. Police were used to break strikes. Sometimes workers were killed by police bullets. Owners used their political power to try to get governments to limit the rights of workers. The trade unions, on their part, became active in areas beyond the workplace. Their first aim was still to ensure fair

wages and good working conditions. But they also dealt with other issues, such as education and the general well-being of all people in Canada.

The efforts of trade unions to improve the lives of working people continue. Today some of the obvious problems of the past have been eliminated. But workers and their unions still work to ensure safe working conditions and good wages. They are also active in community groups, education and Canadian political life.

In 1889, the government called a Royal Commission to enquire into labour conditions. This is some of the testimony.

Question: Have you seen little girls whipped?
Cigar-maker: Yes, sir.
Question: Why were they whipped?
Cigar-maker: Because they were talking among themselves while at work.

Question: Do you think it right to employ children of 12 years at all?
President, Hochelaga Cotton Mills: I think that at 12 years a child should be able to work.
Question: Do you believe a child of 10 is capable of judging exactly the work required of him?
Superintendent, Hochelaga Cotton Mills: Yes.

Free compulsory education
An 8-hour workday
Government inspection of all industry
Public ownership of all utilities
An end to child labour under the age of 14
An end to property qualifications for holding public office
An end to prison labour

Platform of the Trades and Labour Councils Annual Convention, 1891.

Women at the Turn of the Century

Canadian women marched into the twentieth century — several steps behind Canadian men. They could not vote in elections or hold public office. Many jobs and professions were not open to them. Women were paid less than men for doing the same work. Free land for settlement was given to men, but not to women.

Canadian men — like men in most parts of the world at this time — felt that women should not be interested in such things. Women, they said, lacked the judgement to make decisions in political or business life. God had placed women on earth for one purpose — to have babies. The more babies they had, the faster Canada would grow. Women were expected to stay home, look after the house, and care for the family.

Women worked hard in those days. The work of looking after the house and family took much time and energy. On pioneer farms, husband and wife shared the chores. Often, in the West, men would have to leave their families in order to earn money on the railroad or in the towns. While they were away, the women had to look after the farm. They had to cook, clean, make clothing, keep the vegetable garden, tend the stock, operate machinery, and bring in the crops. Even on farms where the men were present all the time, women would work in the fields.

Women Go Out to Work

Nearly one out of every seven Canadian women was working outside the home by 1900. Most of the women holding jobs were single. Women with families would work at home or take in boarders to earn a living. Women were often limited to routine work in factories such as textile mills. Others worked as store clerks or as servants in the homes of the wealthy. These jobs were very poorly paid for the long hours of work involved.

By 1900, some women were finding better jobs. They could work as teachers, nurses, or newspaper reporters. Canada's first woman doctor, Emily Stowe, received her licence to practice medicine in 1880. Dr. Stowe had gone to the United States for training after the University of Toronto had refused to admit her because she was a woman. In 1883, Emily Stowe's daughter Augusta became the first woman to graduate from a Canadian medical school. In the 1890s, Canada's first women lawyers were called to the bar. But many professions — among them engineering — still refused to admit women.

Doukhobor women harvesting.

1200 1300 1400 1500 1600 1700 1800 1900

Dear Madam:
I hear you want suggestions for occupations for women. May I say a few words on the crying need in British Columbia? We want strong, capable women and girls to work in our homes. British Columbia offers splendid wages, from $20 to $35 per month. Our homes are planned to save work. Girls are well cared for and have plenty of liberty. They are able to save and provide money for their old age in case they do not marry. But alas! this is the cry of most mothers and housewives. "I just get a really capable girl, then she gets married!"

Never have I seen better conditions for women and girls than in British Columbia. A good cook commands respect. A good nurse is of the highest value. A woman who will do all kinds of housework is regarded as a treasure. So British Columbia offers good homes, high wages, splendid climate and good prospects for really good, useful women and girls.

I am, faithfully yours,
A LOVER OF BRITISH COLUMBIA
May 27, 1909

Women in the Universities

Many women received little more than a public school education. By the turn of the century, however, women were starting to enter Canada's universities. In 1897, only ten years after the first woman was admitted, one-third of Toronto's University College enrolment was female. But it would be 1912 before Carrie Derick would become the first Canadian-born woman professor.

All Hallows School at Yale, British Columbia, educated Indian girls. Former students often worked as household servants.

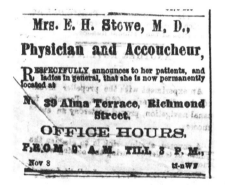

A lobster canning factory at Canoe Cove, Prince Edward Island.

Women in Political Life

Women were becoming active in Canada's social, religious, and political life too. Groups such as the Young Women's Christian Association and the Women's Christian Temperance Union tackled many of Canada's social problems. Women like Adelaide Hunter Hoodless used the YWCA to get better health and nutrition for Canadian children. The WCTU fought to stop the wide-spread drunkenness that affected many Canadian families in the nineteenth century. Members of the WCTU wanted to stop all sales of alcohol in Canada. Other women's groups were started at this time. In 1893, Lady Aberdeen, the wife of Canada's Governor General, launched the National Council of Women. Four years later, the Women's Institute was founded. Some of the most active women's groups were to be found in the Prairies. There women were working side by side with men to open the West.

Few women became active in unions at this time. Those who did worked most to improve working conditions. Equal pay for equal work and the demand to compete with men for better jobs were matters that would wait till later in the twentieth century.

A sweatshop on Spadina Avenue, Toronto, about 1900.

It is true that in most industries where both men and women are employed, women are assigned to less important work. They are not as well trained as men, and are not able to do men's work. This results in lower wages for women. This difference will always remain until women are better trained, and until women are prepared to form strong unions. But this type of co-operation seems foreign to women's nature.

From The Canadian Woman, *1905.*

World War I proved that women could do "men's work." These men and women were machinists at a munitions plant.

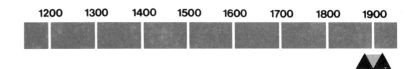

The Right to Vote

The women's groups soon turned to the fact that women could not vote in Canada. Some women had been able to vote in the Maritimes and Quebec in the late eighteenth and early nineteenth centuries. But, with Confederation, Canadian law gave only men the right to vote. The fight to get the vote for women was a bitter one. Sir John A. Macdonald introduced bills to give women the right to vote in 1883, 1884 and 1885. All were defeated. In the 1880s and 1890s, women became able to vote in municipal elections. They began to hold office — usually as school trustees — in many Canadian cities.

Led by women like Nellie McClung, many Canadian women became suffragettes. Suffragettes were women who wanted the right to vote. All across Canada, suffragettes worked hard to get the right to vote in provincial and federal elections. It would be 1916 before the first province, Manitoba, would allow women to vote. The next year, nurses serving with Canada's forces in World War I were allowed to vote in the federal election. In 1920, women were given the right to vote by the Canadian parliament.

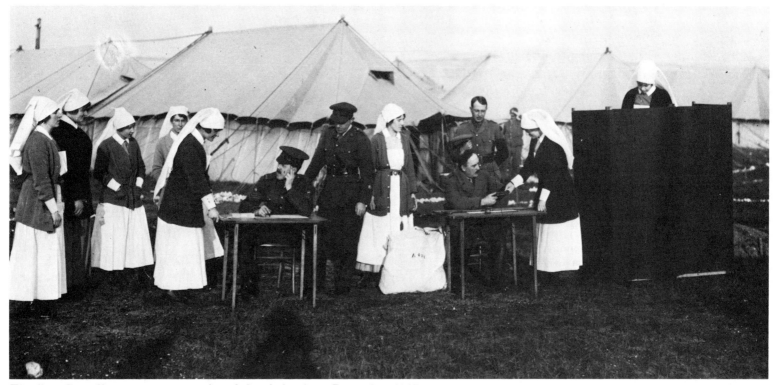

The first Canadian women to vote in a federal election, December 1917.

Schools and Education

In most of the provinces of Canada, children had to go to school only until they were 12 or 14 years old. In Manitoba, education was not compulsory, but children could go to school until they were 14. Often on the Prairies or in other rural areas, there was no school close enough for children to attend.

Very few rural children went beyond Grade Eight. Children were needed at home to work on the farm or to bring in extra money. In planting or harvesting season, they often stayed home to help instead of going to school.

Most cities had public high schools by the 1900s. But even in the cities, most children went to school only until the age of 15. Many children went to work in factories as soon as they turned 14.

Schools taught the children the basic subjects: reading, writing and arithmetic. They also tried to teach a sense of Canadianism and loyalty to the British Empire.

A school in the Timiskaming district, Ontario.

One school board's rules for teachers:

Each teacher will bring a bucket of water and a scuttle of coal for the day's session and will fill lamps, clean chimneys and trim wicks. Men teachers may take one evening each week for courting purposes, or two evenings if they go to church regularly. After school, teachers should spend the remaining time reading the Bible or other good books. Women teachers who marry or engage in other unseemly conduct will be dismissed. Every teacher should lay aside a goodly sum so that he will not become a burden on society. Any teacher who smokes, uses liquor, frequents pool or public halls, or gets shaved in a barber shop will give good reason to suspect his worth, intentions, integrity and honesty. The teacher who performs his labour faithfully and without fault for five years will be given an increase of 25 cents per week in his pay if the School Board approves.

A school near Vulcan, Alberta.

Picture Gallery page 5

1200	1300	1400	1500	1600	1700	1800	1900

Only schools in big cities had facilities like this manual training room in Ottawa in 1901.

We kids got our education at the "Finlander School." It was a log structure chinked between the logs with moss and mortar. It was used in the summer months only at first. Finally they made it good enough for use all year round.

We had a huge box stove that burned a lot of poplar wood. There were about 20 of us from Grade 1 to 8. I never quite knew what I was studying. I was mostly listening to other kids reading. There never was a moment of silence.

I don't seem to have ever spent more than a couple of months per summer at school. I would get nicely interested, when boom! it was haying time, or harvest time, and I had to help. In the spring I was always a month behind time helping put in the crop, but somehow I managed to jump two or three grades a term. At first we didn't have exams anyway.

All the nationalities got along well. The Fauché kids used to point at the food the Herman kids took for lunch, because they ate rye bread.

A French settler in Alberta in the early 1900s.

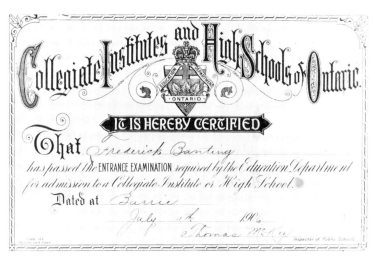

A future scientist is ready to enter high school.

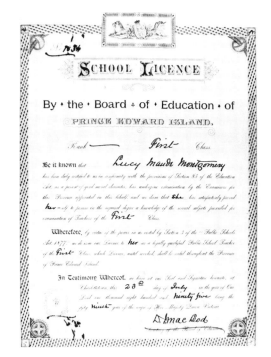

Board of Education members were not always perfect spellers. Lucy Maud Montgomery spelled her second name without an "e."

The Laurier Era

For 18 years after John A. Macdonald's victory in 1878, the Conservatives remained in power. They were defeated in the election of 1896. Wilfrid Laurier and the Liberals won and formed the new government. The Liberals under Laurier would be in power for the next 15 years.

The Laurier period is often looked upon as the "golden age" of Canadian history. Canada's population was growing. The country was prosperous and people were hopeful about the future.

Laurier's Election Promises

Laurier had promised to make some changes if he was elected. He promised to reduce the tariffs. He supported a free trade policy. This policy would have allowed American manufactured goods into Canada without any tariff. It would have been popular with western farmers and with some Maritimers.

But, after they were elected in 1896, Laurier and the Liberals decided to keep the tariff. They felt that Canadian industries still needed protection against American competition. They were afraid that Canadian industries would not be able to sell their products if cheaper goods from the United States and other countries were allowed into Canada without a tariff.

The Liberal government felt, however, that the Canadian Pacific Railway and the railway in eastern Canada needed some competition. Some people felt the CPR could not handle all the West's grain shipments. The railway was charging freight rates that were too high. Laurier and the Liberal government encouraged and supported other railways. Too many railways were built in this time. Some eventually went

This Conservative election poster said that the Liberal free trade policy would mean that "Uncle Sam" would take over Canada. When they were elected, the Liberals decided to keep the tariffs.

bankrupt. In the end, the government had to take them over. They formed the basis for the Canadian National Railway.

New Immigration Policy

The greatest change after the election of the Liberal government was in immigration. Although the Conservative National Policy had supported immigration, nothing much had been done about it. Laurier and the Liberals wanted to see more farmers coming to open up the West. They also wanted more workers in the eastern cities. They thought more people would strengthen the country and provide markets for industry.

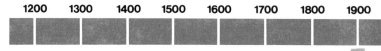

Laurier appointed Clifford Sifton as Minister of the Interior, in charge of immigration. Sifton was from Manitoba, the gateway to Canada's West. He wanted to find hard-working people with farming backgrounds to fill up the West. He began a campaign to bring in settlers from England, Ireland and Scotland, from the United States and from continental Europe.

If there is anything to which I have devoted my political life, it is to try to promote unity, harmony and friendship between the diverse elements of this country.

We have found that our Canadian independence is quite compatible with our dependency as a colony.

Wilfrid Laurier

"HOME. SWEET HOME."

During the period that Laurier was prime minister, people began to think of Canada not only as part of the British Empire but also as their home. They began to be proud of their country, its people and its history.

"NOW THEN, ALL TOGETHER"

The Dutch may have their Holland, the Spaniard have his main,
The Yankee to the south of us must south of us remain;
For not a man dare lift a hand against the men who brag
That they were born in Canada beneath the British flag.

Pauline Johnson, Canadian Born

THE LAURIER ERA   263

Winnipeg in 1895

Curling bonspiels and canoeing, wheat and the railway: this is Winnipeg in 1895. And if you doubt that curling was important, you might note this: a year earlier, the legislature didn't have enough people present for a meeting to be held. Too many members had gone curling.

It was quiet in Winnipeg in the 1890s. The great railway boom had gone. The immigration boom had not arrived. The city was growing at a rate of about five percent a year, from just over 25 000 in 1891 to just over 31 000 in 1896.

Of these, more than a quarter had been born in Ontario. A fifth were born in Manitoba, more than a quarter in Great Britain. Most of the rest were from other parts of Canada, Europe and the United States. And 90 percent of the population was under 45 years of age.

Curling at the turn of the century.

A Prairie Centre

Quiet or not, Winnipeg was still the main city of the prairies. The wide main streets — built originally so Red River carts would not get caught in muddy ruts — took traffic to the grain exchange, the farm equipment dealers and the railway yards.

The unions were growing. In 1895, the Independent Labour Party, the first labour party in Canada, was organized.

And that same year, women were given the right to vote in city elections. Of course, both men and women still had to own a certain amount of property in order to be allowed to vote. And women still could not hold public office.

Main Street with the horse-drawn streetcars of the Winnipeg Street Railway.

Sports and Leisure

Rowing, swimming, cricket, canoeing, yachting, curling: those were the concerns of the residents of Winnipeg who could afford such things. Every summer, they would go to Lake of the Woods, already a growing summer resort. There were other sports too: in 1896, the Winnipeg Victorias won hockey's Stanley Cup.

The city had undertaken a tree-planting program a number of years before. As a result, Winnipeg's first bicyclists could ride along shady streets. Football, baseball and rifle shooting were also popular.

The quiet times were almost over. In 1896, Clifford Sifton's immigration programs would begin to change the face of the west. But for now, the price of grain — 75 cents a bushel — and the time for tennis (four in the afternoon for most businessmen) were the most pressing concerns.

The market and City Hall.

A FAMOUS VICTORY
STANLEY CUP WRESTED
FROM MONTREAL
The Stalwart sons of the Prairie Capital show Easterners How to Play Hockey — Montrealers are shut Out on their Own Ice — Tremendous Local Interest in the Result.

Montreal, Feb. 14. — There is joy in the ranks of the Winnipeg touring contingent tonight. The magnificent Stanley Cup, the emblem of the championship of the Dominion, is theirs. It was presented to the Queen City of the west, as a valentine, won as it was on February 14th. Well and worthy was the victory; long and determined the battle, and for the first time in the history of the hockey champions of the decaying east, they had to submit to a complete whitewash.

The blizzards from the land of the setting sun trouped into Montreal on Wednesday evening. In sporting circles their arrival had been the topic of discussion for several days. While recognizing that their hockey team was to be confronted by a very worthy foe, Montrealers were quite confident that the Winnipeggers would return to the land from which they came without the trophy. Alas, Montreal tonight is draped in mourning and the sports have gone to bed with empty wallets. The "Peg" contingent on the other hand have enough money to start a private bank. No less than 2000 cold beers were passed over the Windsor hotel bar after the match tonight and went down the throats of the Winnipeg supporters.

The Manitoba Free Press, *February 14, 1896*

Immigration

For many people who lived there in 1900, Europe was not a very pleasant place. The continent was crowded with people. Many of these people were poor.

There were more people living on the farms in Europe than ever before. This meant that each farm was being divided into smaller and smaller plots. Some of these plots would no longer support a family.

In the cities, many people were crowded together. In some places, there were more unskilled workers than there were jobs. Both in the country and in the city, there was a wide gap between the rich landholders and factory owners and the poor people.

Persecution

In southern and eastern Europe, most countries were governed by absolute monarchies. This meant that the king or queen could rule absolutely as he or she wished. People who followed religions different from the religions of the ruling class were often treated very badly. For example, many Jews in central and eastern Europe were persecuted just because they were Jews. The Czarist government of Russia permitted *pogroms*. Pogroms were attacks in which people would beat up the Jews and burn their homes.

Many poor or persecuted people had heard that America was a place where the streets were paved with gold. They thought that if they moved to America they could earn money. They could also provide a better life for their children. They could live with more freedom, without persecution because of their religious or political beliefs. Some people hoped that they would find a life that was more exciting than their boring life in the villages.

The cry against non-British immigrants is the most ignorant and absurd thing I have ever heard. I despise racial prejudice because it is not based on reason. You can excite the hatred of one nationality against another simply by hammering away and appealing to their prejudices. In the course of time you will work up an excitement. I cannot imagine a more ignorant and unpatriotic policy.

Clifford Sifton, 1901

Canada: Free Land

Clifford Sifton and the government advertised Canada all over the United States, in the British Isles and in Europe. For many years, people had emigrated from Europe to the United States. But, by the 1890s, almost all the free land in the United States was used up. Posters were hung in the railway stations of many countries saying: "Canada Free Land." The posters promised 160 acres (64 ha) to each settler.

Many families decided to try their luck as immigrants to Canada. Between 1901 and 1911, almost two and a half million immigrants came to settle in Canada. For the first time, more people left the United States for Canada than left Canada for the United States. Most immigrants still came from the British Isles. But a great number now came from the other countries of Europe, many from Austria-Hungary, Germany and Russia.

The Right Kind of Immigrant?

Not everyone thought that Sifton and Laurier's policy of immigration was a good idea. Some thought that bringing in immigrants from non-British countries would weaken Canada. Sifton resigned from his job in 1905. He was replaced by Frank Oliver. Oliver thought that Canada needed "the right class of British immigrant."

These differences of opinion led to tension between the older groups in the Canadian society and the immigrants. Many people thought that all immigrants should learn to speak English and behave like other English-speaking Canadians as quickly as possible. This argument also left French Canadians wondering how they fitted into this image of Canada as a country where everyone must speak English.

Canadian Pacific steamships brought immigrants from Europe.

Of the Anglo-Saxon we are not in the least afraid. But 56% of southern Italians cannot read. Nor can 23% of Russian Jews. And they, perhaps, are the hardest to absorb, even though they are sober and hard working. Everyone agrees that drunkenness is the great curse of the Slav.

Many foreigners are atheists and socialists. They will work for little pay, driving out Canadian workers. They apply for charity in our cities. They expose healthy people to disease. They herd themselves together in small districts, creating slums.

How should we receive immigrants? We must bring in stricter rules to keep out undesirables. The question we must ask ourselves is, will the foreigners corrupt us or will we Christianize them?

A Presbyterian minister, 1913

Settlers on the Prairies

The great flood of immigrants from Europe and the United States made the Prairies the fastest growing area of Canada at the end of the nineteenth century. The railway carried the European settlers from the ports of eastern Canada to cities like Winnipeg.

On their arrival at Winnipeg, the new immigrants were housed for a short time in Immigration Hall. There they were fed and clothed until they were able to find land or jobs. At Immigration Hall, Canadian doctors checked the newcomers carefully. Some of the immigrants might have become sick during their long trip from Europe. No one wanted an epidemic of sickness to spread.

Some of the immigrants stayed in the cities. Others became farmers on the cheap or free land that was available. Some of the immigrants who wished to farm came on their own. Others were brought in groups by colonization companies. Some groups came together because they came from the same country. Others were members of the same religious groups.

Ukrainian Settlers

A number of immigrants came from the area we now know as the Ukraine. This is a flat region, similar in climate and landscape to the Prairies. Wheat and other grains are grown there.

The Ukrainians would usually settle together in the same area. They would share such tasks as clearing the land, building houses and barns and harvesting the crops. They continued to speak their own language, dress according to their own ways and keep their own religion. They wanted to preserve their own culture. This sometimes meant that English-speaking people did not like them because they were different.

Doukhobors built villages like those they grew up with in Europe.

Religious Groups

Many immigrants came in order to be able to practise their religion freely. Among them were the Mormons, the Hutterites, the Mennonites and the Doukhobors.

The Mormons came from the United States. The Hutterites, Mennonites and Doukhobors fled from Europe. They were pacifists and refused to fight as

Ukrainians reaping grain.

American settlers on the way to Alberta.

soldiers in the armies of Russia and Prussia. A large number of Jews also moved to Canada. Since Jews were not allowed to own land in many parts of Europe, they were not usually farmers. They tended to settle in the cities.

The Homestead Act

Often, when these people arrived in the West, they did not have enough money to start farming right away. They would stay in Winnipeg, where they would work building sewers, railways and roads. They saved their money until they had enough to move to a farm.

In 1872, the Homestead Act had been passed. Under this act, would-be settlers could obtain free land on the Prairies. The land was surveyed into townships. Each township was six miles (9.7 km) square. Each square mile — called a section — was subdivided into four quarter sections of 160 acres (64 ha) each.

The Homestead Act said that anyone over 21, or anyone who was the head of a family, could claim a quarter section of land. Some sections were reserved for schools, some for the Hudson's Bay Company and others for land settlement companies. A settler could claim any other unclaimed section.

Stores of Jewish merchants on Main Street, Winnipeg.

The Prairies at the Turn of the Century

For their first year or so on the Prairies, the new settlers might live in a sod house. These houses were made of grass and earth cut from the ground like bricks. Later, if times were good, the farm family would be able to build a wood-frame house. It could take three years or more to bring a prairie farm into production. But once the farm was established, it was worth the struggle. The 1880s and 1890s saw great world demand for wheat. Prices were high and the prairie farmers prosperous. Homemade ploughs and horses gave way to machinery pulled by tractors.

In the Northwest Territories and in Manitoba, the farmers were doing well. At first, the early frosts and short growing season of this area made growing wheat risky. Development of new types of wheat such as Red Fyfe and Marquis changed things. These were scientifically created for the western prairie conditions. They grew very quickly and could be harvested before fall frosts set in.

Breaking sod with a steam-powered tractor, Saskatchewan.

Towns and Cities

Towns grew quickly all across the Prairies. Cities like Winnipeg, Regina and Calgary were along the railway. Edmonton grew from an NWMP post to a flourishing city. Smaller centres grew up at grain collection points along the way. The towns and cities were places where farmers could buy seeds, equipment and other supplies. They were places where one could buy a newspaper, collect mail, or see a play. Doctors, dentists and lawyers set up their practices in the towns to meet the needs of the settlers.

By the turn of the century, buildings of brick and stone began to replace the earlier wooden false-front stores of the 1880s. Dirt roads and wooden sidewalks remained in the small towns and villages. But in the big cities of Regina and Winnipeg there were fine paved avenues lined with trees. By the turn of the century there were streetcars, electric lights and telephones in the cities.

Merchants and professionals prospered. They built large homes and rode in fine carriages. They could take the CPR to newly built resorts in the Rocky Mountains, west of Calgary. The railroad brought them the best goods from the stores of New York and Toronto.

Saskatchewan

The Crees called the river which flowed across their lands on the Prairies *Kisikatchewan* or "swift current." Early explorers and mapmakers wrote this as Saskatchewan. The province takes its name from the river.

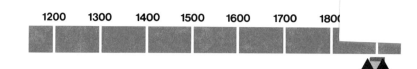

Problems for Immigrants

Not all newcomers prospered. Many of the Eastern Europeans immigrants had come from cities. They had no farming background, and some failed as farmers. Others who stayed in the cities, could not speak English, and so found it hard to get a job. Even doctors and other professionals found themselves working as labourers, on the railroads or in construction. The pay was $1.75 a day for ten hours of work. The immigrants would often crowd into boarding houses meant to accommodate much smaller numbers. Immigrants came to the Prairies faster than housing could be built.

By 1905, over a million immigrants had come to the prairies to stay. In that year, the Canadian government decided to create two new provinces out of the Northwest Territories. Alberta had its capital at Edmonton and Saskatchewan had its capital at Regina. Canada now had nine provinces.

A new town, Manitoba, 1910.

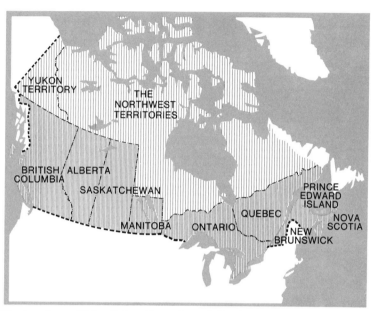

The borders of Manitoba, Ontario and Quebec were extended north in 1912. Newfoundland, the tenth province, joined Confederation in 1949.

Alberta

The Marquis of Lorne was Governor General of Canada from 1878 to 1883. He was married to Princess Louise Caroline Alberta, a daughter of Queen Victoria. In 1882, he went to Blackfoot Crossing to bring the Queen's greetings to the Blackfoot nation's council meeting. He named the territory after his wife.

The station, grain elevator and main street of Wetaskiwin, Alberta, 1898.

The Maritimes and Central Canada

The end of the nineteenth century brought major changes for the Maritimes. In the 1880s and the 1890s, farming, fishing and lumbering had been doing well. The coal mines on Cape Breton Island prospered because steamships and trains used coal for fuel. In 1882, the Nova Scotia Steel company was established at Sydney near the coal mines. Its factories used the coal to make steel for the railway and other new industries. The coal mines prospered and expanded.

In the 1880s, wooden sailing ships made in Nova Scotia and New Brunswick were in demand all over the world. Saint John was one of the largest centres of shipbuilding in the world. But ships with steel hulls were developed. This marked the end of wooden ships. The centre of shipbuilding shifted to the Clyde River in Scotland. Shipbuilding declined in the Maritimes.

Maritime Resentment

Other Nova Scotia industries were unable to compete successfully with industries in Ontario and Quebec. Many Maritimers resented the tariff which made American goods more expensive. Some Maritimers began to question the whole idea of Confederation. What had Canada done for the Maritimes? Some felt the Maritimes' natural trade was with the Atlantic countries of Britain and the United States, not with the rest of Canada. Ontario and Quebec seemed to be getting all the benefits from Confederation.

Central Canada

Quebec and Ontario were experiencing a period of great economic growth. In the cities, the factories were busy turning out a wide range of modern goods. They were making cars, telephones, electric lights, and many other products that were the symbols of the new twentieth century. Montreal was still the leading industrial centre in Canada. Toronto was catching up.

In the countryside, things were also good. Farmers enjoyed reasonable prosperity. Around Montreal and Toronto, dairy farming dominated the agricultural scene. The dairy farmers sold their milk, butter and other products to feed the fast-growing populations of the cities. In the Niagara peninsula, the fruit industry was developing. Tobacco was also an important crop. Families like the Macdonalds made their fortunes in tobacco and cigarette making. Quebec and Ontario were losing out to the Prairies as wheat-growing regions.

Mines and Forests

Copper and nickel ores had been found together in the Sudbury, Ontario area in the 1880s. But it wasn't till the early 1900s that a way was found to separate them. Smelters to process the ore were built and a mining boom was underway. In the Eastern Townships of Quebec, asbestos had been found. A major mining industry developed at Asbestos and Thetford Mines.

The forests of the Canadian Shield were the source of lumber for the timber and pulp and paper industries of Central Canada. The forests had been used for sawn timber for nearly a century. At the turn of the century, great rafts of logs and timber still came down the Ottawa and St. Lawrence Rivers. But the trees of Central Canada were smaller after nearly a century of logging. Those that were left were excellent for pulp and paper making. By 1900, Canada had become the world's leading exporter of pulp and paper products.

Top: Nova Scotia Steel and Coal Company, New Glasgow.
Middle: Woodstock Woodworking Company, New Brunswick.
Bottom: Fishermen, Souris, Prince Edward Island.

Top: Magpie Mine underground station, Sault Ste. Marie, Ont.
Middle: Open hearth furnaces, Hamilton, Ontario.
Bottom: Logging sleds, Quebec.

British Columbia

By 1900, British Columbia's native people found their old ways of life changing. At first trade in sea otters and other furs had brought them new wealth. But by now the sea otter had been wiped out by overhunting. Iron tools had brought a new dimension to Northwest Coast art. Tall totem poles and other fine carvings could be made using iron chisels, axes, and knives. Some of the coastal tribes continued salmon-fishing. Canneries were built in some villages and the catch sold.

Native peoples were moved into reservations or into missionary villages. This was done even though there were no treaties. Laws were passed by the Canadian parliament outlawing the potlatch and other native ceremonies. Native languages and religion were wiped out by missionaries and government schools.

The Railway

Vancouver was created by the Canadian Pacific Railway. Before the railway came, there was only the small village of Granville where Vancouver stands today. Granville was a logging and sawmill town, with only a few hundred people.

In 1885, the railway stopped in Port Moody, 20 km east of Granville. The CPR knew that Granville had a better harbour than Port Moody. The railway company entered into secret negotiations with the British Columbia government. A deal was arranged that would give the CPR over 4000 ha of the best land in Granville at no cost. In addition, all the landowners in Granville had to give the CPR one-third of their lands. As soon as the deal was signed in February 1886, the CPR announced that it was extending the line 20 km to the west. The president of the CPR, William Van Horne, renamed Granville, Vancouver.

Bella Coola.at the turn of the century.

1200 1300 1400 1500 1600 1700 1800 1900

The completion of the railway brought new life to British Columbia. Vancouver had the finest harbour on North America's west coast. Ships from all over the world came to the harbour. There they met trains from the Prairies carrying loads of grain and flour for world markets. Timber and lumber products from the forests and sawmills of the province were shipped all over the world. In turn, imported goods from England, the United States and the Orient were unloaded.

The Cities

The cities — Vancouver, Victoria, New Westminster — were growing. There were streetcars, electric lights and a few tall buildings as high as five or six storeys. The stores were full of fine goods from eastern Canada, Europe and the United States. The telegraph allowed businessmen to get messages to Montreal or Toronto in minutes. The train left every day for eastern Canada. Fast steamships could carry passengers to San Francisco, the Orient or Europe.

Felling timber.

The mission church at Metlakatla, 1899.

Not everyone could enjoy these things. Many worked for only a few dollars a month. These workers and their families lived in crowded rooming houses or small shacks. Young women worked as cooks or maids for the wealthy families of Shaughnessy or Beacon Hill.

Immigration to British Columbia

The gold rush was over. But the mines in British Columbia were still busy. Gold had given way to silver, lead, zinc, copper, and coal. Giant smelters were built to turn the raw ore into metal. On Vancouver Island, Robert Dunsmuir owned and operated many large coal mines in the Nanaimo-Wellington area. Dunsmuir's coal mines made him rich and powerful. He soon became premier of the province. Dunsmuir was as ruthless as he was rich. When the United Mine Workers Union went on strike for better wages and safer working conditions, he fired all the miners. Dunsmuir brought in Chinese labourers from Hong Kong to work the mines.

The Chinese miners were among many immigrants to come to British Columbia from all over the world. The new province was populated with people from Europe, Canada, the United States, India, Japan and China. There were Hawaiians living on Saltspring Island; blacks were also on Saltspring and in Victoria. The new immigrants worked in the mines, the forests, on the farms and in the cities of British Columbia.

Danger at Work

Working in the mines, sawmills, forests and on early steam boats was dangerous. Mine collapses, boiler explosions and other accidents were frequent. Men were often killed or badly crippled. Women and children worked hard too. They worked on the farms, in the canneries, in the stores and in other businesses. Medical care was limited. There were few doctors or hospitals. There were no insurance plans, pensions, or worker's compensation to help accident victims. Women died young, often in childbirth. Many children died in the first few years of their lives. Outbreaks of flu and other diseases could take many lives.

Other Problems

The Chinese and other Asian immigrants faced other problems. White Canadians resented them, because they worked hard for low wages. Many could not speak English. They kept to themselves, living in their own "Chinatown" area. Often the Chinese were beaten up or called names by the Canadians. They were not allowed to become citizens.

The Canadian government made rules for immigrants that would discourage Asians. These Sikhs from India were not allowed to enter Canada. Their ship, the *Komagata Maru*, sat in Vancouver harbour for two months in the summer of 1914 before they were finally turned away.

Chinese immigrants to British Columbia.

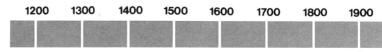
A Japanese grocery store on 9 September 1907 after a night of anti-Asiatic riots.

The Chinese quarter in Vancouver.

Vancouver in the late Nineteenth Century

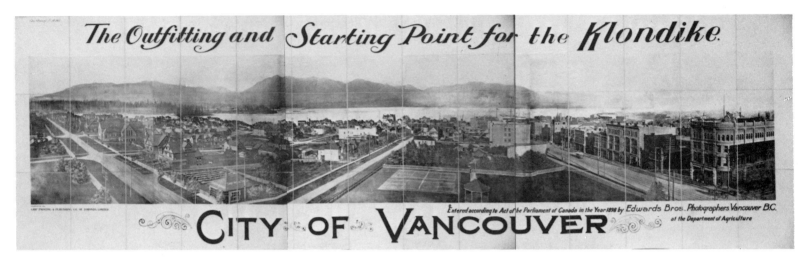

The Outfitting and Starting Point for the Klondike.

CITY OF VANCOUVER

Entered according to Act of the Parliament of Canada in the Year 1898 by Edwards Bros. Photographers Vancouver B.C. at the Department of Agriculture

The new city of Vancouver was incorporated in April 1886. In the same month, a hospital was built. There were many accidents in the forests and saw mills — so many that the hospital had to put up tents to house the injured workers. Houses and other buildings were going up all over the city.

On June 13th, 1886, disaster struck the fast-growing new city. Fire swept through the newly built wooden buildings. In minutes the whole city was on fire. Twenty people died in the fire. The town lay in ruins.

Recovery and Growth

A week later, 100 new buildings had been built. Vancouver never looked back. By spring 1887 it was a bustling young city with many stores, warehouses, hotels and houses. Wooden sailing ships stood side by side with steel-hulled steam ships at the many docks along the harbour. There was a roller-skating rink. An opera house was under construction.

Twenty years later, this float in the Labour Day parade of 1906 reminded Vancouver citizens of the great fire. In the days that followed the fire, City Hall was a tent like this.

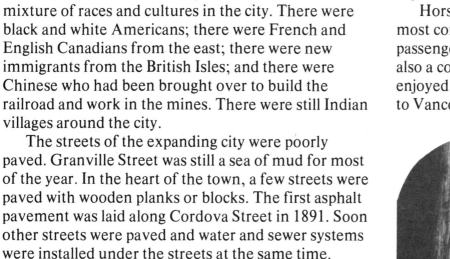

| 1200 | 1300 | 1400 | 1500 | 1600 | 1700 | 1800 | 1900 |

And there was a railroad station. In May of 1887, the first passenger train from Montreal arrived in Vancouver. The passengers were met by excited crowds, brass bands, and flags and streamers flying everywhere.

Vancouver's population grew quickly. People came by train and ship to find work in the forests, mines and the new businesses of the city. There was a rich mixture of races and cultures in the city. There were black and white Americans; there were French and English Canadians from the east; there were new immigrants from the British Isles; and there were Chinese who had been brought over to build the railroad and work in the mines. There were still Indian villages around the city.

The streets of the expanding city were poorly paved. Granville Street was still a sea of mud for most of the year. In the heart of the town, a few streets were paved with wooden planks or blocks. The first asphalt pavement was laid along Cordova Street in 1891. Soon other streets were paved and water and sewer systems were installed under the streets at the same time.

A Modern City

Vancouver prided itself on being a modern city. The first electric lights were installed in 1886. By 1890 nearly every store, hotel and many private homes had electric lights. There were also several telephones. In 1890, Vancouver's first "rapid transit" service began with four or five electric streetcars.

The first automobile came to Vancouver in 1899. It was thought to be too heavy and clumsy to be practical. After one trip it was never used again. Later, Vancouver acquired a motorized ambulance. Its first passenger was an American tourist, run over by the ambulance at an intersection. The tourist died in the ambulance on the way to hospital. In 1908, Canada's first gasoline station was built in Vancouver.

Bicycles were a popular form of transportation in late nineteenth-century Vancouver. There were "driving schools" where one could learn to ride bicycles.

Horse-drawn wagons and carriages remained the most common means of transportation, carrying passengers and goods throughout the city. Walking was also a common means of going places. Families enjoyed strolling through Stanley Park at the entrance to Vancouver's inner harbour.

A stroll through the Douglas firs in Stanley Park.

Canada's Role in International Affairs

Laurier on the campaign trail.

Laurier strengthened Canada's position as an independent nation while he was Prime Minister. Canada was still officially a British colony. Despite becoming a nation in 1867, Canada still had to let Britain run her foreign affairs. The new nation had no diplomats in other countries, no army or navy. British diplomats handled Canada's relations with other countries. The British army and navy took care of Canada's defence.

Most English-speaking Canadians thought that loyalty to Canada meant loyalty to the British Queen and Empire. In 1898, May 24, Queen Victoria's birthday, was declared a public holiday. Every year Canadians would celebrate with parades and pageants.

Not all felt loyalty to the Empire. French-speaking Canadians still regarded Britain as the nation that had conquered them in 1759. They felt loyalty to Canada — especially French Canada — but little to the Queen and Empire.

Several events while Laurier was Prime Minister led to Canada's standing on her own feet in international affairs. These were the Alaska boundary dispute, a series of Imperial conferences, the creation of the Canadian navy, and the Boer War.

A roadhouse in the Yukon.

The Alaska Boundary Dispute

The Klondike gold rush brought up the question of who owned the Alaska Panhandle. The Panhandle is a strip of land running along the British Columbia coast, south of Alaska. The United States had bought Alaska from the Russians in 1867. Many Americans thought this should be the first step in taking over all of northwestern North America. When Alaska became an American territory, no one worried much about the Panhandle and the boundary between Canada and the United States. But the gold rush meant that Canada wanted access to the Yukon by way of a Pacific coast port.

An international commission was set up in 1903 to settle the boundary dispute. The negotiations were really between the United States and Britain. Britain

1200 1300 1400 1500 1600 1700 1800 1900

named two Canadians to the commission but a British diplomat was the third member. Three Americans, appointed by President Teddy Roosevelt, represented the United States.

Teddy Roosevelt was famous for his policy of "Speak softly and carry a big stick." He was always ready to use troops — his big stick — to back American policy. Roosevelt warned that he would send troops to Alaska if Britain voted against the Americans. He also suggested that other pressures would be applied.

The British diplomat on the commission voted for the Americans. The ports were awarded to the United States. Canadians protested bitterly. They thought that Britain had sold out Canada. Strong anti-American feelings followed. Even stronger was the feeling that Canada could no longer count on Britain to act in Canadian interests. Canada had to obtain the power to carry out its own foreign policy.

The Imperial Conferences

A series of conferences between Britain and her overseas colonies — Canada, Australia, New Zealand, India, Hong Kong, the West Indies, and South Africa — was held in 1897, 1902 and 1907. Laurier represented Canada at those conferences. Britain wanted to create an Imperial council that would bring the colonies under greater British political control. The colonies would contribute money to support the British navy.

Laurier strongly rejected the idea of an Imperial council. He wanted more political control for Canada, not less. He wanted Canada to be an independent country, not a colony.

In 1909, Canada set up its own Department of External Affairs. Britain still set foreign policy for the colonies. But it was a small step toward control of Canada's own affairs. The same year saw the creation of the International Joint Commission. This group was set up to deal with Canadian-American relations. For the first time, Canada was represented only by Canadians. Meetings were held in Washington and Ottawa, not London. Canada was coming of age as a nation.

But the process of coming of age was costly to Laurier's career. It had involved a great deal of compromise. The compromises had satisfied neither English nor French Canadians. In the election of 1911, this dissatisfaction would drive Laurier out of power.

The Creation of the Canadian Navy

Great Britain and Germany were heading toward war in the early 1900s. The two countries were in a race to build the biggest and most powerful navy. A special conference of all the British colonies was called in London in 1909. Britain asked the colonies for money to help build her navy. Laurier agreed to help Britain. But he would not give Britain money. Instead, Canada would develop its own navy. Eleven warships, five cruisers and six destroyers, would be built in England for Canada's navy. Canada would make her navy available to help Britain if there was a war.

Laurier's policy of compromise made no one happy. The French thought he had given too much support to Britain. The English Canadians accused Laurier of letting down Britain. They made fun of his "tin pot navy." People in the Maritimes were upset that the ships were being built in England.

CANADA'S ROLE IN INTERNATIONAL AFFAIRS   281

The Boer War

The day after a battle. This little farmhouse at Paardeberg Drift, South Africa, was used as a field hospital. Tents and a stable nearby were also crammed with wounded soldiers.

The Boer War saw the first involvement of Canadian soldiers in a foreign war. The Boers were Dutch settlers in South Africa. They lived in the republics of the Transvaal and the Orange Free State. These two republics had come under British control only a few years earlier, in the late 1870s. The Boers were an independent group of farmers who had lived in South Africa for over two hundred years.

At first, after the British take-over the Boers were allowed to keep on running their own affairs. Then, huge amounts of gold and diamonds were found in the Boer lands. The British decided to take firm control.

The Boers rebelled against Britain. In 1899, Britain sent troops to South Africa to put down the rebels. The British also asked Canada, New Zealand, and Australia to send troops to South Africa.

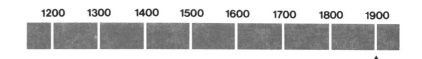
Disagreement in Canada

Laurier found himself in an awkward position. English Canadians approved of sending troops to South Africa. French Canadians opposed it strongly. They argued that this was a British war, not a Canadian one. The people of Quebec had a great deal of sympathy for the Boers. They remembered what had happened to them when the British conquered Quebec. The French Canadians were not the only ones to oppose Canada's entrance into the Boer War. Many Irish Catholic immigrants to Canada supported the Boers. They too remembered the conquest of their country by the British many years before. Some Irish Canadians felt that any enemy of Britain was a friend of Ireland.

Prime Minister Laurier tried to satisfy both groups. He arranged for a Canadian force to go to South Africa. The Canadian troops would serve as a unit. They would fight as Canadians, not as part of the British army. However, all the Canadians who went to South Africa had to be volunteers. Canada would not send any of the regular Canadian militia units to fight.

The Volunteers

Many English-speaking Canadians volunteered to go to the Boer War. Among them were a large number of North West Mounted Policemen. The most famous Canadian unit of the war, the Lord Strathcona's Horse, was led by Sam Steele, a top-ranking Mountie.

The Canadians fought well in a war that is not remembered as one of Britain's greatest moments. Canadian newspapers were full of stories about their bravery. Canadian children of the period played Canadian soldiers and Boers instead of cowboys and Indians.

In the end, Laurier failed to satisfy either the English or the French. The English Canadians felt that he had not done enough to help Britain. The French Canadians thought he had done too much. One result of the Boer War was an increase in tensions between English and French Canadians. But a second result was a stronger identity for Canada as a country in its own right, not just a British colony.

Sam Steele

BORN: Purbrook, Simcoe County, Ontario, 1849
DIED: Putney, England, January 30, 1919

1866— member of Canadian militia, involved in defence of Canada against threat of Fenian raids.

1870 — member of Red River expedition during first Riel Rebellion.

1873 — one of the first three recruits to join new NWMP. Made sergeant major on swearing in.

1882-85 — followed the railway west, patrolling the route and protecting workers from bootleggers and gamblers. Present at the driving of the last spike. Rode first train through Rockies to Vancouver.

1885 — led Alberta Field Force in second Riel Rebellion.

1896 — sent to the Klondike to keep peace during the gold rush.

1899 — commanded Lord Strathcona's Horse in South Africa during the Boer War.

1914 — promoted to major general. Recruited soldiers for Canadian forces in World War I. Commander of Second Canadian Division, sent to France in 1915.

Calgary in 1912

Can Tom Three Persons master Cyclone? Or, has the master cowboy from the Blood Indian Reserve near Cardston finally met his match in the black bucking horse from below the border?

That's the question on everyone's lips this morning as the first ever Calgary Stampede begins. Some 5000 Indian tipis are already clustered on the outskirts of town. Two hundred Mexican longhorn cattle have been brought in from Medicine Hat. There's even a replica of Fort Whoop-up, that notorious whiskey-traders' fort of 50 years ago, built on the edge of the fair grounds.

Boom Years

And everyone is feeling good. These are Calgary's boom years. More than $20 million in building permits have been issued this year. Although no one knows it, that's a record that won't be matched until 1950. The population is booming, too. In the past five years, the city's population has tripled, to close to 45 000 people.

Close to half of these people were born in Canada. And almost half of those were born in Ontario, with only 5000 native Alberta sons and daughters. Some 25 000 people have come to Calgary from outside Canada. Of these 15 000 are from Great Britain, with just over 3000 each from Germany and the United States.

The building industry in the city is at a peak. Almost one quarter of the work force is in construction. The largest brickworks in Calgary is turning out up to 80 000 bricks a day. The Palliser Hotel is being built and the Canadian Pacific Railway

Calgary's Eighth Avenue in 1910.

sheds are well underway. Last year, a new power plant was finished, and now Calgarians are sure of cheap power. There are 50 cars on the 100 km of track for the street railway, and a new city hall has the people of the city cheering. The city ranks fourth in North America in building construction.

The same corner of Eighth Avenue during the 1925 Stampede. In the parade drove "the World's largest team (40 horses and 10 wagons Grain)."

A street scene during the 1914 oil boom.

Problems

Some people aren't quite as happy. Women's groups are trying to get city council to censor movies being shown in the city. And the fact that the Chinese have formed their own YMCA hasn't made them forget that only last year, Calgary cooks went on strike to protest the employment of Chinese in restaurants.

But all that's forgotten in the excitement of the stampede. A cowboy band from Oregon leads the parade. Original members of the North West Mounted Police are marching there too. And Tom Three Persons defeats Cyclone in the bucking bronc event.

It gives Calgarians something pleasant to remember over the next few years. The next year, 1913, sees the start of a depression. Population grows slowly. Construction slows. Oil is discovered near the city in 1914, creating a minor flurry of interest. But after that, the city won't see such boom days again for another 40 years.

The gardens on the left were landscaped by the CPR for the people of Calgary to enjoy.

Canada Looks Ahead

Barn raising, Roland, Manitoba, 1912.

The end of the Laurier era marked the end of a long process by which Canada became a country. Canada entered the twentieth century as a modern nation. There were nine provinces from the Atlantic to the Pacific Ocean. Millions of people from all parts of the earth had come to settle the new country. There were factories in cities, turning out a wide range of manufactured goods; brass beds, ploughs, stoves, suits, and many other things. The grasslands of the prairies had been transformed into rich wheat farms. Railways ran from sea to sea. The first airplanes had flown in Canadian skies.

Canada was still a country of shaky compromise. There were tensions between French-speaking and English-speaking Canadians. Many English-speaking Canadians looked down on foreign immigrants who were not white or who did not speak English. There were also religious conflicts. Women still could not vote.

A Sense of Identity

Despite these tensions, Canada was slowly becoming a nation. People began to think of themselves as Canadians first, rather than British, or Irish, or Ukrainian, or Italian. It was harder for some groups — the Chinese and the French for example. There were still many immigrants coming to Canada, increasing the country's population.

Douglas McCurdy flies Alexander Graham Bell's *Silver Dart* at Baddeck Bay, Nova Scotia, 1909.

It was a young growing nation. Farms were still being cleared. Men and women moved to the frontiers of the country, clearing land, working the mines, and cutting the forests. Roads and rail lines were still being built to bring settlers to new areas of the country.

The Wonderful Century

Looking back from 1900
Let us reverse the wheels of progress to 100 years ago. Many of today's "necessities" disappear. As we go back to 1800, the electric light goes out. The telephone, phonograph and telegraph disappear. Sewing machines, harvesters, gas engines, passenger elevators and steam fire-engines are no more. No longer are there photographs. The printing press dwindles to a clumsy hand machine. There are no cash registers or typewriters, no india rubber or celluloid goods, no aluminum, steel or great suspension bridges. All pasteurizing, knowledge of germs, sanitary plumbing, antiseptics, anesthetics, X-ray machines and artificial limbs disappear. There are no air brakes, dynamos, steamships, storage batteries, dynamite, lucifer matches or soda water. In 1800 it will be 25 years before a single mile of railway track will be laid anywhere in the world.

From an article in The Vancouver Province, *December 15, 1900*

These people were also pioneers; their lives were very similar to those of the pioneers who settled the Canadas a century before.

But Canada in the 1900s was rapidly becoming an urban country. More and more people were living in cities. Electric lights lit the streets. Electric streetcars ran alongside automobiles on city streets. Tall buildings were being built. But most people still lived in small homes or rented flats. Factory workers were often very poor. Immigrants often lived in ghettos, faced with problems of poverty and prejudice. Schools were filled with children learning to be Canadians.

Canada and the World

Canada was beginning to assert its independence in the larger world community. No longer was Canada regarded as merely an extension of Britain. It would still be some time before Canada would be completely free of British control. But Canada was on its way to being seen as a separate country by other nations.

The twentieth century appeared to offer even greater promise for Canada. Modern industry and science seemed to offer a good life for everyone. Poverty and isolation would be eliminated. Canada was a nation rich in resources. It had the best of everything. It seemed obvious that, in Laurier's words, "the twentieth century shall be the century of Canada."

Questions

Can You Recall?

1. What were the three major aims of Macdonald's national policy?
2. What was Canada's population in 1900?
3. In the 1800s, how long was the average work day? How many days did people work each a week?
4. Why were children employed in mines and factories in the 19th century?
5. Why did Canadian workers form trade unions?
6. State three things that women could not do in 1900 that men were able to do?
7. In what province and in what year did women first get the right to vote?
8. What important part did Clifford Sifton play in the history of western Canada?
9. When did Alberta and Saskatchewan become provinces?
10. What important change in shipbuilding affected the Maritimes in the 1880s? How did it affect the region?
11. What role did the Chinese play in the early history of British Columbia? What problems did they face?
12. Why did some people in Quebec not want to fight in the Boer War?

Ideas for Discussion

1. Discuss the role of labour unions in Canada today. Compare working conditions for men, women, and children in the nineteenth century with those of today.
2. Discuss changes that have taken place in the rights and roles of women since the 1880s. Why do you think women had so few rights 100 years ago? How do you think women felt about this condition?
3. Describe the changes that took place in the lives of Canadians between 1867 and 1900. Select five events or inventions you feel brought about the most important changes during this time. Discuss the importance of these events and inventions. Compare your list with the lists of other students.
4. Discuss Laurier's efforts to make Canada less of a British colony. Explain why, in the end, his efforts appeared to satisfy nobody.

Do Some Research

1. Interview someone from a trade union and someone from a business about working conditions in Canada today. Find out how they view the role of unions.
2. Prepare a report on one of the following inventions:
   a) the airplane   d) the telephone
   b) the automobile   e) the motion picture
   c) the electric light   f) the phonograph
   Find out how the invention affected the lives of people around 1900.
3. Prepare an oral report on one of the following women:
   a) Emily Stowe   c) Lucy Maud Montgomery
   b) Nellie McClung   d) Emily Carr
4. Prepare a research report on the contributions to Canadian life of one of the following immigrant groups:
   a) Italian   d) Ukrainian
   b) Mennonite   e) Chinese
   c) Hutterite   f) Japanese
5. Prepare a research report on the Boer War and Canada's role in it.
6. By 1905, Canada had nine provinces. What British colony was to become Canada's tenth province? When did this colony join Confederation and why?

Be Creative

1. Draw a series of cartoons showing working conditions in the 1800s in Canada.
2. Write a letter from an eastern European immigrant arriving on the prairies at the turn of the century.
3. Imagine you are a suffragette. Write a letter to a newspaper telling how you feel about not being allowed to vote.
4. Write a song or poem about one of the following things in 19th century Canada:
   a) immigration   b) child labour   c) women's rights
5. Prepare a mural showing the changes in Canadian life from 1867 to 1900.
6. Reread "The Wonderful Century" on page 287. Write an article like this listing inventions that have come into use since 1900. Explain how these inventions have changed our way of life.

A Class History

Canadians come from many different backgrounds. They arrived in this country at different times. Here are some examples:
A native person whose family has been here for thousands of years;
A French colonist who came across the Atlantic with Champlain;
A Loyalist who came north from the United States after the American Revolution;
Someone who left Ireland after the Irish Potato Famine;
A European or Asian who came to help build the railway;
Someone who came to settle the West at the turn of the century;
An immigrant who came in the period just after World War II;
A political refugee from Hungary, Uganda or Vietnam.

1. Interview your relatives to find out as much as you can about your family's history. Here are some questions you could ask. (Not all questions may apply to your family.)

a) When did the family come to Canada?
b) What country did they come from?
c) Why did they decide to come?
d) Did they live in a rural area or in a town in the old country? What kind of work did they do?
e) Did they live in a rural area or in a town in Canada? What kind of work did they find?
f) Have the family moved from one part of Canada to another? Why or why not?
g) What difficulties have your family had in Canada? What do they like about living here?

Include an entertaining family story or a "biocard" of a family member who particularly interests you. If you can, illustrate your report with photographs. (Be careful with these; they must be returned to your family's collection.)

2. Assemble the reports into a class history book. Use it to put together some class statistics.

a) Make a timeline for the years 1600 to 2000. Start with an indication of the number of native families in your class who were already in Canada in 1600. Mark on the timeline when other families arrived in Canada. Are the times of arrival spread out over the timeline? Or are they grouped together at one or two points on it?

b) What countries did class members or their families come from? Show this information on a bar graph like the one below. Remember that some class members may have relatives from two or more countries.

What do these statistics tell you about your class and your community? Do you think your community is typical of Canada? List some advantages and disadvantages of living in a community like yours.

Ethnic groups in Canada.

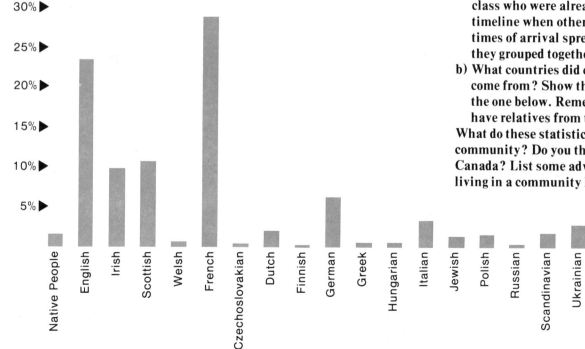

Recreation

The cast for "The Cake Walk" at the carnival, Carleton Place.

At the Montreal Curling Club.

Ascending the Illecillewaet Glacier, B

Mountaineering, British Columbia.

On a caribou hunt, New Brunswick.

McGill University students play hockey, Montreal.

Backlot baseball, Winnipeg.

Community picnic.

Field hockey, Manitoba.

Junior swimming class, Peterborough, Ontario.

The brass band, Metcalfe, Ontario.

Commerce

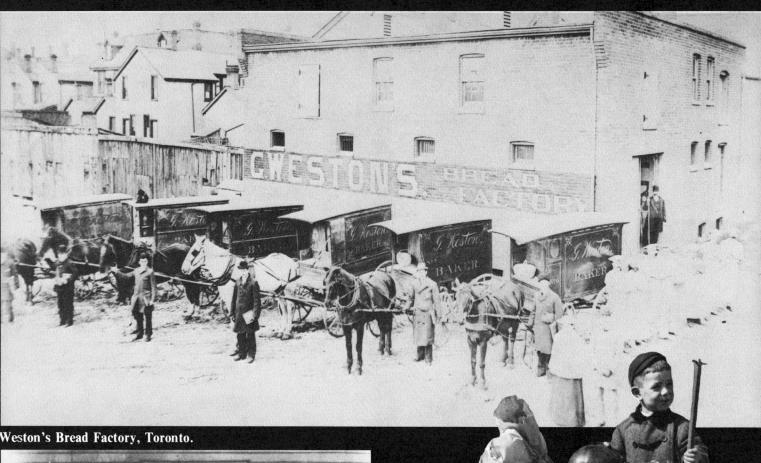

Weston's Bread Factory, Toronto.

The blacksmith's shop.

Delivery boy.

A good place for business? Lethbridge, Alta.

Kingston Market.

The general store.

Delivering oil, Winnipeg.

Paying with gold dust, the Klondike.

Land and Sea

The beginning of better things.

Clearing the land, Saskatchewan.

Breaking new soil.

Cutting clover.

The harvest, Manitoba.

The fishing weir, St. Andrews, New Brunswick.

Lumbering, Nova Scotia.

Building fishing schooners, Lunenburg, Nova Scotia.

Sorting timber at the lower boom, Fort William, Quebec.

The timber coves, Sillery, Quebec.

People

The Klondike miner.

CPR survey party, British Columbia.

Off to school, Saskatchewan.

Sugaring off, Ontario.

The spinner, Quebec.

Immigrant, Saint John, N.B.

A Japanese family, Vancouver.

Immigrant family, Manitoba.

NWMP band, Fort Walsh, Alberta.

Boys in a kayak.

Glossary

(*n.*) = noun; (*v.*) = verb

---

abolish   to put an end to, to do away with

absentee landowner   one who owns land and rents it to other people, but does not live on or near that land

absolute   complete; without any limits

abuse   *1)* to treat badly; *2)* to make bad use of

access   a way in; a way to reach something

advisor   one who gives others advice on an important matter

agricultural   matters to do with farming

ally   friend; nations that fight on the same side in a war are allies

amend   to change

artillery   large, heavy guns, such as cannons

assembly   see **legislative assembly**

asylum   *1)* place of safety; *2)* hospital for people who are considered insane

banish   to send out of the area or the country as a punishment

bankrupt   to have lost one's money in business; being unable to pay one's debts

barbarity   rude, coarse or cruel behaviour

barricade   structure that bars the way, that keeps people out

Basque   one who comes from the Basque region between Spain and France

bee   meeting of pioneers to do work together, such as quilting or building a barn

bill of rights   official list of things people have a right to. Most bills of rights list such rights as the right to say what you want to, the right to vote and the right to own property

binder   farm machine that ties bundles of grain together

bison   large, shaggy animal with a humped back. The American buffalo is a member of the bison family.

blacksmith   one who makes iron tools by hand

boarding house   house where you pay for meals and a place to sleep, as in a hotel

boom   sudden growth; sudden activity that makes prices rise. A housing boom occurs when many houses are bought and sold and the price of these houses goes up.

booty   goods taken from an enemy

boundary   imaginary line marking the end of something, *e.g.* the boundary (border) of a country

bribe   money or other valuables offered to someone to persuade them to do something

brick kiln   oven where clay bricks are baked to make them hard

bucket brigade   line of people passing buckets of water from one to another to put out a fire

campaign   series of activities that are put together to achieve a goal. A political campaign is planned to get someone elected; a military campaign is planned to win a war.

canal   inland waterway built for transportation purposes

caravan   group of people travelling together, usually with several vehicles, such as wagons

carding mill   mill where wool is combed to make it ready for spinning

chandler   one who makes and sells candles

chinking   material such as mud or plaster used between logs, bricks or stones in the walls of a house to keep heat in and cold out

cholera   serious disease of the intestines that spreads easily among people

churn   to stir and shake in a churn, usually to make butter

civilian   someone not in the armed forces

civil law   law that has to do with the rights of people. (*Civil*

law deals with matters between people about such things as money or land. *Criminal* law deals with crimes against the law, such as theft or murder.)

civil servant   one who has a job with the government

civil war   war between people who live in the same country

claim   to say that someone owns or has a right to something

Classics   usually, the languages, literature and arts of the ancient Greeks and Romans

clearing   open area, *e.g.* a clearing in the forest

coalition government   government formed by two or more political parties, usually when one party does not win enough seats in Parliament to outvote the other parties (form a majority)

colonist   one who helps to found a colony; one who lives in a new colony

colony   settlement of people who have left their country to live somewhere else, on land claimed by the country they left

commerce   buying and selling in large amounts; the practice of business

common   *1)* belonging to everyone; *2)* usual

community   group of people living in the same area

competition   contest between two or more participants for power, money, land or other goals

compromise   agreement to end an argument. Each side gives up something so that both sides meet part way.

conditions   things that can make an activity easy or hard, *e.g.* good (or bad) driving conditions.

confederacy   a joining together of countries, states or tribes

confederation   the joining together of several political units into one large unit or country

conference   meeting to discuss something

conflict   fight or struggle

conform   to do the same as everyone else

conquer   to win in war; to gain by fighting

conservative   wanting to keep things as they are, not wanting change; careful

constitution   written laws that say how a country will be governed

continent   one of the seven large land masses on earth. North America and Europe are continents.

contract   official (usually written) agreement between people or companies

control   to have complete power over

controversy   difference of opinion; argument

convert   to persuade someone to change his or her religion

corduroy road   road made of logs

coronation   act of crowning a king, queen or emperor

council   group of people who make decisions for a larger group, *e.g.* a city council decides things for all the people in that city

create   to make; to bring into being

criticism   finding fault with something

culture   habits, arts and way of life of a group or nation

custom   habit shared by a group or nation

customs   department of government that collects taxes on things brought into the country

cycle   series of events that repeats itself; the seasons of the year are a cycle

decade   period of 10 years

debt   something owed to someone else, usually money

decisive   *1)* In connection with a person — able to make decisions quickly; *2)* in connection with an action — a firm move that solves a problem once and for all

defence   protection against attack

depression   time when business is not going well and many people lose their jobs

delegates   people who represent larger groups, usually at meetings

dependent   relying on someone else for support and help

deport to send someone considered dangerous or living without permission in a country, out of that country

desert to run away from

detachment group of soldiers

develop *1)* to grow; to change with time; *2)* to make something grow and change

diplomat one who officially represents his or her country in another country. The Canadian ambassador to the United States is a diplomat.

discipline (*n.*) strict training; (*v.*) to train or punish

discontent unhappiness

dominate to control by strength or power

drawbridge bridge that can be raised and lowered

drill group of exercises or lessons repeated over and over again

drought long-continued dry weather; lack of rain

duty *1)* something which must be done; *2)* tax on imported or exported goods

dyke wall of raised earth or other material that keeps water from flooding an area

economic having to do with money

editor person in charge of a newspaper, magazine or other publication, who decides what will go into that publication

eliminate to get rid of

emerge to come out of something that surrounds, *e.g.* to emerge from water

emigrate to leave your own country to live in another country

enforce to make sure something happens; if you enforce a law, you make sure that everyone obeys it.

engage to take part in

epidemic rapid spreading of a disease

equality being equal; having the same rights

establish to set up; to bring into being

exclusive licence the right to be the only one to do something. If you have exclusive licence to

trade furs in a certain area, you are the only one allowed to trade there.

exile (*n.*) separation from one's native country; (*v.*) to send someone out of the country as a punishment

expand to grow larger

expedition voyage, journey or march for a special purpose

expel to force someone to leave

explorer one who explores, who travels into new lands to find out what is there

export to send something out of the country for sale elsewhere

extinction total doing away with; wiping out

factory place where goods are made using labour and machinery

federal having to do with the central government of a country that is made up of smaller parts, such as provinces

federal union joining together of a number of units such as provinces under a central government, where the units each keep their own local governments.

fertile able to help things grow well. Fertile soil produces a large crop.

flax plant whose stems are used for making linen

fleur-de-lis French word for the lily — the floral emblem of France and Quebec

fodder food for animals

fort strong place or group of buildings that can be defended against an enemy

fortress large, well-protected fort

foundry place where metal is melted and made into various things

freeman *1)* person who is not a slave; *2)* citizen with full rights

freight goods carried by truck, train, ship, plane or other means of transportation

fulling mill place where cloth is cleaned and thickened

garrison soldiers living in a town or fort to defend it

gold field area where gold is found

government people who officially run a country, province, region, city, etc.

governor official appointed to rule a colony

governor-general official appointed by the king or queen to represent him or her in a country such as Canada

grant (*n.*) gift; (*v.*) to give away

grievance reason for being angry

grist mill place where grain is ground into flour

guerrilla tactics type of warfare where a small group of fighters carries out sudden raids and ambushes

habitant farmer of New France

habitation French word meaning a place to live

handbill printed notice passed out by hand

hardship difficulty; something that makes life hard

harness leather straps used to attach a horse to a wagon or plough

harrow farm tool with teeth or sharp discs which is pulled across the earth to break it up

headquarters place from which an organization such as an army is controlled

homespun cloth made of yarn spun at home

homestead piece of public land given to settlers in the Canadian West

horizon line where the earth and sky seem to meet

hull ship's frame

Ice Age one of several periods, many thousands of years ago, when ice covered much of the earth's surface

identity special features that, taken together, make a person or a group different from others; special character of a person or group

immigrate to move to a new country from one's home country

immigrants people who come to live in a new country

imperial having to do with an emperor or an empire

implements tools

import to bring goods for sale into a country

impose to officially put something onto something or someone. A tax can be imposed on goods. A fine can be imposed on people.

impress to have a strong effect on someone's mind or feelings; to cause high admiration

incorporate to make something part of something else

independent managing by one's self; free; not under another's power

indigo plant from which blue dye is made

industry general name for any large-scale making or harvesting of goods for sale, *e.g.* the clothing industry; the mining industry

influence (*n.*) the power to mould or sway someone else's opinions or actions; (*v.*) to mould or sway another's opinions or actions

inland away from the sea

insecure *1)* not safe or strong; *2)* feeling unsafe or weak

insubordination refusal to obey someone who should be obeyed

intercolonial connecting two or more colonies

intendant French word meaning the person in charge; the director

interfere *1)* to take part in the affairs of others without their invitation; *2)* to get in the way

interior the area of a country away from its seacoasts or borders

intermarriage marriage between members of different groups

international having to do with two or more countries

invader one who comes to take something not his or hers by force; usually refers to attacking armies

invasion the act of invading

invest to lend money to a business or bank in the hopes of making more money

investigate *1)* to look into something in a detailed way; *2)* to study and examine officially

irregular forces soldiers who are not in the regular army

isolation being alone

knight (*n.*) man who is entitled to use the word "Sir" before his name; (*v.*) to make someone into a knight

labourer worker who does physical labour

legend story about something said to have happened in the past, which is passed down through generations. A legend may or may not be true, but many people think that the story behind a legend is true.

legislative assembly group of peple elected to make the laws; people elected to the legislature

liberal one who favours change and progress

liberation the act of setting free

lime kiln place where limestone is changed into lime by heating and burning. Lime is used for mortar and as a soil improver.

loyal faithful. Someone who is loyal to a government accepts that government and agrees to do what that government tells him or her to do.

Loyalist one who remained loyal to Britain during the American revolution

loyalty loyal feelings; promises to be loyal

lure (*n.*) attraction; (*v.*) to attract

mainland main part of a body of land, not including off-shore islands

maize corn

majority more than half; 50 percent plus one

manufacture the making of goods in a factory

manufacturer owner of a company that makes goods in a factory

maritime of or by the sea

mast long, upright pole that supports a ship's sails and rigging

medicinal having the qualities of a medicine; healing

merchant one who sells goods

Métis one of mixed European and Indian ancestry; child of marriage between Indian and European parents

migration large-scale movement of people or animals from one place to another

militia army made up of ordinary citizens who only become soldiers during times of war or emergency

minister *1)* preacher or similar religious leader; *2)* member of the Cabinet in a parliamentary government

missionary one who sets out to convert others to his or her religion

molasses dark, sweet syrup made from sugar cane

monarch ruling king or queen

morale state of mind; mood

municipal local level of government for villages, towns and cities

muskeg marshy, swampy land

mutineer one who turns against army or navy authority and tries to take control by force; rebel

mutual affecting two people or groups equally

nationality the state of being a citizen of a certain country, *e.g. We are of Canadian nationality; My nationality is Canadian.*

natural resources things found in nature that human beings are able to use. Water, forests, iron ore and petroleum are all natural resources.

naval having to do with the navy

navvy labourer in railroad or other construction work

negotiation discussions between people or groups who are trying to reach agreement on an issue

network organization of connected things or people spread out like a fishnet, *e.g.* a network of fur forts; a spy network

neutral not taking sides, especially in war; neither for nor against

nutrition the effects of food on our health

oath important pledge or promise, often given while placing a hand on the Bible

offset make up for; balance

oppose disagree with; argue against

Opposition in Parliament, the party or parties that lost the election. The Opposition sits on the opposite side of the House from the governing party.

oppression unjust putting down of a person's rights or freedom; harsh, cruel actions used to keep others powerless

overland over, or via land

parallel of latitude a series of imaginary lines running east to west round the globe. The 49th parallel of latitude forms much of the boundary between Canada and the U.S.A.

pardoned forgiven

parliament name given to the national legislature of Britain or Canada. There are two Houses to Canada's parliament, the Commons and the Senate.

patriot one who is strongly loyal to his or her country

Patriotes group of French Canadian and Irish Catholic patriots who opposed the British in Lower Canada in the 1830s

pemmican dried buffalo meat

pension regular payment of money to people who are past the official age to stop working (retirement age)

permafrost in very cold regions, a layer of earth — just beneath the ground's surface — which remains frozen even in summer

permanent unchanging; lasting a long time

persecute to purposely make life difficult and unpleasant for innocent people because of their race, religion, or beliefs

pioneer one who does something new or goes somewhere few people have gone before

policy things a government or group says they wish to do

political having to do with politics or politicians

population all people living in a given area; the number of people living there

potlatch special celebration of the Northwest Coast Indians

prejudice hatred for or bad opinion of all people of a certain race, religion or nationality; an opinion formed without examining all sides beforehand

proclamation official public announcement

production *1)* the making of things in a factory or industry; *2)* the amount of things made by a factory or industry

profession type of work which requires a high level of training, *e.g.* medicine, law, engineering, teaching

profit money made from business activities; the difference between the cost of something and money made selling it

proposal idea; suggestion; plan of action

prospector one who searches for valuable minerals such as gold

prosperous rich, well-to-do

province one of several large political units within a country. Canada is made up of 10 provinces.

provisional intended to last a short time, until something permanent takes its place; temporary

provisioner one who sells or supplies food and other goods

provisions food and other basic necessities

public service service such as police, road building and mail delivery provided by the government

quilt bed-covering made up of many small pieces of cloth sewn together

rebel (*n.*) one who rises against an authority or government because he or she thinks it's unjust; (*v.*) to rise against an authority or government because one thinks it's unjust

rebellion battle of rebels to change or overthrow an authority or government they think is unjust

recommend   suggest that something be done
red ochre   red paint made from minerals
reform   (*n.*) change made to make society or government better than it was before; (*v.*) to make society or government better than it was before
reformer   one who wants to better society or government through change
Reformer   name given to politicians who opposed the Family Compact in Upper Canada in the 1830s
regiment   large body of soldiers under one commander
region   area of land, identified by what it is near, or contains, *e.g.* the Atlantic region; a hilly region
remedy   cure or medicine
repeating rifle   rifle that can fire several shots before being reloaded
representative   one who acts on behalf of another person or group
republic   form of government where the head of state (usually a president) is elected by the people
resentment   stored-up angry or unhappy feelings
reserve   area of land set aside for native peoples
resist   oppose; defend
resistance   defence against an attack or invasion
resort   scenic area with hotels and recreation facilities
restrict   *1)* to set up limits; *2)* to keep something or someone within limits
revenge   getting back at someone for some harm done
revolution   armed overthrow of a government by the people so that they can set up a new government
ridicule   (*n.*) words or actions that make another person look stupid; (*v.*) to make fun of someone
right   power or freedom that all people share, *e.g.* the right to own land or the right to vote in elections
riot   wild, usually violent, public outburst or disturbance

ritual   solemn event or ceremony, usually religious
road houses   in early Canada, inns or hotels at regular distances along much-travelled roads
roaming   wandering
rocker box   device used to separate gold from river gravel
route   pathway or course
routine   *1)* fixed way of doing things; *2)* a regular act or habit
Royal Engineers   division of the British Army responsible for building roads and bridges
rural   of the country or farm, as opposed to the city or town

sachem   member of the Iroquois ruling council
saint's day   in Roman Catholic religion, a special day set aside to honour a saint
salary   money earned for work
salt pork   pork preserved by pickling in salt and water
sandbar   ridge or island of sand formed by tides or currents
school trustee   one of the elected officials who oversee the running of local schools
scurvy   disease caused by a lack of Vitamin C in the diet
section   unit of farmland 2.6 km²
seigneur   in New France, a lord who owned large areas of land rented out to farmers
settlement   area of country newly lived in by people who have come to start a community there; colony; small, isolated community
settler   one who comes to live in a new area; pioneer; colonist
shaman   native Indian religious leader or healer
shanty   crude wooden hut or lean-to
shipyard   place where boats and ships are built
siege   surrounding of a town or fort by an enemy army to cut off supplies while attacking
skirmish   small battle
smelter   place where ores are heated to produce metals such as copper or lead
source   place something starts from, *e.g.* a river's source
spar   pole, attached to the mast, used to support a sail

spiritual   having to do with matters of a religious nature
spoilage   loss of food or supplies caused by spoiling, mould or rot
stalemate   stage of conflict when neither side seems able to win; deadlock
strategy   *1)* plan of action in war; *2)* carefully designed plan for achieving something
subsidy   money paid to support a company or person, usually by the government
suffragette   woman who worked to gain women the right to vote (suffrage)
support   assist, help; prop up
surrender   to give up; to admit defeat
survey   measuring and mapping of land
surveyor   one who measures and maps an area of land
survivor   one who remains alive, *e.g. There were two survivors of that plane crash.*

tannery   place where animal hides are made into leather
tariff   tax paid on goods brought into one country from another country; usually to protect local industries from competition from foreign countries
tax   money collected by a government to pay for the services it provides to the public
technology   general name for all the tools and machines that people invent in order to do things faster or better
telegraph   method of sending messages along wires, using electrical currents
tenant   one who rents housing and/or land from a landlord
tension   mental strain, worry
territory   *1)* large area of land; *2)* area over which someone claims power
textile   cloth
thatch   straw used to make roofs for houses
threaten   to put in danger
title   legal document that shows a person or company owns a particular piece of land

Tory   name given to Conservative politicians
township   piece of land with an area of 36 square miles (100 km²)
trade union   organization that protects the rights of workers to fair wages and good working conditions
traditional   done in the same way for a long period of time
trait   special mark or characteristic of a person or thing
traitor   person who double-crosses or betrays his or her country or cause
transcontinental   reaching across a continent
travois   wood frame pulled by a dog or horse, used by Plains people to move their possessions
treason   the act of double-crossing or betraying one's country
treaty   agreement that ends a state of war or conflict between two countries or groups
tundra   treeless arctic landscape of shrubs, low bushes and ground plants
tunic   shirt-like jacket

unemployment   the condition of being without a job
united   joined together
union   *1)* a combining or joining *2)* see **trade union**
urban   of the city or town, as opposed to the country or farm

Venetian   person from Venice, Italy
vie   compete, challenge
Vikings   sailors and sea-raiders from Scandinavia of the 10th and 11th centuries
violate   break a rule, law, or agreement
volunteer   *1)* one who freely chooses to go on a military expedition; *2)* one who does a job without expecting pay
vying   see **vie**

worker's compensation   money paid to workers injured on the job; a form of insurance paid for by employers and government
workplace   place of work, such as a factory, office, or store

Index

Aberdeen, Lady, 258
Acadia, 68-77, 78, 100, 103, 108, 111
Alaska, 20, 21, 26, 185, 280
Alexander, William, 74, 101
American Civil War, 177, 194, 201, 202, 232
American Revolution, 48, 107, 118-123, 128, 160, 161, 165, 166, 167
Amundsen, Roald, 63
Arctic, 19, 21, 36-37, 48, 50, 194
Argall, Samuel, 71, 72
Arnold, Benedict, *123*
Asbestos, P.Q., 272
Australia, 163, 281, 283
Austria-Hungary, 267

Baffin Island, 54
Barkerville, B.C., 188
Basques, 50, 103
Batoche, battle of, 237
Beaver Dam, battle of, 157
Begbie, Matthew, 219
Bell, Alexander Graham, 233, 287
Beothuk, 41, 48
Bering, Vitus, 185
Biencourt, 71
Big Bear, 236, 237
Bjarni, 54
Blackfoot, 34, 226, 227
Blacks, 92, 99, 131, 177, 276, 278
Boer War, 241, 247, 280, 282-283
Booker, Colonel, 203
Boston, 74, 99, 102, 119, 120, 122, 185, 233
Brant, Joseph, *129*
Brantford, 129, 233
British North America Act, 204
Brock, Isaac, 155, 156
Brown, George, 177, 195, 199, 200, 249, 253
Brulé, Etienne, 80, *81*
Bytown, 232

Cabot, John, 51, 58
Calgary, 271, 284-285
California, 20, 21, 26, 185, 197
Canadian National Railway, 262
Canadian Pacific Railway, 228-231, 237, 239, 253, 262, 270, 274, 284
Cape Breton Island, 59, 76, 251,

Caribbean, 50, 58, 128, 129
Cariboo, 6, 175, 188, 189, 196, 218
Carmack, George, 242
Cartier, George, Etienne, 195, 199, 200, 207, *249*
Cartier, Jacques, 51, 60-61, 65, 78, 88, 249
Cataraqui, 132, 133
Champlain, Hélène Boulle, *79*
Champlain, Samuel de, 51, 64, 65, 68, 70, 78, 80, 84, 88, 90
Charlottetown, 101, 103, 220, *Conference*, 200, 203, 220
Chateau Clique, 160
Chateau Richer, 8
Chateauguay, battle of, 157
China, 56, 58, 63, 80
Chinese, 229, 276, 278, 285, 286
Churchill River, 180
Columbia River, 26
Columbus, Christopher, 50, 55, 58
Company of One Hundred Associates, 84
Confederation, 168, 192-209, 259
Constitution Act, 1867, 204
Cook, James, 174, 184, 185
Cormack, William Epps, 41
Craigellachie, B.C., 229
Cree, 21, 226, 236, 237
Crooked Lake, Sask., 236
Crowfoot 226, 227
Crozier, Leif, 236, 237
Cypress Hills Massacre, 225

Declaration of Independence, 122, 128
Deganawidah, *47*
Denys, Nicolas, 73
Derick, Carrie, 257
Detroit, 118, 155
Dollard des Ormeaux, 89
Donnacona, 60, 61
Dorion, Antoine Aimé, 197
Douglas, James, 175, 186
Doukhobors, 256, 268
Duck Lake, battle of, 236, 237
Dumont, Gabriel, *235,* 236, 237
Dunsmuir, Robert, 276
Durham, Lord, 167, 168-169, 200
Dutch, 77, 89, 99, 132

Eastern Townships, 129, 136, 272
Eastern Woodlands people, 19, 21, 32, 35, 42-47
Eaton, Timothy 223, 243
Edmonton, Alta., 243, 270, 271
Eric the Red, 54, 55
Ericson, Leif, 54, *55*
Eskimo, *see* Inuit

Family Compact, 164, 165, 166
Fenians, 202-203
Fenton, Faith, 243
Fils de la Liberté, 161
Fish Creek, battle of, 236, 237
Fleming, Sandford, 233
Florida, 107, 118, 120, 197
Fort Beauséjour, 111
Fort Carlton, 237
Fort Duquesne, 110, 111, 112, 113
Fort Erie, 11, 203
Fort Frontenac, 109, 133
Fort Garry, 13
Fort Henry, 170
Fort Langley, 186
Fort Niagara, 112, 117
Fort Prince of Wales, 180, 181
Fort Vancouver, 175, 186
Fort Victoria, 175, 186-187
Fort Whoop-up, 225, 284
Franklin, Benjamin, *121*
Franklin, John, 17
Fraser, Simon, 174, 177, 181
Fraser River, 175, 187, 188, 229
Fredericton, 130
Frobisher, Martin, 51, *63*
Frontenac, Louis, 85, 133
Fuca, Juan de, 184

Galt, Alexander, 195, 198, 200
Gama, Vasco da, 58
Gaspé, 60, 88, 114
George III, 118, 122
Georgian Bay 80, 88, 239
Germans, 77, 99, 132, 267, 284
Grand Banks, 74, 102
Grand River, 129
Granville, 274
Great Lakes 19, 40, 42, 44, 109, 111, 213
Greenland, 36, 50, 54
Groseilliers, Médart, 96, *97*
Gudred, 55
Gulf of Mexico, 80, 194

Haldimand, Frederick, 132
Haliburton, Thomas, 121
Halifax, N.S., 76, 100, 119, 158-159
Hamilton, Ont. 170, 232, 251, 253
Hawaii, 184, 276
Heart's Content, Nfld., 232
Hébert, Louis, *71*
Heina, B.C., 16
Helmcken, John, 219
Henday, Anthony, 97, 180
Hiawatha, *47*
Hochelaga, 61
Holland, 63

Hong Kong, 276, 281
Hoodless, Adelaide Hunter, 258
Howe, Joseph, 199, *201*
Hudson, Henry, 51, 63, 96
Hudson Bay, 40, 63, 75, 96, 109, 174, 180, 182, 212
Hudson's Bay Co., 96-97, 108, 138, 180-181, 182, 183, 186, 212-213, 269
Hull, General, 155
Huron, 42-47, 48, 75, 80, 88-89
Hutterites, 268

Iceland, 50, 54
Ile d'Orléans, 90, 92, 114
Ile Royale, 76
Ile St. Jean, 76, 101
India, 21, 56, 58, 61, 110, 281
Indians (East), 276
Ingstad, Helge and Anne, 55
Inuit, 19, 21, 36-37, 48, 55
Ireland, 59, 160, 178, 202, 232
Irish, 99, 103, 178-179, 182, 202
Iroquois, 42-47, 60, 61, 75, 80, 84, 87, 88, 89, 129
Italian, 58, 184, 286

Japanese, 63, 276, 277
Jews, 266, 269
Johnson, Pauline, 263

Kelsey, Henry, 97, 180
Kingston, Ont., 133, 170-171, 206
Kirke, David, 84
Klondike, 6, 242-243, 280

Labrador, 55
Lachine, P.Q., 80
Lagimodière, Marie-Anne Gaboury, 216
Lake Champlain, 80
Lake Erie, 129
Lake Huron, 39
Lake Manitoba, 82
Lake of the Woods, 265
Lake Ontario, 129, 132, 166, 170
Lake Superior, 126, 237
Lake Winnipeg, 82
L'Anse aux Meadows, 55
Larsen, Henry, 63
La Salle, Sieur de, 80
Laurier, Wilfrid, 241, 262-263, 280, 281, 283, 286, 287
Laval, Francois de, 84, 92
La Vérendrye, Pierre, 82, 97
Lepine Ambrose, 217
Lévis, General, 115, 117
Lexington, battle of, 122

l'Incarnation, Marie de, 87
London Conference, 204
Long Sault, 89
Louisbourg, 76, 109, 110, 112, 114
Louisiana, 77, 80, 197
Loyalists, 7, 128-133, 136, 140, 155, 164, 171, 176
Lundy's Lane, battle of, 157
Lunenburg, 6, 77

Macdonald, John A., 177, 195, 196-199, 200, 207, 213, 225, 228, 238, 248-249, 253, 259, 262
Mackenzie, Alexander (explorer), 177, 181
Mackenzie, Alexander (politician), 228, 248
Mackenzie, William Lyon, 164-167
Mackenzie River, 20, 32
Magellan, Ferdinand, 60
Mance, Jeanne, 88
Marconi, Guglielmo, 4, 233
Massachusetts, 98, 99, 107, 120
Massey, Daniel, 251
McClung, Nellie, 259
McDougall, William, 214
McGee, D'Arcy, 197, 200, 203, 249
Mennonites, 268
Mercier, Honoré, 241
Métis 182, 183, 212-217, 234-239, 241
Mexico, 20, 21, 32, 97, 197
Micmac, 39, 41, 65, 72, 75, 76, 77
Miramichi River, 101
Mississauga Indians, 132
Mississippi River, 20, 80, 82, 109
Molson, 139
Monck, Governor, 200, 202, 206, 207
Montcalm, Louis Joseph, 112, 113, 114, 116, 117
Montgomery, Lucy Maud, 261
Montreal, 10, 61, 90, 93, 117, 119, 122, 139, 162, 170, 179, 232, 240-241, 254, 272
Monts, Sieur de, 64, 65, 70
Mormons, 268
Murray, James, 117

Nanaimo, B.C., 186, 253, 276
New Caledonia, 186, 187, 188, 219
New France, 65, 78-95, 109-117, 134, 136
New Orleans, 109
New Westminster, B.C., 189, 275
New York, 119, 122, 128, 130, 270
New Zealand, 281, 283

Niagara, 12, 132, 156, 157, 202, 222
Nicolet, Jean, 80
Nootka Sound, 170, 184, 185
North West Co., 138, 174, 180-183
North West Mounted Police, 224-225, 235, 236, 237, 243, 283, 285
Northwest Coast people, 21, 22-29, 174, 184, 185, 274, 278
Northwest Passage, 17, 63, 64, 184
Northwest Rebellion 48, 234-241

Ohio River, 20, 42, 109, 110, 118, 120, 154
Ojibwa, 40, 43
Oliver, Frank, 267
Onderdonk, Andrew, 229
O'Neill, Colonel, 203
Order of Good Cheer, 70
Ottawa, 206-207, 281
Ottawa River, 89, 179, 206, 207
Owen Sound, Ont. 222, 239

Pacific Scandal, 228, 229
Papineau, Louis Joseph, 161, 162, 163
Patriotes, 160-163, 168
Peace River, 243
Peterborough, Ont., 178
Placentia, Nfld, 76, 102, 103
Plains of Abraham, 107, 114, 116
Plains people 21, 32-35, 48, 227, 235-237
Plateau people, 21, 28, 30-31, 33
Polo, Marco, 56
Pontiac, 118
Port aux Basques, Nfld., 102, 103
Port Moody, B.C., 229, 274
Port Royal, 65, 70, 71, 72, 78, 108
Portugal, 50, 56, 58, 60, 98, 103
Potato Famine 178, 202
Poundmaker, 226, 237
Prince Albert, Sask., 237

Quadra, Bodega y, 185
Quebec City, 65, 78, 80, 84, 90-92, 108, 112-117, 123, 134, 139, 179, 206, 253; Q. Conference, 201, 203, 204
Queen Charlotte Islands, 24
Queenston Heights, battle of, 156

Radisson, Pierre, Esprit, 96, 97
Rebellions of 1837, 7, 160-168, 194
Red River, 177, 182-183, 186, 214-217, 234
Reformers, 165-168, 195, 253
Regina, 211, 238, 241, 270, 271

Reid, Mary, 142
Ridgeway, battle of, 203
Riel, Louis, 215-217, 234-241
Riel Rebellion (1870), 214-217, 234
Rindisbacher, Peter, 183
Roberval, Marguerite de, 65
Robinson, Peter, 178
Rocky Mountains, 30, 32, 79, 82, 186, 229, 270
Roosevelt, Teddy, 280
Rupert's Land 180, 212-213, 248
Russia, 185, 266, 267
Ryerson, Egerton, 147

St. Boniface, Man., 13
St. Charles, battle of, 162
St. Croix River, 64
St. Denis, battle of, 162
St. Eustache, battle of 162-163
Saint John, N.B., 7
St. John Island, 101
St. John River 101, 130
St. John's, Nfld., 4, 233
St. Lawrence River, 9, 42, 64, 78, 80, 112-114, 132, 138, 194, 214
Ste. Marie among the Hurons, 88-89
Ste. Foy, battle of, 117
Salaberry, Charles de, 157
San Francisco, 187, 242, 272
Saskatchewan River, 110, 234-236, 241
Schubert, Catherine, 187
Scott, Thomas, 215, 216, 239
Scottish, 77, 100, 177, 182
seigneurial system, 8, 72, 86-87, 95, 132, 135, 136
Selkirk, Lord, 174, 177, 182, 210
Shadd, Mary, 177
Shawanahdit, 41
Shelburne, N.S., 130, 131
Sierra Leone, 131
Sifton, Clifford, 263, 265, 267
Signal Hill, 4, 233
Simcoe, Elizabeth, 129, 133
Simpson, George, 180
Six Nations, 46, 227
Skagway, 280
slaves, 24, 45, 92, 99, 131, 177
Slick, Sam, 121
Smith, Donald, 228, 229
Snorri, 55
Sons of Liberty, 119, 120, 161
South Africa, 281, 282-283
Spain, 58, 60, 98, 174, 185
Stadacona, 61, 65, 78
Steele, Sam, 283
Stoney Creek, battle of, 157

Stowe, Emily, 257
Strickland, Samuel and Emma, 142
Subarctic people, 21, 38-41
Sudbury, Ont., 222, 272
Swiss, 77, 132, 183
Sydney, N.S. 272

Taché, Bishop, 216
Taché, Etienne, 198
Talon, Jean, 85, 86, 87
Tecumseh, 154, 155
Texas, 32, 197
Thetford Mines, P.Q., 272
Thompson, David, 181
Three Persons, Tom, 284, 285
Tilley, Samuel, 196
Toronto, 133, 157, 179, 222-223, 232, 270, 272
Traill, Catherine, 143, 145, 149
Trent River, 132
Trois Rivières, 93, 136
Tupper, Charles, 197, 201

Underground Railroad, 177
Ukrainian, 268, 286

Vancouver, 243, 274, 275, 278-279
Vancouver, George, 185
Vancouver Island, 15, 184, 186, 218, 276
Van Horne, William, 229, 274
Vaudreuil, Governor, 112, 114, 117
Verchères, Madeleine de, 89, 249
Victoria, 186, 189, 242, 275, 276
Victoria, Queen, 205, 206, 207, 280
Vikings, 52, 54-55, 58
Vineland, 55

War Hawks, 154
War of 1812, 154-159
Washington, George, 110, 122
Washington, D.C., 157, 232, 281
West Indies, 85, 194, 281
Williams, Eunice, 109
Windsor, Ont., 165, 222
Winnipeg, 13, 264-265, 268, 269, 270
Wolfe, James, 114, 115, 116, 117
Wolseley, Colonel, 216
Woodside, H.J., 243
World War I, 259

Yale, B.C., 188, 256
York, 133, 157, 166
Yorktown, battle of, 122
Yukon, 242, 243

Acknowledgements

Picture Credits

Illustrations are listed as they appear from top to bottom in each column on the page, and are separated by semicolons. The following abbreviations have been used:

AGO — Art Gallery of Ontario
ANQ — Archives Nationales du Québec
BCPM — British Columbia Provincial Museum
CAG — Confederation Centre Art Gallery and Museum
GA — Glenbow-Alberta Institute
HBC — Hudson's Bay Company
JRR — John Ross Robertson Collection, Metropolitan Toronto Library
MA — Manitoba Archives
MM — McCord Museum, McGill University
MTL — Metropolitan Toronto Library
NGC — National Gallery of Canada
NMC — National Museums of Canada
NA — Notman Archives, McCord Museum
OA — Ontario Archives
PAA — Provincial Archives of Alberta
PABC — Provincial Archives of British Columbia
PAC — Public Archives of Canada
PANS — Public Archives of Nova Scotia
QUA — Queen's University Archives
ROM — Royal Ontario Museum
SA — Saskatchewan Archives
SFUM — Simon Fraser University Museum
UC — United Church of Canada

20 ROM 78CUR213; 21 ROM 78CUR622; ROM 78ETH354; ROM 78CUR208; 22 PABC 948; 23 PAC F-2036; Oregon Historical Society 45452; 24 PABC 33784; 25 PAC C-24378; BCPM PN9689; 26 PABC 74728; 27 PABC 74550; SFUM; SFUM; PABC 74224; 28 BCPM 4579; 29 PABC 74499; 30 Penthouse Studios; Roy Carlson; 31 American Museum of Natural History 42946; 32 GA; ROM 912.150; MTL; 33 GA NA1344-2; 34 PAA B768; PAC C-18696; 35 Stark Museum of Art, Orange, Texas; 36 ROM 78ETH349; 37 ROM 70ETH422; ROM 70ETH418; ROM 78ETH355; 38 MTL 919.8R37.11 p.377; 39 AGO; NMC; 40 MTL 970.1C13.4 pl.14; 41 Newfoundland Museum; 44 MTL 970.1S17.4 v.3; 45 PAC C-16336; 46 NMC; New York Historical Society; 47 ROM; 52 Penthouse Studios; 53 Culver Pictures; 54 Universitetes Oldsaksamling, Oslo; 55 Library of Congress; 56 NFGC, Venice; 57 British Museum; 58 JRR 1156; 60 PAC C-8029; 62 ROM 76CAN782; 63 JRR 1658; 64 PAC F-2268; 66 PAC; 67 New York Historical Society; 71 PAC; PAC C-16952; 72 ROM 73166; 75 Stokes Collection, New York Public Library; 76 JRR 2433; 78 ROM 70CAN121; 79 Quebec Tourist Branch; 80 Penthouse Studios; 81 PAC C-73635; 82 PAC C-6881; 83 ROM 75CAN913; ROM 75CAN926; 84 PAC C-11925; 86 PAC F-2411; 87 PAC C-8070; PAC C-7100; 88 ROM 66CAN141; 89 PAC C10687; 90 MTL 971.01B11 p.232; 91 PAC C-2960; ROM 69CAN113; 92 JRR 2026; 93 PAC C-28405; PAC C-15784; 94 PAC F-2462; Redpath Library, McGill University; 95 PAC; 96 HBC; 97 PAC; 98 New York Historical Society; 100 Nova Scotia Museum 8020; 101 ROM; 102 ROM 70CAN27; 103 PAC C3686; 104 MTL; 108 ROM 75CAN917; 110 ROM 67CAN54; 112 JRR 73; 113 ROM 75CAN798; JRR 1715; 114 PAC C-785; 115 JRR 2057; JRR 2129; 116 ROM 67CAN154; 117 ROM 72CAN81; 120 MTL; 121 PAC C-5838; 122 Connecticut Historical Society; 123 ROM 68CAN107; PAC C-14831; 124 ROM 76CAN316; 128 Library of Congress; 129 OA Simcoe Sketch 206; 130 ROM 64CAN97; 132 PAC C-2001; 133 OA Simcoe Sketch 204; 134 ROM 69CAN101; 136 NGC 2036; 137 ROM 66CAN78; 138 JRR 2014; 139 JRR 113; 140-141 PAC C-17; 142 PAC PA-45005; 143 MTL M1-17; 144 UC J32K562; 145 MTL; 146 PAC; 147 JRR 3338; 148 MTL 1461; 149 ROM 942.48.7; PAC C-41067; 150 JRR 262; 151 NGC; 154 PAC C-69455; PAC C-69467; PAC; 155 JRR 3358; 156 JRR 229; 158 JRR 53; 160 ROM 951.158.11; 161 ANQ GH1070-166; 162 MM M4777.3; 163 MM M4777.5; PAC C-66899; 164 JRR 1556; 166 MTL; 167 JRR 4667; OA No. 6; 169 Nova Scotia Communication and Information Centre 11655; 170 QUA PG-K109-8; QUA PG-K116-12; 171 Hastings County Historical Society L3512; QUA PG-K79-18; 176 PAC C-4987; 178 CP 836; 179 PAC; 180 HBC A425; GA L.67.10.20; 181 JRR 2368; NGC; 182 PAC C-1906; 183 MA; PAC C-1938; 184 PABC 7928; 186 PABC 19657; 187 PABC 61162; PABC 22527; 188 MTL; PABC 763; 189 PABC 5189; GA NA-674-45; PABC F-2088; PABC 761; 190 PAC C-20848; PABC D-8352; ROM 78CUR361; BCA D-8360; 191 PAC C-3610; 196-199 Information Canada; 200 PAC C-733; 201 PANS; 202 PAC C-18737; 203 PAC C-51976; 204 JRR 3407; 205 PAC C-18292; 206 PAC C-3039; 209 NA 69,929; PAC PA-49675; ROM 73CAN160; MTL; Massey-Ferguson; 212 JRR 2386; 213 PAC C-1229; 215 MTL; 216 MTL 819.13R37.01; 217 GA Wa-47-9; 218 JRR 34; 220 CAG 78.24; Illustrated Historical Atlas of Prince Edward Island, p.159; ibid., p.70; 221 Picturesque Canada, p.856; 222 PAC C-4448; Picturesque Canada, p.406; 223 ibid., p.421; Eaton's of Canada; 224 PAC C-10097; GA NA-1434-12; 226 SA A-1009; SA; 227 GA NA-29-1; 228 CP; 229 MTL; CP 8889; 230 PAC PA-38679; NA 2117; 231 PAC PA-66576; PAC C28860; CP; 232 PAC C-4992; 233 PAC PA-70872; PAC C-14128; 234 OA 2381 S5441; 235 GA 1033-3; GA NA1829-5; MTL; 236 SA D284S; GA NA3205-5; 237 SA B7380; 238 MTL 971.05R37575 p.338; 239 OA 9814 S15961; 240 PAC C-70905; PAC C-7903; 241 PAC PA-16124; 243 PAC PA-17213; Eaton's of Canada; 244 NA 70020I; 245 PAC C-17633A; 248 MTL; MTL; 249 PAC C-6166; 250 Massey-Ferguson; 251 Massey-Ferguson; 252 PAC C-127; 253 General Motors; 254 PAC C-30944; 257 PAC C-56774; The Globe, 1867-11-11; CAG H-120; 258 UC; PAC C-18864; 259 PAC PA-2279; 260 OA S13671; GA NA-748-41; 261 PAC PA-28236; University of Toronto Library; CAG; 262 PAC C-6541; 263 MTL; PAC C-8427; 264 PAC C-14082; PAA B2320; 265 PAC PA-20568; PAC C-34885; 266 PAC C-89542; PAC C-89534; PAC C89535; 267 CP; 268 PAC C-683; 268-269 MA Sisler 192; 269 MA Immigration 14; PAC PA-20567; 270 AS B-329; 271 MA Settlement 222; PAA B-2627; 273 PAC PA-29322; PAC PA-10679; PAC C-37550; PAC PA-29346; PAC PA-24646; PAC C-29821 (International Labour Organization); 274 PABC 66363; 275 PAC PA-83142; PAC PA-11629; 276 PAC PA-34014; 277 PAC PA-118195; PAC C-84291; PAC PA-9561; PAC C-14118; 278 PAC PA-29292-4; PAC C-46571; 279 PAC PA-24827; 280 PAC C-5600; Suzzallo Library, University of Washington; 282 PAC C-6097; 283 PAC; 285 PAC PA-40674; PAC PA-96367; PAC PA-20562; 286 GA NA-406-3; PAC PA-61741; 290 PAC C-88234; Library of Congress 17038; PAC C-30144; PAC C-18908; 291 PAC C-17831; PAC C-30940; PAC; PAC C-30935; PAC C-6955; PAC PA-103924; 292 MTL 971971.20.1; PAC; PAC PA-10628; 293 PAC PA-59483; GA NA-922-1; OA S-13894; PAC; PAC C-79334; PAC C-5393; 294 PAC C-5123; SA B-3031; PAC PA-38567; PAC PA-21482; MA; 295 PAC C-7914; PAC PA-41837; PAC C-26966; PAC C-8599; PAC C-4777B; 296 Vancouver Archives N-751; PABC F-2106; Western Development Museum, George Sheppard; 297 PAC; PAC C-63524; PAC PA-66890; MA Foote; GA NA-98-14; ROM 78CUR690.